Vegetarian Cooking For Dummies®

D0691059

Vegetarian Recipe Substitutions

Use the following lists to adapt nonvegetarian recipes to vegetarian versions. You may have to experiment a couple of times to find the right substitute for a particular recipe, so have patience! Look through your recipe files or flag the pages of favorite recipes in your nonvegetarian cookbooks to get started. Mark the changes you'd like to try with a pencil. Erase and make adjustments as needed until you get the recipe to come out just the way you like it. You'll be surprised to see how easy it can be to create great-tasting vegetarian foods out of traditional nonvegetarian recipes.

Egg substitutes

In baked goods, in place of one whole egg, use

- ½ small ripe banana, mashed
- ¼ cup applesauce, canned pumpkin or squash, or pureed prunes
- ¼ cup tofu blended with the liquid ingredients in the recipe
- 1½ teaspoons powdered vegetarian egg replacer, such as Ener-G brand, mixed with 2 tablespoons water
- 1 heaping tablespoon soy flour or bean flour mixed with 1 tablespoon water
- 2 tablespoons cornstarch beaten with 2 tablespoons water
- 1 tablespoon finely ground flaxseeds whipped with ¼ cup water

In veggie burgers, loaves, and casseroles, in place of one whole egg, use

- 2 to 3 tablespoons quick-cooking rolled oats or cooked oatmeal
- 2 to 3 tablespoons mashed potatoes, mashed sweet potatoes, or instant potato flakes
- 2 to 3 tablespoons fine breadcrumbs, cracker meal, or matzo meal
- 2 to 3 tablespoons flour — whole-wheat, unbleached white, or oat
- 2 to 3 tablespoons arrowroot starch, potato starch, cornstarch, or vegetarian egg replacer mixed with 2 tablespoons water
- 2 to 3 tablespoons tomato paste
- ¼ cup tofu blended with 1 tablespoon flour

In other recipes, use tofu in place of egg whites to make

- Almost-egg salad sandwich filling (see Chapter 14)
- Scrambled tofu (see Chapter 11)
- Spinach salad topping

For Dummies: Bestselling Book Series for Beginners

Vegetarian Cooking For Dummies®

Vegetarian Recipe Substitutions (continued)

Meat substitutes

Instead of meat, use

- Textured vegetable protein (TVP) to replace ground meat
- Bulgur wheat to replace ground meat
- Tofu, tempeh, or seitan
- Meatless hotdogs, veggie burger patties, meatless sausages, or bacon alternatives
- Beans — rehydrated, canned, or dried flakes

Dairy substitutes

Instead of cow's milk, use

- Soy, rice, oat, or potato milk or a soy/rice milk blend
- Pureed potato with vegetable broth or pureed soft tofu in cream soups

Instead of dairy cheese, use

- Soy- or nut-based cheese alternatives
- Tofu mashed with a few teaspoons of lemon juice to replace ricotta cheese or cottage cheese in recipes for lasagne and stuffed shells

Instead of dairy yogurt and sour cream, use soy yogurt (plain or flavored).

Instead of butter, use soy margarine or vegetable oil.

Hidden Animal Ingredients

To avoid hidden animal ingredients in the foods you buy and eat, scan ingredient lists for the following terms:

- Albumin
- Anchovies
- Animal shortening
- Carmine
- Casein
- Gelatin
- Lard
- Natural flavorings
- Whey

Hungry Minds™

For Dummies: Bestselling Book Series for Beginners

Vegetarian Cooking

FOR

DUMMIES®

Vegetarian Cooking FOR DUMMIES®

by Suzanne Havala, RD

Hungry Minds™

HUNGRY MINDS, INC.

New York, NY ◆ Cleveland, OH ◆ Indianapolis, IN

Vegetarian Cooking For Dummies®

Published by:
Hungry Minds, Inc.
909 Third Avenue
New York, NY 10022
www.hungryminds.com
www.dummies.com

Library of Congress Control Number: 00-112157

ISBN: 0-7645-5350-X

Printed in the United States of America

10 9 8 7 6 5 4 3 2 1

1B/QY/QV/QR/IN

Distributed in the United States by Hungry Minds, Inc.

Distributed by CDG Books Canada Inc. for Canada; by Transworld Publishers Limited in the United Kingdom; by IDG Norge Books for Norway; by IDG Sweden Books for Sweden; by IDG Books Australia Publishing Corporation Pty. Ltd. for Australia and New Zealand; by TransQuest Publishers Pte Ltd. for Singapore, Malaysia, Thailand, Indonesia, and Hong Kong; by Gotop Information Inc. for Taiwan; by ICG Muse, Inc. for Japan; by Intersoft for South Africa; by Eyrolles for France; by International Thomson Publishing for Germany, Austria and Switzerland; by Distribuidora Cuspide for Argentina; by LR International for Brazil; by Galileo Libros for Chile; by Ediciones ZETA S.C.R. Ltda. for Peru; by WS Computer Publishing Corporation, Inc., for the Philippines; by Contemporanea de Ediciones for Venezuela; by Express Computer Distributors for the Caribbean and West Indies; by Micronesia Media Distributor, Inc. for Micronesia; by Chips Computadoras S.A. de C.V. for Mexico; by Editorial Norma de Panama S.A. for Panama; by American Bookshops for Finland.

For general information on Hungry Minds' products and services please contact our Customer Care department; within the U.S. at 800-762-2974, outside the U.S. at 317-572-3993 or fax 317-572-4002.

For sales inquiries and resellers information, including discounts, premium and bulk quantity sales and foreign language translations please contact our Customer Care department at 800-434-3422, fax 317-572-4002 or write to Hungry Minds, Inc., Attn: Customer Care department, 10475 Crosspoint Boulevard, Indianapolis, IN 46256.

For information on licensing foreign or domestic rights, please contact our Sub-Rights Customer Care department at 212-884-5000.

For information on using Hungry Minds' products and services in the classroom or for ordering examination copies, please contact our Educational Sales department at 800-434-2086 or fax 317-572-4005.

Please contact our Public Relations department at 212-884-5163 for press review copies or 212-884-5000 for author interviews and other publicity information or fax 212-884-5400.

For authorization to photocopy items for corporate, personal, or educational use, please contact Copyright Clearance Center, 222 Rosewood Drive, Danvers, MA 01923, or fax 978-750-4470.

Library of Congress Cataloging-in-Publication Data

Hungry Minds™ is a trademark of Hungry Minds, Inc.

About the Author

Suzanne Havala, MS, RD, LDN, FADA, is a nationally recognized author and consultant on food, nutrition, and public policy. Suzanne brings reliable, sound guidance to consumers and organizations on diet and its impact on health. Her advice has been quoted in *Parade, SELF Magazine, Shape, Vegetarian Times, The New York Times, Runner's World, New Woman, YM, Omni, Sassy,* and *Harper's Bazaar* and in appearances on *Good Morning America, Weekend Today in New York,* and *The Susan Powter Show.*

Suzanne is the author of *Being Vegetarian For Dummies, The Natural Kitchen, Good Foods, Bad Foods: What's Left to Eat?, The Vegetarian Food Guide and Nutrition Counter, Shopping for Health: A Nutritionist's Aisle-by-Aisle Guide to Smart, Low-fat Choices at the Supermarket, Being Vegetarian,* and *Simple, Lowfat & Vegetarian.*

Suzanne is a licensed, registered dietitian and Fellow of the American Dietetic Association. She is based in Chapel Hill, North Carolina, where she is a Public Health Leadership Doctoral Candidate in the Department of Health Policy and Administration in the School of Public Health at the University of North Carolina. She has been a full-fledged vegetarian for more than 26 years.

For more information, please visit www.suzannehavala.com.

Dedication

For my mother, who taught me to cook from scratch and present it with flair.

Author's Acknowledgments

Please join me in a round of applause for the following people in appreciation of their magnificent contributions in transforming the vision of this book into reality: Editor Linda Ingroia, who shepherded this book through from proposal to final product; Project Editor Pam Mourouzis and the talented editorial, design, and production crew at Hungry Minds; my agent, Patti Breitman; and Laurel Robertson, for her support and kindness. Special thanks to my sous chef and able assistant, Barbara Hobbs, and tireless taste-testers Mike and Henry Hobbs. Finally, a standing ovation, please, for my mother, Kathleen Babich. It was she — always ahead of her time when it came to matters of food, health, and ethics — who introduced me to the vegetarian alternative when I was very young. She taught me the value of fresh, unprocessed fruits, vegetables, and whole grains, the joy of good food cooked from scratch, and the art of presentation. For this, I am eternally grateful.

Publisher's Acknowledgments

We're proud of this book; please send us your comments through our Online Registration Form located at www.dummies.com.

Some of the people who helped bring this book to market include the following:

Acquisitions, Editorial, and Media Development

Project Editor: Pamela Mourouzis

Senior Acquisitions Editor: Linda Ingroia

Acquisitions Coordinator: Erin Connell

Recipe Tester/Technical Editor: Emily Nolan

Illustrator: Elizabeth Kurtzman

Photographer: David Bishop

Cover/Insert Art Director: Michele Laseau

Food Stylist: Roscoe Betsill

Prop Stylist: Donna Lawson

Cover Photo: David Bishop

Production

Project Coordinator: Jennifer Bingham

Layout and Graphics: Amy Adrian, Barry Offringa

Proofreaders: John Greenough, Nancy Price, Marianne Santy, TECHBOOKS Production Services

Indexer: Maro Riofrancos

General and Administrative

Hungry Minds, Inc.: John Kilcullen, CEO; Bill Barry, President and COO; John Ball, Executive VP, Operations & Administration; John Harris, CFO

Hungry Minds Consumer Reference Group

> **Business:** Kathleen Nebenhaus, Vice President and Publisher; Kevin Thornton, Acquisitions Manager

> **Cooking/Gardening:** Jennifer Feldman, Associate Vice President and Publisher, Anne Ficklen, Executive Editor; Kristi Hart, Managing Editor

> **Education/Reference:** Diane Graves Steele, Vice President and Publisher; Greg Tubach, Publishing Director

> **Lifestyles:** Kathleen Nebenhaus, Vice President and Publisher; Tracy Boggier, Managing Editor

> **Pets:** Dominique De Vito, Associate Vice President and Publisher; Tracy Boggier, Managing Editor

> **Travel:** Michael Spring, Vice President and Publisher; Suzanne Jannetta, Editorial Director; Brice Gosnell, Managing Editor

Hungry Minds Consumer Editorial Services: Kathleen Nebenhaus, Vice President and Publisher; Kristin A. Cocks, Editorial Director; Cindy Kitchel, Editorial Director

Hungry Minds Consumer Production: Debbie Stailey, Production Director

◆

The publisher would like to give special thanks to Patrick J. McGovern, without whom this book would not have been possible.

◆

Contents at a Glance

Cartoons at a Glance

By Rich Tennant

"I'LL HAVE A PIECE OF THE DEATH-BY-SKIM-TOFU."

page 147

"I'm not actually buying this stuff, I'm just using it to hide the fruit, legumes, and greens until we get checked out."

page 57

"Do I like arugula? I *love* arugula!! Some of the best beaches in the world are there."

page 7

"First it was the cattle, now it's a tempeh mutilation. I just wish I knew what these weird other-worldly vegetarian aliens wanted."

page 289

"I'm pretty sure it's pizza dough that gets tossed, not pasta dough."

page 103

Cartoon Information:
Fax: 978-546-7747
E-Mail: richtennant@the5thwave.com
World Wide Web: www.the5thwave.com

Recipes at a Glance

Salads

Bean Entrees

Grain Entrees

Pastas

Other Entrees

Chocolate and Carob Desserts

Other Desserts

Table of Contents

Introduction

● ●

*B*ecause you picked up this book, I know you or someone who loves you knows that vegetarian foods are good for you. Research has established that vegetarian diets are associated with substantial health advantages. For example, vegetarians have lower rates of coronary artery disease, high blood pressure, diabetes, and some forms of cancer. Vegetarians are less likely to be overweight, and they have fewer kidney stones and gallstones. Eating healthful vegetarian foods is like putting premium unleaded fuel into your automobile: It keeps your body in top form and running at its best. The investment is wise, considering the value of the machine.

Of course, eating well isn't just about health. It's also about the power of a seductive aroma and a colorful table loaded with tantalizing dishes. Eating well is one of life's simplest and most rewarding pleasures. We all love good food. So whether you're ready to be a full-time vegetarian or you just want to decrease your dependence on animal products, this book is here to guide the way.

About This Book

The aim of *Vegetarian Cooking For Dummies* is to provide you with practical information and guidance in preparing delicious vegetarian meals in your own kitchen. Lots of ready-made vegetarian foods are available at supermarkets and natural foods stores, and they're fine for once in a while or when you're in a pinch. Nobody wants to make a steady diet out of convenience foods, though — not when homemade foods are so much more satisfying. This book shows you how to make vegetarian meals at home from scratch, with the following criteria in mind:

- ✔ **The recipes are quick.** The majority of the recipes in this book can be prepared in 30 minutes or less, and many can be prepared in 5 minutes.

- ✔ **The recipes are simple rather than gourmet.** If you have basic cooking skills, you can master these recipes. The ingredients are relatively easy to find and don't necessitate complex instructions. The rare exceptions (such as Goat Cheese and Arugula Salad with Lavender-Vanilla Vinaigrette in Chapter 14) are well worth the few extra steps — a walk on the wild side of flavor.

  The recipes run the gamut from familiar favorites (always a good place to start) to those that may require a couple of tries to fully appreciate. No risk, no return, right?

✔ **The recipes are scrumptious and don't cost a lot to make.** A study in the October 1998 issue of the *Journal of the American Dietetic Association* reported that people give the most consideration to taste and cost when they decide what to eat. No problem. The recipes in this book are up to the task.

✔ **The recipes are nutritious but do not sacrifice taste or cost.** Like I said, taste and cost are of primo importance, but that doesn't mean that foods can't be decidedly good for you, too. Even the desserts in this book have many redeeming nutritional qualities.

In a few cases, flavor and nutrition battle. When that happens, I opt for taste but offer alternative instructions for those who want to boost the food's nutritive value even higher than that of the original recipe. You will eat guilt-free — I insist.

✔ **The recipes are versatile to meet the preferences of different kinds of vegetarians (and nonvegetarians).** Some vegetarians eat dairy products and eggs. Some eat no eggs but include dairy products in their diets. Others avoid all foods of animal origin, including honey and ingredients that may be processed with animal products, such as white table sugar. Some people aren't vegetarian at all but do want to cut down on meat, or they may be lactose intolerant and want to avoid milk products.

Throughout this book, I present recipes in the form that results in the best product overall — albeit a subjective judgment. However, wherever possible I give instructions for modifying the recipes to suit your diet. For example, I may present a recipe for pizza with part-skim mozzarella cheese, with instructions that you can substitute soy cheese if you desire. Alternatively, recipes for pudding are listed with soymilk instead of cow's milk as a primary ingredient. Highly nutritious soymilk, which is readily available at supermarkets, can replace cow's milk cup for cup in recipes with excellent results. You can use cow's milk instead of soymilk, however, if you prefer to do so.

✔ **The recipes are descriptive.** They include clues about how the finished products should smell, taste, and look, along with suggestions for what to serve them with.

Conventions Used in This Book

In the interest of keeping ingredient lists and directions concise, the recipes in this book follow certain conventions:

✔ All temperatures are in degrees Fahrenheit. For information about converting from degrees Fahrenheit to degrees Celsius, see this book's appendix.

✔ All butter is unsalted.

✔ All eggs are large.

✔ All soymilk is fortified.

✔ All flour is all-purpose unless otherwise noted.

✔ All sugar is granulated unless otherwise noted.

✔ All black pepper is freshly ground.

✔ All herbs are fresh unless otherwise noted.

✔ All citrus juices are freshly squeezed.

✔ All fruits and vegetables are medium-sized unless otherwise noted.

How This Book Is Organized

This book is divided into five parts. Each part focuses on a different aspect of vegetarian cooking, beginning with the basic question "What's a vegetarian?" Then I move on to the nutritional underpinnings of a diet that excludes meat and other animal products, how to plan vegetarian meals and integrate them into your culinary repertoire, how to stock your vegetarian kitchen, and how to master vegetarian cooking fundamentals. Together, the first three parts of this book lay the foundation for the fourth part: the recipes. The last part of the book — the Part of Tens — consists of helpful lists of quick tips and resources for vegetarian cooks.

Part 1: A Whirlwind Guide to Vegetarian Basics

This part is your ticket to understanding the fundamentals of vegetarianism. I define the various vegetarian diets, revealing once and for all what the word *vegan* means (and how to pronounce it). I look at what vegetarians *do* eat rather than stopping at what they *don't* eat. This part also discusses the reasons people adopt vegetarian diets and explains the myths and realities of vegetarian nutrition. You even get a helping hand in planning healthful vegetarian meals, as well as suggestions for seamlessly incorporating meatless dishes into your menus.

Part II: Your Vegetarian Kitchen

This part presents a step-by-step plan for transforming your kitchen into Vegetarian Command Central. I talk about beans, grains — the backbone of vegetarian cooking — and tofu and other soy foods. Which foods can serve as substitutes for meat? What's vegetarian egg replacer and how do you use it? Where do hidden animal ingredients hang out? You can find the answers to these questions and more, along with tips on how to stock your fridge, freezer, and cupboards.

Part III: Tools and Techniques

In this part, you get a few tricks of the trade for working vegetarian magic in the kitchen. I tell you which kitchen tools are the best investments and talk about adapting recipes to make them vegetarian. (Amaze your friends with surprising substitutions and tips!) I also cover simple cooking techniques for preparing fine vegetarian foods, such as how not to cook the life out of your vegetables. Included too are many timesaving tips and ideas for weekend cooks who want to get a jump on the week ahead.

Part IV: The Recipes

This part's title is coyly understated for such a stellar collection. I carefully selected the 100 recipes contained here for their unique contributions to your fledgling but soon-to-be-growing cache of delectable vegetarian dishes. Some are earthy. Some are sophisticated. All will tempt your senses. Simply stated, these recipes are fabu. Also included are sample menus for breakfast, lunch, dinner, and snacks, as well as vital information about planning for holidays, parties, and other special occasions.

Part V: The Part of Tens

These quick chapters make your foray into meatless cuisine that much easier. Here you can find great vegetarian Web sites, mail-order sources of vegetarian ingredients, worthwhile vegetarian organizations and publications, and more.

Icons Used in This Book

Throughout this book, you'll run across the following icons. These eye-catching little images help reinforce ideas presented in the text or point out little extras that I thought you'd be interested to know. Here's what each icon means:

Check the text next to these icons for definitions of new or important terms.

These tips and bits of advice smooth the way, saving you time or effort.

You definitely want to read these words to the wise. They'll help you avoid pitfalls or mistakes that you might otherwise stumble into.

This icon marks information that's especially for vegans — those vegetarians who consume no animal products whatsoever. I also mark vegan recipes with this symbol: ☽.

This icon points out interesting facts and other information that, although not vital to your understanding of vegetarian cuisine, may be fun to know.

Author's Note

The information in this book is general and is not meant as medical advice for an individual's specific health problems. If you are seriously ill or you are on medication, please check with your health care provider before changing your diet.

Where to Go from Here

How you approach this book is up to you. You can read it from cover to cover, or you can surf, opening it up to whichever sections catch your interest. If you're an accomplished cook, you may want to skip directly to the recipes in Part IV. If you need a primer on the basics of vegetarian nutrition, Part I is the place to start. Feeling a little less than confident about working with vegetarian foods? Read about how to stock your kitchen and all about tools and techniques in Parts II and III. Part V, of course, contains all sorts of great resources that you can pursue at any time. The bottom line: Do it whichever way works best for you. Enjoy!

Part I

A Whirlwind Guide to Vegetarian Basics

The 5th Wave   By Rich Tennant

"Do I like arugula? I _love_ arugula!! Some of the best beaches in the world are there."

In this part . . .

"I skate to where I think the puck will be."

—Wayne Gretzky, hockey great

You have to know where you're heading (and why) to be successful. The degree to which you want to work animal products out of your diet, the nutritional goals you hope to achieve, and the manner in which you integrate vegetarian foods into your culinary repertoire will guide your strategic planning in the kitchen.

What better place to start than with the basics? The chapters in this part reveal the who, what, why, and how of the vegetarian way.

Chapter 1

What Vegetarianism Is

In This Chapter

▶ Knowing who's who and what they do and don't eat

▶ Figuring out what's left to eat if you don't eat meat

▶ Building a healthy body one forkful at a time

Can you visualize a meal without a piece of meat at the center of the plate? Most Americans were raised in the great American tradition that says, "A meal without meat is not a meal." Your mother probably told you that if you couldn't eat all of your dinner, you should "at least finish your meat."

Most people learn to plan meals around the type of meat they plan to prepare. Chicken tonight? Fix green beans and rice to go with it. Roast beef? Have a baked potato and a small salad on the side. Leave out the meat, and all many people can imagine is a gaping hole at the center of the plate. If you don't eat meat, what on earth can you have for dinner?

The answer, of course, is "plenty," but that may not be apparent to nonvegetarians at first. Vegetarian diets, common in some parts of the world, are outside the culture of the majority of Americans. Undoing a lifetime of habits and traditions and adapting to a new eating style takes time and practice.

Once you break out of the meat-and-potatoes rut, you'll discover that your meals are more interesting, more healthful, and more diverse. Making the switch, however, requires a change of mindset. Most people find that getting there is an evolutionary process. The good news is that there's never been a better time to start. With this book in hand, you're on your way!

In this chapter, you find out what it means to be a vegetarian and what the different types of vegetarians eat. I also explore the many reasons people elect to go vegetarian.

Laboring Over Labels

We use lots of different labels to describe people. With just a few words, a label can speaks volumes about a person:

- ✔ She's a yuppie Boomer.
- ✔ He's a white Anglo-Saxon Protestant.
- ✔ They're New Age radicals living in California, land of juice bars and alfalfa sprouts.

When people use labels to describe vegetarians, different terms correspond to different sets of eating habits. For example, *lacto-ovo vegetarians* avoid meat but eat dairy products and eggs. *Vegans,* on the other hand, eat no animal products at all. In fact, a vegan not only avoids foods made from animal products but also eliminates all products made from animals, such as leather, wool, and cosmetics and toiletries made with animal byproducts. In general, the label used to describe a vegetarian has to do with the extent to which that person avoids foods of animal origin.

Label logic

A 1992 survey conducted by *Vegetarian Times* magazine found that almost 7 percent of Americans considered themselves vegetarians. However, a closer look at the eating habits of those "vegetarians" found that most of them were eating chicken and fish occasionally, and many were eating red meat at least a few times each month. That finding prompted many strident vegetarians — those who never eat meat, fish, or poultry — to pose the question, "Since when do chicken, fish, and cows have roots?"

Many people today use the term *vegetarian* loosely to mean that they're cutting back on meat. The term has a positive connotation because many people understand that there are health advantages associated with a vegetarian lifestyle.

"What about true vegetarians?" you may ask. "Who are they, and what exactly do they eat?"

A Roper Poll conducted in 1994 for the Baltimore-based Vegetarian Resource Group found that about 1 percent of American adults never eat meat, fish, or poultry. The group repeated the poll in 1997, and the results were unchanged. The VRG conducted another poll in 2000, and this time the results showed that the ranks of vegetarians had grown to 2.5 percent of the U.S. population. Most vegetarian activists believe that these figures reflect reality.

The definition of *vegetarian* most widely accepted by vegetarians is this: A vegetarian is a person who eats no meat, fish, or poultry. Thanksgiving turkey-eaters aren't vegetarians. Neither are the "I only eat chicken and fish" imposters. Vegetarians consistently avoid all flesh foods as well as byproducts of meat, fish, and poultry. They avoid refried beans, piecrusts, tortillas, and biscuits made with lard. They avoid soups made with meat or fish stock, foods made with gelatin (such as Jell-O), many brands of candy, and most marshmallows.

Vegetarian diets differ according to the extent to which they exclude animal products. The major types are the following:

- ✔ **Lacto-ovo vegetarian:** A *lacto-ovo vegetarian* diet excludes meat, fish, and poultry but includes dairy products and eggs. Most vegetarians in the U.S., Canada, and Western Europe fall into this category. Lacto-ovo vegetarians eat such foods as cheese, ice cream, yogurt, milk, and eggs. They also eat foods made with byproducts of these ingredients, including whey, casein, skim milk solids, and egg whites.

- ✔ **Lacto vegetarian:** A *lacto vegetarian* diet excludes meat, fish, poultry, and eggs as well as foods containing byproducts of these ingredients. For example, a lacto vegetarian wouldn't eat the pancakes at most restaurants because they contain eggs. However, a lacto vegetarian does eat dairy products such as milk, yogurt, and cheese.

- ✔ **Vegan:** Technically, the term *vegan* (pronounced "VEE-gun") refers to more than diet. A vegan is a vegetarian who avoids eating or using all animal products, including meat, fish, poultry, eggs, dairy products, wool, silk, fur, leather, and food and nonfood items made with animal byproducts, such as many types of personal care products. Some vegans also avoid honey and certain sweeteners that may be processed with animal products, such as refined white sugar and maple syrup.

  There's no better way to demonstrate the extent to which we have become dependent on animal products than to try to adopt a vegan lifestyle. Go vegan for a day or a week and you'll see what I mean. It's not impossible, but it takes effort. Vegans deserve admiration.

Although one could argue that many additional forms of vegetarianism exist, this book focuses on cooking for the most common forms — vegan, lacto, and lacto-ovo vegetarian diets. All three of these variations are nutritionally adequate and are associated with health advantages.

For more information about the various types of vegetarian diets, check out my book *Being Vegetarian For Dummies* (also published by Hungry Minds, Inc.).

Resources for vegans

Despite the obstacles to living a vegan lifestyle, most vegans are strongly motivated by ethics and rise to the challenge. Networking with other vegans and tapping into the right organizations for support helps. A large part of maintaining a vegan lifestyle has to do with being aware of where animal products are used and knowing about alternatives.

Vegetarian and animal rights organizations have many materials to help people maintain a vegan lifestyle. Here are two particularly good sources of information for vegans:

The Vegetarian Resource Group (VRG)
P.O. Box 1463
Baltimore, MD 21203
410-366-8343
www.vrg.org

People for the Ethical Treatment of Animals (PETA)
501 Front Street
Norfolk, VA 23510
757-622-PETA
www.peta.com

The limitations of labels

Labels are a start, but they have their limits. That's because people don't always fall neatly into the categories in which you place them. For example, what would you call a person who avoids flesh foods but occasionally eats very small amounts of eggs and dairy products, usually as minor ingredients in a baked good, such as a muffin or cookie? The person is a lacto-ovo vegetarian, right? Technically, that's correct. But this person's diet borders on vegan. This person might even identify herself as a vegan but have a toe in the lacto or lacto-ovo vegetarian camp. Ah, the subtleties of labels.

Variations in people's eating habits — even within the same category of vegetarian diet — are common. You might say that vegetarian diets fall somewhere along a continuum, ranging from a diet that contains a large proportion of animal products to one that includes only plant matter (see Figure 1-1). One lacto-ovo vegetarian may eat heaping helpings of cheese and eggs, while another may use eggs and dairy products only in very small amounts — as condiments or minor ingredients in foods.

The moral of the story: Labels are only a starting point. They have limitations. Even if you know what type of vegetarian a person is, there can be a lot of variation in the degree to which he or she consumes or avoids animal products.

Figure 1-1:
The range of vegetarian diets, from a diet that contains a large proportion of animal products (left) to one that contains no animal products (right).

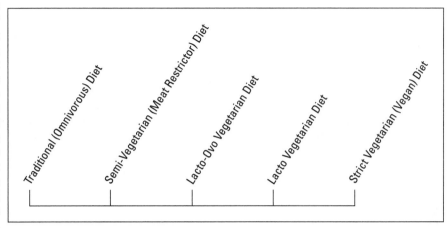

Traditional (Omnivorous) Diet

Semi-Vegetarian (Meat Restrictor) Diet

Lacto-Ovo Vegetarian Diet

Lacto Vegetarian Diet

Strict Vegetarian (Vegan) Diet

TIP

If you find yourself in the position of preparing a meal for a vegetarian, it pays to speak to that person to find out precisely what he or she does and doesn't eat. Doing so can save you time, expense, and anxiety and help ensure that everyone has an enjoyable meal.

Finding Foods to Eat in Place of Meat

"If you don't eat meat, what do you eat?" Vegetarians laugh when they hear that question . . . or they grit their teeth.

Nonvegetarians often just don't get it. When they think of a vegetarian diet, they visualize a plate with a gaping hole in the center — a big bare spot where the meat used to be. They think in terms of what's missing rather than what's there.

That's understandable when you think about the meat-and-potatoes mindset. The meat is the "main dish," the focal point of the meal around which the remainder of the meal is built. The vegetables and salad are the "side dishes." Relegated to the hinterlands, their small serving sizes are dwarfed by Flintstones-sized hunks of chicken, beef, or fish. Fruit, if it's present at all, is a garnish teetering on the edge of the plate.

The truth, of course, is that vegetarians enjoy more variety in their diets than meat-eaters do. That's because their meals are based on foods from the abundant, colorful, fragrant, delicious, nutritious, and varied plant world. Meat-eaters rotate their meals around a handful of different kinds of meat. Other dishes rely heavily on dairy products and eggs. Vegetarians, on the other hand, have a virtually unlimited repertoire that makes use of hundreds of different types of fruits, vegetables, grains, *legumes* (dried beans and peas), seeds and nuts, and other plant-based foods served in various combinations.

Many of the foods that vegetarians enjoy have their origins in other cultures. Many restaurants serve traditional vegetarian dishes that have their roots outside North America and Western Europe. Experimenting with some of these dishes can serve as a good introduction to healthful cuisines from other cultures, as well as to vegetarian cuisine. Some of the dishes you might try include the following:

- ✔ Spring rolls (China)
- ✔ Stir-fried tempeh (Indonesia)
- ✔ Samosas (Malaysia)
- ✔ Spaghetti with marinara sauce (Italy)
- ✔ Hummus, or garbanzo bean dip (Middle East)
- ✔ Lentil soup (Syria)
- ✔ Stir-fry with noodles (Cambodia)
- ✔ Vegetables stir-fried with spices (Bangladesh)
- ✔ Lentils and curried vegetables (Nepal)
- ✔ Bean burritos (Mexico)
- ✔ Spanakopita, or spinach pie (Greece)
- ✔ Couscous (Morocco)
- ✔ Peanut soup (West Africa)

 You'll find lots of vegetarian choices at Chinese, Indian, Ethiopian, Mexican, Italian, Greek, and Middle Eastern restaurants. Go in the spirit of adventure and sample a range of ethnic dishes that are new to you. It's cheaper than a plane ticket!

Eating for the Health of It

Compelling reasons exist for going vegetarian. Chief among them for many people are the health advantages of a diet that excludes meat.

Compared to nonvegetarians, vegetarians have lower rates of coronary artery disease, high blood pressure, obesity, diabetes, some forms of cancer — even gallstones and kidney stones. Most people with health problems would benefit from adopting a vegetarian diet, and anyone who is healthy will stay healthy longer if he or she avoids meat. The reason: Plant matter has protective qualities. The more plant matter your diet contains, the healthier you're likely to be.

Getting the fat and cholesterol out

Vegetarian diets tend to contain less total fat than nonvegetarian diets do. And the more you limit animal products in your diet, the less fat the diet usually contains. Vegan diets, for example, tend to be lower in fat than lacto vegetarian and lacto-ovo vegetarian diets. Diets that are low in total fat, saturated fat, and cholesterol are the healthiest. They are associated with a reduced risk of cancer, coronary artery disease, diabetes, high blood pressure, and obesity.

Fat is a concentrated source of calories. Gram for gram, it has more than double the calories of carbohydrate or protein. Consequently, diets that are high in fat are usually high in calories, and diets that are low in fat tend to be lower in calories. Red meat, chicken with skin, and full-fat cheese, cream, and ice cream are ultra-high in fat. It should come as no surprise, then, that vegetarians tend to be slimmer than nonvegetarians.

Much of the fat that animal products contribute is *saturated fat.* A distinguishing feature of saturated fat is that it's usually firm at room temperature, like a stick of butter. Foods that are high in saturated fat include red meats, butter, the skin on poultry, sour cream, ice cream, bacon, cold cuts, cheese, yogurt made with whole milk, and whole and 2% milk.

Vegetarian diets tend to be lower in saturated fat than nonvegetarian diets. Saturated fats come primarily from animal products, especially high-fat dairy products and meats. In fact, two-thirds of the fat in dairy products is saturated. Even so-called low-fat dairy products contain a substantial amount of saturated fat.

There are a few plant sources of saturated fat. Tropical oils such as palm oil, coconut oil, and cocoa butter are high in saturated fats. These oils are most often found in candy, pastries, and other desserts — foods that everyone should limit for good health. Another source of saturated fat is stick margarine and other *hydrogenated oils,* which are hardened into saturated fats through processing and act like saturated fats in the body. They're most often found in processed foods, peanut butter, and commercial baked goods.

Saturated fats stimulate your body to produce more cholesterol. Everyone needs some cholesterol, but your body manufactures what you need; you don't need more from outside sources. For people who are predisposed to heart disease, too much cholesterol can contribute to hardening of the arteries. The waxy substance collects on the walls of arteries, making it difficult for blood to flow.

Cholesterol is produced in the liver of humans and other animals. That's why it's found only in foods of animal origin. Plant products never contain cholesterol. Think of it this way: Have you ever seen a mushroom with a liver?

If you think that chicken and fish are "safe" choices, think again. Even though chicken and fish contain less saturated fat than red meat, they contain just as much cholesterol. Vegetarian diets are lower in both saturated fats *and* cholesterol than nonvegetarian diets.

A lacto-ovo vegetarian diet has the potential to be high in total fat, saturated fat, and cholesterol if you don't take care to limit eggs and high-fat dairy products. If you switch to a lacto-ovo vegetarian diet, be careful not to get caught in the cheese-and-eggs rut, depending on cheese and eggs as the primary ingredients in your foods (grilled cheese sandwiches, cheese omelets, macaroni and cheese, and so on).

Making friends with fiber

The part of a plant that the body can't digest completely is called *dietary fiber*. Even though you don't digest it, you need it. Your inability to digest dietary fiber provides health benefits. Because vegetarians tend to eat a greater proportion of plant products, they tend to get more fiber than non-vegetarians do, and that's a good thing.

Fiber binds with environmental contaminants and helps them pass out of the body. When your diet is high in fiber, waste material passes out of your body more quickly, too. The benefit to keeping things moving is that potentially harmful substances — such as cancer-causing agents — have less time to be in contact with the lining of your intestines.

Another feature of fiber that is advantageous is bulk. High-fiber foods tend to make you feel full before you've eaten too many calories. Think, for example, about how many apples you could eat before you'd feel full. Three medium-sized apples have about the same number of calories as a small candy bar. Which would fill you up faster? People who eat lots of fiber-rich foods tend to take in fewer calories and have an easier time controlling their weight.

Fiber has other benefits, too. People who get plenty of fiber in their diets are less likely to have trouble with constipation, hemorrhoids, varicose veins, *hiatus hernias* (a protrusion of the diaphragm into the esophagus), and *diverticulosis* (a condition in which herniations or small outpouchings form in the large intestine, which can fill with debris and become inflamed). Getting plenty of fiber (and water) in your diet keeps your stools large and soft and easy to pass. Diabetics have an easier time controlling their blood sugar levels, too, when they eat a diet that's high in fiber.

Pointing out the truth about protein

Vegetarians usually get enough protein, but they don't go overboard like many nonvegetarians do. That leads to several health benefits. For starters, when you moderate your protein intake, you help your body conserve calcium. A diet that's high in protein — especially from animal sources — increases the amount of calcium that passes through the kidneys into the urine and out of your life. That's part of the reason that recommendations for calcium intake for Americans are so high: They try to compensate for the large amount of calcium that nonvegetarians lose each day as a result of their meat habit.

When you eat less protein, you also cause less wear and tear on your kidneys. Vegetarians have fewer kidney stones and less kidney disease than nonvegetarians do. And just in case you need another reason to push the meat off your plate, know this: A high intake of animal protein is linked with higher blood cholesterol levels and more coronary artery disease, as well as a greater incidence of some types of cancer.

Getting high on phytochemicals

Vegetarian diets are as healthful for what they *have* as for what they don't have. Plants contain a host of substances that promote health. As a group, these substances are called *phytochemicals,* most of which have only recently been discovered. When gold was discovered in California, people rushed for the hills. When phytochemicals in foods were discovered, people rushed to the salad bar.

Thousands of phytochemicals probably exist, and scientists have identified only a small number. You may have heard of some of them: beta carotene, lycopene, lignins, genistein, daidzein, and many more. Some phytochemicals are *antioxidants,* which are believed to help reduce the risk of cancer, coronary artery disease, lung disease, cataracts, and other diseases. Examples of antioxidants include beta carotene, vitamins A, E, and C, and the mineral selenium. All of these antioxidants are found in abundance in plants.

Because plants are rich in the phytochemicals that promote and protect health, it's important to eat enough plant foods. The more animal products you include in your diet, the less room there is for plant matter. Whether you go all the way to a vegetarian diet or only part of the way, you'll benefit greatly from radically increasing the ratio of plant to animal products in your diet. Think about the ratio of plant to animal foods that you're eating now, and then look to Figure 1-2 for the ideal ratio for vegetarians.

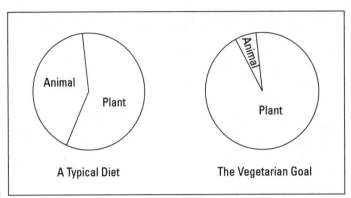

Figure 1-2:
What's your
ratio?

Taking Care of Mother Earth and All Her Creatures

Humans aren't the only ones who benefit from a vegetarian diet. Our land, seas, and air would be cleaner and healthier if more people ate less meat. That's because a disproportionate amount of the planet's natural resources is used to produce meat and other animal products. For example, growing 1 pound of wheat takes about 25 gallons of water, but producing 1 pound of beef takes about 390 gallons of water. A cow has to eat 7 pounds of protein from grain and soybeans to produce 1 pound of beef. Think of how many more people could have been fed had they eaten the grain and legumes themselves rather than feeding them to Bessie first.

Livestock grazing also causes desertification of the land by causing the topsoil to erode and the land to dry out. We need rich, abundant supplies of topsoil to ensure that we'll have enough arable land to grow the food that we need to survive and feed the world's rapidly growing population. Without our topsoil . . . well, visualize a Mad Max movie.

Our meat habit is depleting our trees and forests as well. Forests in Latin America, Central America, and South America are disappearing at breakneck speed to make way for cattle grazing. It doesn't matter that it's happening "over there" and we're "over here." We're all affected, regardless of where we live. The Earth's tropical rainforests act like lungs. Trees help keep the air clean by exchanging carbon dioxide for fresh oxygen. In other words, the trees take our waste and convert it to a product we need to survive. No trees, no oxygen, no life.

Judging from the amount of blue you see when you look at a map of the world, it's hard to imagine that we could run out of wet stuff anytime soon. Problem is, most of what you see is salt water. For drinking and irrigation, we need *fresh* water. Our supply of fresh water is at great risk due to animal agriculture. Great *aquifers* — giant pools of fresh water — lie deep below the Earth's surface. These pools are dwindling rapidly. We're sucking up vast quantities of precious fresh water to irrigate the huge tracts of land being used to graze cattle.

To add insult to injury, our water supply is also being polluted with the pesticides, herbicides, and fertilizers used to grow feed for animals. Worse, the nitrogen-filled fecal waste produced by the animals is washed into our streams, rivers, lakes, and bays. All for greasy, artery-clogging cheeseburgers!

Animal agriculture and the large-scale production of meat, eggs, and dairy products require the intensive use of fossil fuels, including petroleum. These natural resources are being depleted in order to transport animals and animal feed, to run farm machinery, and to operate the factory farms where the animals are raised.

Few Americans actually see the true cost of animal agriculture when they check out at the supermarket. That's because the government subsidizes businesses that produce meat and dairy products and protects them with price supports. Look at the bright side: If meat-eaters play their cards right, they might get out of having to pay for the real costs of their diet. After they're gone, their children and grandchildren will get stuck with the bills for cleanup and rehabilitation. Assuming, of course, that it's not too late.

Of course, vegetarianism also promotes the kind treatment of animals. Leonardo da Vinci (1452–1519) said, "I have from an early age abjured the use of meat, and the time will come when men such as I will look on the murder of animals as they now look on the murder of men." Suffice it to say that many vegetarians are motivated by the horrors inflicted upon helpless, innocent creatures and take a stand for nonviolence instead.

Chapter 2

Nutrition Myths and Realities

· ·

In This Chapter

▶ A primer on protein

▶ The bare-bones facts about calcium

▶ The nuts and bolts of iron

▶ A pinch of vitamin B12

▶ Rounding up the rest

· ·

*T*his chapter contains fodder for those earnest discussions with family and friends about the merits of a vegetarian diet. Here, I take on all the questions you've ever heard about where vegetarians get their protein, calcium, iron, and vitamin B12, among other nutrients.

"If you don't eat meat, where do you get your protein?"

"How do you get enough calcium if you don't drink milk?"

"Do you need supplements?"

Let them ask. After reading this chapter, you'll have the answers.

Getting the Particulars on Protein

Protein is a vital part of all living tissues, including muscles, blood, bodily fluids, bones, and teeth. Never mind that protein is the easiest nutrient to get in a vegetarian diet. It's still the subject that people ask about first when they meet a person who doesn't eat meat.

It's understandable. If you're old enough to be reading this book, you learned the old "Basic Four Food Groups" approach to nutrition. You clipped photos of hamburgers and roast beef and glued them to a poster in the square labeled "protein foods." Eggs sunny-side-up or a chunk of cheese may have joined them in the protein corner. Animal products were the best sources of protein. Everyone knew *that.*

Like you, nutrition science has grown up a lot. Ideas about meal planning and the foods that make up a healthy diet have been turned on their heads.

Protein essentials

What you need to know about protein boils down to a few key facts. The first is background.

Protein is made up of building blocks called *amino acids.* There are 22 amino acids. Linked together, they form proteins. Of those 22 amino acids, your body can manufacture 13. The remaining nine, known as *essential amino acids* or *indispensable amino acids,* have to come from your diet. They include

- ✔ Histidine
- ✔ Isoleucine
- ✔ Leucine
- ✔ Lysine
- ✔ Methionine
- ✔ Phenylalanine
- ✔ Threonine
- ✔ Tryptophan
- ✔ Valine

Amino acids, including all the essential amino acids, are found in varying amounts in almost all foods, including animal products, vegetables, grains, legumes, seeds, and nuts. The exception is fruits, which contain very little, if any, protein. To get enough protein in your diet, all you really need to do is to eat a reasonable variety of foods, including vegetables, grains, legumes, seeds, and nuts, and get enough calories to meet your energy needs.

Measuring up

Most vegetarians get enough protein, but they don't go overboard. Most of the people who eat a typical North American diet, on the other hand, get excessive amounts of protein in their diets. Too much of a good thing *is* possible, and protein is a case in point.

Too much protein increases your body's loss of calcium and makes your kidneys work harder. It increases your blood cholesterol level and boosts your risk of cancer and coronary artery disease. We all need protein, but most nonvegetarians need far less than they typically get.

Putting the pieces together

If you became a vegetarian in the 1960s or 1970s, the first thing you probably learned was how to complement your proteins. Not compliment, as in, "Hey, looking good today!" but *complement,* as in putting proteins together like puzzle pieces. *Complementary proteins* (or *complete proteins*) were the goal. Complementing was a tricky business, but conscientious vegetarians took the task very seriously.

We carefully combined our bread with our peanut butter, and we took pains to eat beans with rice or to eat lentil soup with a slice of whole-wheat bread. There were charts you could follow to help you get it right. To vegetarians, it seemed that one false move could send them over the edge to protein deficiency. Without a degree in chemistry, some people decided not to bother to try.

The idea behind combining certain foods with others was to maximize their amino acid profiles. You combined a plant food that has a short supply of one or more of the essential amino acids with a food that has a good supply of the amino acids that the first one lacks. It certainly seemed sensible at the time.

Nutritionists have since realized that, in real life, getting insufficient amounts of essential amino acids in *any* diet would be very difficult. Most foods contain all the essential amino acids in varying amounts. Assuming that your diet contains a reasonable variety of foods and enough calories to meet your energy needs, your diet should contain more than enough of all the essential amino acids. No conscious combining of foods is required. Your body does it all for you automatically.

Body builders who flood their bodies with protein from powdered supplements, high-protein shakes, and meals centered about big pieces of meat are making a mistake. Protein doesn't build muscle; *work* builds muscle. Your body can make muscle from the moderate amounts of protein in vegetables and grains, and you'll be far healthier for it.

For more information about how to calculate your individual protein needs, as well as a list of recommended intakes of protein, calcium, iron, vitamin B12, and other nutrients, see *Being Vegetarian For Dummies* (Hungry Minds, Inc.).

The protein pros

Almost all plant foods contain some protein, but those that are especially rich sources include legumes, nuts and seeds, and soy foods such as tempeh and tofu.

Tempeh is a traditional Indonesian soy food made from whole soybeans. It's fermented and pressed into a rectangular block. *Tofu* is a traditional Asian soy food. It's white, nearly odorless, and bland in flavor. See Chapter 5 for more information about these common vegetarian ingredients.

Examples of protein-rich vegetarian dishes include the following:

- ✔ Bean burritos (see Chapter 15)
- ✔ Barbecued tofu
- ✔ Black bean soup (see Chapter 13)
- ✔ Vegetable stew with tempeh
- ✔ Bean nachos
- ✔ Almond butter on toast
- ✔ Mixed green salad with garbanzo beans and sunflower seeds
- ✔ Hummus (a Middle Eastern garbanzo bean spread — see Chapter 12)
- ✔ Three-bean salad (see Chapter 14)
- ✔ Tofu salad (see Chapter 14)
- ✔ Tofu-stuffed shells or manicotti
- ✔ Spinach-tofu lasagne

Making the Calcium Connection

Nothing requires humans to drink milk from cows — even adult cows don't drink cow's milk! Our preference for dairy milk is based on tradition and habit. Nevertheless, cow's milk *is* loaded with calcium, an essential nutrient.

Confirmed cow's milk drinkers who enjoy their cross-species habit need read no further. They get more than enough calcium from the concentrated supply found in milk. However, those who can't tolerate cow's milk or don't want to include it in their diets can read on about the food sources of calcium that nature intended for people to eat.

Humans share their calcium supply with many other plant-eating species. Horses, elephants, zebras, giraffes, and monkeys rely on foods that come from the soil to meet their calcium needs in adulthood. Even adult cows — yes, cows! — build their impressive skeletons by eating plenty of greens and other vegetation. Just like you.

You can get plenty of calcium by eating generous servings of the following foods each day:

- ✔ Dark green leafy vegetables such as kale, collard greens, mustard greens, turnip greens, Swiss chard, and Chinese cabbage or bok choy
- ✔ Broccoli
- ✔ Tofu processed with calcium

- ✔ Dried figs

- ✔ Legumes such as black-eyed peas, black beans, garbanzo beans, pinto beans, and navy beans

- ✔ Almonds

- ✔ Sesame seeds

- ✔ Calcium-fortified orange juice and soymilk

Examples of vegetarian dishes that are rich in calcium include the following:

- ✔ Stir-fry with bok choy, broccoli, carrots, and tofu

- ✔ Vegetarian chili (see Chapter 13)

- ✔ Navy bean soup

- ✔ Broccoli with almonds

- ✔ Sliced apple and fig salad

- ✔ Garbanzo bean salad (see Chapter 14)

- ✔ Cooked turnip greens

- ✔ Pizza with mushrooms, onions, and broccoli florets

- ✔ Cereal with fortified soymilk

Too much protein isn't the only thing that can cause your body to lose calcium. (Refer to the section on protein earlier in this chapter.) Sodium has an even greater effect on your calcium stores. To preserve their bodies' stores of calcium, vegetarians and nonvegetarians alike can improve their diets by reducing their intakes of salty foods such as snack chips, soy sauce, ketchup and mustard, table salt, and processed foods.

Mining for Iron

As with protein, most people were taught from an early age that the best source of iron is meat — especially red meat. So if you don't eat meat, where do you get your iron?

Everywhere!

Iron is widespread throughout the plant world. Vegetarians get plenty of iron — usually more than nonvegetarians — from a wide range of foods. The bonus to getting your iron from plants rather than meat is that plants are a good source of fiber, phytochemicals, and other vitamins and minerals that everyone needs, and they don't contain the saturated fat and cholesterol that meat does. Although getting enough iron is not difficult for vegetarians, you may want to keep a few pointers up your sleeve for the next time family and friends inquire.

Iron is everywhere!

Good plant sources of iron include legumes, nuts, seeds, dark green leafy vegetables, broccoli, whole-grain and enriched breads and cereals, watermelon, and some dried fruits. Examples of iron-rich vegetarian dishes include

- Vegetarian chili (see Chapter 13)
- Braised kale with sesame seeds (see Chapter 16)
- Oatmeal with raisins
- Peanut butter sandwich
- Lentil soup (see Chapter 13)
- Bean burritos (see Chapter 15)
- Cuban black beans with rice (see Chapter 15)
- Broccoli with slivered almonds
- Split pea soup
- Cooked collard greens

Not only is it easy to get enough iron on a vegetarian diet, but it's healthier, too. Iron from meat is in a form that the body absorbs very readily. In meat-centered diets, too much iron is thought to contribute to hardening of the arteries, or *atherosclerosis,* because iron converts cholesterol into a form that the arteries absorb more easily.

The C factor

Vegetarians tend to get plenty of iron in their diets, but one of the secrets to ensuring that your body has good iron stores is to get plenty of vitamin C. Vitamin C helps your body absorb the iron that's present in your diet. So if you include vitamin C–rich foods at meals, your body will absorb the iron that's present in your meals more efficiently.

Foods that are high in vitamin C include citrus fruits and juices, kiwi fruit, strawberries, tomatoes, broccoli, cabbage, potatoes, green bell peppers, and cauliflower. You may have noticed that some of the foods that are high in vitamin C are also high in iron.

Too much tea can inhibit iron absorption

Tea contains *tannic acid,* a substance that inhibits your body's ability to absorb dietary iron. If you drink more than a glass of hot or iced tea per day, you may be markedly decreasing the amount of iron your body can absorb. If you're an avid tea drinker, consider switching to herbal varieties, because most of those don't have the same effect as regular teas.

If you stop to think about it, you might also realize that serving vitamin C–rich foods with iron-rich foods is common. You probably do it every day without realizing it. Examples of vegetarian meals that are high in both vitamin C and iron include

- ✔ Veggie burger with tomato slices and home fries
- ✔ Vegetarian chili with cornbread and cole slaw
- ✔ Tofu lasagne and steamed broccoli
- ✔ Pasta with tomato sauce
- ✔ Breakfast cereal, toast, and orange juice
- ✔ Oatmeal with sliced strawberries
- ✔ Three-bean salad with minced onion and green bell pepper
- ✔ Lentil loaf with cooked carrots and cauliflower

Disputing over a Little Vitamin Called B12

Your body's requirement for vitamin B12 is extremely small, but there is some question as to whether people who never eat animal products can get enough. It's much ado about very little, but a deficiency of vitamin B12 can cause serious problems. That's why, as a vegetarian, you need to understand what all the fuss is about. You also need to understand the extent to which vitamin B12 may be a relevant issue for you.

What's the fuss?

Vitamin B12 is produced by microorganisms (bacteria) that live in ponds, streams, and rivers, in the soil, and even in the guts of animals, including humans. When you eat animal products such as eggs, cheese, milk, and meat, you get a dose of vitamin B12. If you drank water from a stream or ate unwashed produce from your backyard garden, you might get a dose of vitamin B12. Of course, most people don't live such a natural lifestyle anymore, and drinking water from streams can be hazardous in these days of chemical dumping and waste runoffs.

Instead, our drinking water is chlorinated, and we buy our produce in the supermarket, washed free of any vitamin B12–containing soil that may have clung to it at the farm. Of course, pesticides and other chemicals applied to the crop had probably already killed off any bacteria that were in the soil in the first place. After all, it's been a long time since Old MacDonald ran the farm.

Because we can't rely on getting vitamin B12 from our water, and we can't rely on getting it from foods growing from the soil anymore, the only place we might naturally and reliably find vitamin B12 is in foods of animal origin. For vegetarians who rarely or never eat foods of animal origin, that presents a bit of a dilemma.

What's a vegan to do?

Where can a vegan or near-vegan find a reliable source of vitamin B12? Fortunately, the solution is simple and straightforward. First, vegans should make it a point to include a reliable source of vitamin B12 in their diets on a regular basis. Many options don't entail eating an animal product.

Reliable vegan options for vitamin B12 include the following:

- An over-the-counter vitamin B12 supplement (check natural foods stores for vegetarian sources)

- Fortified soymilk or rice milk

- Fortified commercial breakfast cereals (read the ingredient labels to be sure)

- Red Star brand Vegetarian Support Formula (T-6635+) nutritional yeast

    Nutritional yeast has a nutty, Parmesan cheese–like quality. Sprinkle it on popcorn, hot vegetables, and other savory foods. The brand that's fortified with vitamin B12 is Red Star T-6635+. If you can't find a store near you that carries it, you can order it from The Mail Order Catalog, P.O. Box 180, Summertown, TN 38483 or call 800-695-2241.

- Fortified meat substitutes, such as some brands of veggie burgers and veggie sausages

When you read food labels to check for vitamin B12 content, look for the word *cyanocobalamin*. Several forms of vitamin B12 exist, but this is the form that's physiologically active for humans. When you see cyanocobalamin on the label, you know that you're getting the form your body needs.

Scientists disagree about the extent to which vegans risk vitamin B12 deficiency if they don't regularly consume vitamin B12 supplements or fortified foods. Because vitamin B12 is produced in the human intestines, some scientists believe it's logical to conclude that what is produced must be available to the body if the need arises. Other scientists doubt that vegans can get enough B12. Until more is known, it's best for vegans to err on the conservative side and include a reliable source of the vitamin in their daily diets.

. . . And All the Rest

No nutrients available in a meat-and-dairy–based diet can't also be found in a plant-based diet. In fact, the nutrients found in a plant-based diet come with the added advantage of *not* being accompanied by cholesterol, saturated fat, and animal protein. Plant-based diets are also extra-rich sources of fiber and phytochemicals that too often are lacking in nonvegetarian diets.

Nevertheless, it's hard to shake old habits and relearn the nutrition facts that you thought you knew. In addition to protein, calcium, iron, and vitamin B12, the nutrients most often associated with animal sources are vitamin D, riboflavin, and zinc. Take a look at where these nutrients come from when a person's diet doesn't include meat. (For more complete nutrition information, see *Being Vegetarian For Dummies.*)

Making D while the sun shines

Vitamin D helps regulate the body's calcium balance and plays a major role in bone health. It isn't really a vitamin — it's a hormone. Your body produces it when your skin is exposed to sunlight. In fact, sunshine is the natural source of vitamin D; few foods contain any. The only foods that naturally contain vitamin D are liver and egg yolks, and neither of these foods is recommended for health reasons.

Too little vitamin D can result in *rickets,* a disease that causes a deformity of the bone, or *osteomalacia,* a disease characterized by softening of the bones.

Vitamin D is a fat-soluble vitamin, so you store what you make. The vitamin D that you produce in the summer months is stored and helps carry you through the winter months, when you get less exposure to sunshine. To produce enough vitamin D, you need 20 to 30 minutes of summer sun on your hands and face two or three times a week. (People with dark skin need longer exposure to sunlight than people who have fair skin.)

In the United States, dairy products are routinely fortified with vitamin D as a public health measure to protect people who may not get adequate exposure to sunlight. Several vegan foods on the market are fortified with vitamin D as well, such as some brands of soymilk, rice milk, and other milk substitutes. People who are especially vulnerable include people living in smog-filled cities (especially in the North), people who are home-bound or otherwise don't go outdoors, people who wear a lot of sunscreen, and people with dark skin who live in northern latitudes. Vegans or other vegetarians who don't use dairy products and who think they may be at risk of a vitamin D deficiency should consult a registered dietitian or other healthcare provider. In certain cases, the health professional may recommend a supplement.

If you take a vitamin D supplement, do not take more than the Recommended Dietary Allowance for adults of 5 micrograms or 200 International Units (IU) per day. Too much vitamin D is toxic and can cause serious liver damage. If you're unsure about whether you need a supplement, check with a registered dietitian, your doctor, or your pharmacist.

Reviewing your needs for riboflavin (or vitamin B2)

Riboflavin is another in a long line of nutrients found in a wide range of foods but especially concentrated in animal products. Milk, cheddar cheese, and cottage cheese are particularly rich sources. Organ meats, other meats, and eggs are also high in riboflavin.

Vegetarian sources of riboflavin include green leafy vegetables, enriched breads and cereal products, and legumes. Some forms of seaweed also have high concentrations of riboflavin, but most North Americans haven't acquired a taste for seaweed yet. Vegetarians can get what they need by including plenty of these wholesome foods in their daily diets.

Going from A to zinc

Zinc is another of those "shaky" nutrients — for vegetarians and nonvegetarians alike. Many people don't meet the recommended intake, and there is some debate among scientists about the level at which recommended intakes are set. Recommendations in other parts of the world are set much lower than in North America, in part due to varying opinions about how well zinc is absorbed. In general, vegetarians appear to have satisfactory zinc levels, even when their intakes of zinc are marginal.

How much riboflavin is enough?

Many scientists and nutritionists feel that the current recommendations for riboflavin intake for North Americans are too high. Populations consuming considerably less than the recommended amount have not been found to suffer from deficiency symptoms. Until scientific consensus is reached, however, I encourage you to aim for the current recommendations of 1.1 mg/dl for adult females or 1.3 mg/d for adult males. As always, a good way to ensure that you get what you need is to limit sweets and junk foods that displace nutrient-dense foods from your diet.

TIP

Eating bean sprouts and sprouting seeds, soaking and cooking legumes, and cooking or serving foods in combination with acidic ingredients such as lemon juice or tomato sauce can make zinc more available to the body.

Rich sources of zinc for vegetarians include

- ✔ Bran flakes
- ✔ Cooked millet
- ✔ Kale
- ✔ Legumes
- ✔ Oatmeal
- ✔ Shredded wheat
- ✔ Tempeh
- ✔ Tofu
- ✔ Wheat germ
- ✔ Yogurt

CAUTION!

If you take a calcium supplement, take it between meals or at bedtime. Calcium supplements taken with meals can interfere with zinc absorption because the two nutrients interact with each other.

THE LAST BITE

The siren song of supplements

Many people find nutritional supplements irresistible. Supplements offer a feeling of insurance: If you know that you aren't eating right, popping a pill to cover your bases is comforting. But do you really need supplements? Unfortunately, the experts split on that issue.

No one, however, would argue with the following advice: Do your very best to get what you can from your diet. Eat plenty of fresh fruits, vegetables, whole-grain breads and cereals, legumes, nuts, and seeds. Limit the junk. Limit the sweets. Get plenty of sleep, fresh air, and exercise. If you do your best to live as healthfully as you can, you minimize your need for supplements, and you're probably better off than you would have been by relying on supplements to give you what you weren't getting from food.

If you have questions about your need for supplements, you may want to seek guidance from a registered dietitian. You can locate a dietitian near you by calling the American Dietetic Association's referral service at 800-366-1655. Be sure to ask for a dietitian who is knowledgeable about vegetarian diets. You can also find more information about supplements for vegetarians in *Being Vegetarian For Dummies.*

If you do decide to take supplements, taking a *multi*vitamin and mineral supplement is usually better than taking separate vitamins and minerals. Buy one that has roughly 100 percent of the recommended dietary allowance (RDA) per tablet, rather than a high-potency formula that may have several times the RDA for some nutrients. You might also consider taking "daily" supplements a few times a week rather than every day.

Chapter 3

Moving to Meat-Free

● ●

In This Chapter

▶ Finding the right approach: gradual or overnight?

▶ Handling family, friends, and significant others

▶ Getting a crash course in vegetarian PR

● ●

Some people have been surrounded by vegetarianism all their lives. They may have been raised within a culture for which going meatless is the norm, or they may have close vegetarian friends or family members whom they've observed for years. For them, going vegetarian — if they aren't vegetarians already — can be a relatively easy transition. They model their own eating patterns after those they know.

For other people, however, going vegetarian is a whole new personal challenge. They may be the only vegetarians in the house or in their entire circle of family and friends. For them, making the switch is tantamount to going for a hike in the Himalayas without a map or a walking stick. They could use a little help.

If you're new to a vegetarian diet, there are some things you should know to help ease the transition and ensure your success. Think of this chapter as your personal coaching session.

Making the Switch: Gradual or Cold-Tofu?

There's no one right way to make the change to a vegetarian diet. How you do it is a matter of practicality and personality.

Some people prefer the all-at-once, wake-up-in-the-morning-and-I'm-a-vegetarian approach. Anything less leaves them too much room to waffle. Others need to get their big toes wet before they jump in. They need to inch their way along, maybe cutting back on meat for a while and then gradually increasing the number of days per week that they go totally meatless.

Whichever approach you choose, keep this in mind: There is no right or wrong way to make the transition. Do what feels comfortable for you. The advice that follows can help make whichever route you choose a little smoother.

Although there's no right or wrong way to go vegetarian, the people who choose the overnight approach face the greatest likelihood of "relapse." That's due to the steep learning curve involved in developing new habits and acquiring a new skill set. Feeling totally comfortable with the new lifestyle takes most people a long time, so "overnighters" may experience frustration at the outset.

Instant Vegetarian

It's a remarkable thing. One day, your best friend is eating a rack of ribs at your favorite haunt. The next day — presto! — he's ordered a veggie burger, hold the cheese. What inspires people to make such a drastic change so rapidly?

It could be any number of things: He made the connection between the ribs he was eating and his own, or maybe someone said something that struck him right. Maybe, like a slot machine in Vegas, things he'd heard and read and ruminated about for years suddenly came together, and the bells and whistles went off.

Whatever compels some people to go vegetarian instantly, there are advantages to their approach:

- ✔ **They achieve their goal right away.** For the impatient type, this can be all-important. Anything short of right away would wear on their nerves.

- ✔ **They feel better sooner.** A vegetarian diet provides many health benefits. By going all the way sooner, you may find that you lose weight, stop experiencing heartburn, stop being constipated, and lower your blood sugar and possibly your blood pressure, and you may even have more energy. People who go vegetarian all at once may notice a more pronounced effect as compared with people who drag out the change over a longer period.

- ✔ **They don't get lost along the way.** People who don't make the change all at once tend to get derailed along the way. These are the same folks who can't have a gallon of ice cream in the house without eating the whole container in three days. They can't have just a little bit of meat. They need to get it all out of their lives today to keep from lapsing back into old patterns.

People who publicly state their intentions tend to fulfill them. For that reason, it's a good idea to begin describing yourself to others as a vegetarian as soon as you've made the decision to avoid meat. Doing so increases the likelihood that the change will stick.

Of course, the overnight approach also has some disadvantages. The danger in going vegetarian instantly is that you're unlikely to have all the necessary supports in place. You'll probably need to relearn what you know about nutrition, and you'll have to develop skills in meal planning, eating out, cooking, dealing with social situations, and so on. If you opt for the instant approach to vegetarianism, promise yourself that you'll take steps to put these pieces in place as soon as possible.

If you switch to a vegetarian diet overnight and find yourself tired and hungry, you aren't getting enough to eat. Cereal and soymilk, bean burritos, pasta with marinara sauce, and pizza with vegetable toppings are all quick and easy. Get something to eat — quickly — and then educate yourself about vegetarian diets. A good place to start: *Being Vegetarian For Dummies* (Hungry Minds, Inc.).

The slow boat to Beanland

If you have the time and patience, most people find a gradual approach to going vegetarian to be more comfortable than an abrupt change. They educate themselves and master new skills in increments as their knowledge and confidence increase.

The advantages of a gradual approach include an increased likelihood that the change will stick. The people who are most likely to give up are those who make the switch overnight with no supports in place. Moving at a gradual pace, on the other hand, permits you to progress according to your ability to handle the change. A gradual approach may also be less disruptive to your routine because it's easier to adjust to small changes over a longer period.

Some people find it helpful to map out a game plan for switching to a vegetarian diet. For example, you might use a calendar to mark the steps in your transition that you want to have accomplished by certain dates. Doing so can help keep you moving along and prevent you from getting stuck in a rut. Set goals and a realistic timeline.

The primary disadvantage of taking the gradual route is the risk that you'll never arrive at your destination. You have many opportunities to get sidetracked or stuck in a comfortable rut. Before long, a year has passed and you're still in chicken-and-fish-mode.

Your best defense against never reaching your destination is to have a system in place that encourages you to monitor your progress and keep moving. Refer to *Being Vegetarian For Dummies* for a suggested timeline for gradually making the transition to a vegetarian diet.

Paving the Way to Success

Whether you're taking the overnight approach or the gradual approach, if you're new to the vegetarian lifestyle, there are some things you'll need to learn and some tried-and-true tips for getting there.

Get educated

You have a lot to learn, and many good resources can help you. Read everything you can get your hands on. Many books about vegetarianism are available, and each author explains things a little differently. Hearing the same material presented in different ways can be helpful.

Chapter 22 includes a list of my favorite vegetarian cookbooks, which are full of recipes that are sure to inspire you. In Chapter 23, you can find ten Web sites that provide information about a variety of vegetarian issues.

Many people like to collect vegetarian cookbooks. Don't be surprised, however, if only one or two recipes in each book become favorites. That's common. Look at it this way: For the cost of the book, you get a couple of dishes that may become traditions in your home. Plus, you can pass them on to family and friends. It's worth it!

Get involved

Many cities are home to local vegetarian societies that can be a great source of inspiration and practical assistance. Check your phone book or inquire at vegetarian restaurants or natural foods stores to find out whether there is a vegetarian society where you live. Attending its monthly meetings and potluck dinners can be a good way to sample vegetarian food and get to know other vegetarians. Many vegetarian societies plan special events for holidays and other times of the year. Some sponsor regular restaurant outings.

If you don't have a vegetarian society in your town, consider starting one yourself. The Vegetarian Resource Group (www.vrg.org) provides individuals with information about forming local vegetarian groups.

Get experience

The best way to hone your skills is to practice. When you hit snags and work through them, your expertise and confidence grow. Try your hand with new recipes such as those in this book, experiment with new vegetarian foods and products, and practice dealing with social situations such as meals at friends' homes and hosting meals at your own. Eat out at restaurants and practice ordering meals at both vegetarian and nonvegetarian restaurants. Make it a habit to shop at a natural foods store at least once a month to expose yourself to new food options.

When you're just starting out, make a list of all the foods you already enjoy that happen to be vegetarian, and serve them often. Examples may include pizza with vegetable toppings, pasta primavera, minestrone soup, spaghetti with tomato sauce, vegetable lasagne, bean burritos, lentil soup, peanut butter and jelly sandwiches, and vegetable stir-fry.

Vegetarian convenience foods also can help ease the transition to a meat-free diet. Products such as veggie hotdogs, veggie burgers, veggie cold cuts and breakfast meats, and vegetarian frozen entrees are quick, convenient, tasty, and familiar. You can find a huge variety at natural foods stores, and many are also sold at regular supermarkets.

Avoiding Food Fights at Home and in Others' Homes

Chances are very good that if you're a vegetarian, you're the only vegetarian in your family and you're a minority among your friends and acquaintances. You need a strategy for keeping the peace and fitting in. This section discusses some strategies for keeping those relationships intact.

Deciding whether to cook one meal or two

The first dilemma that usually strikes is what to do when meat-eaters and vegetarians live under the same roof and eat meals together. Which takes precedence — the meat or the plants?

In this situation, what frequently happens — especially when the vegetarian is outnumbered — is that a meat-based meal is prepared, and the vegetarian simply eats everything but the entree, doubling up on vegetable and salad side dishes. This scenario isn't satisfactory to many vegetarians for long, however.

Many vegetarians begin to be repulsed by the presence of meat in the kitchen. Some take the position that a meat-free meal is "the least common denominator." In other words, why not make the meal meatless, because both the vegetarian and the meat-eater can eat the food? That way, you don't need to fix two separate meals.

Because every family situation is different, you need to negotiate this one on a case-by-case basis. You may be able to set some ground rules if you're entering a new relationship, but if you change your eating habits after a precedent has already been established, you may need to compromise.

Vegetarian diets are healthful for children of all ages. As long as you don't overly restrict fat and you adhere to the basic principles of good nutrition, vegetarian and vegan diets are nutritionally adequate and can help instill good eating habits that a child will carry over into adulthood. *Being Vegetarian For Dummies* provides much more information about vegetarianism for children.

When you have guests

What you serve when company comes to visit is another situation that you have to work out with your family if you're not the only person with a say in the matter. Depending on the circumstances, however, you have several options to consider:

- ✔ **Serve a fabulous vegetarian dinner and knock their socks off.** If you have the confidence and skill, put together a delicious, sophisticated vegetarian meal and bask in the applause. Many guests would not only be impressed but also enjoy the change of pace.

- ✔ **Serve a sneaky vegetarian meal.** You can always lean on an old favorite, such as vegetable lasagne or pasta primavera — a familiar favorite for vegetarians and nonvegetarians alike. Serve it with a loaf of good bread and a beautiful mixed green salad, with a delectable dessert. Nobody is likely to notice that the meal doesn't contain meat.

- ✔ **Go out to eat.** In some cases, going out to a restaurant for a meal rather than eating in may be entirely appropriate. That way, all the guests can choose what they prefer to eat.

I won't even suggest that you prepare a meat-based dish for your guests. Most vegetarians wouldn't want to do so, and it really isn't necessary.

If social situations have you stumped, consider talking to other vegetarians about how they have handled similar situations. Talk with members of your local vegetarian society, or go online and join a vegetarian chat room or discussion forum. See Chapter 23 for suggested sites.

When you are the guest

When the tables are turned and you are the guest in someone else's home, the dynamics are different. The first major decision to make is whether to tell your hosts that you don't eat meat (or dairy, or eggs).

As always, there's no right answer in this case. What you do largely depends on how comfortable the situation feels. Many people think that it's best to tell your hosts up front that you're a vegetarian so that they don't go to the trouble of fixing you a steak. You can assure them that you'll find enough other foods to eat without the need for a substitute. You might even ask if they'd like you to bring a vegetarian dish of your own to share.

If you don't know your hosts very well, you may feel uncomfortable drawing attention to your food preferences. In that case, keep the following tips in mind:

- ✔ Take large servings of the meatless dishes served at the meal. Make your plate look full so it doesn't appear that anything is missing.

- ✔ If someone notices that you haven't taken the entree, or if someone points out to the others that you're a vegetarian, take pains to let it be known that you have plenty to eat and that no fuss is necessary.

- ✔ If there's little for you to eat because the potato salad is made with mayonnaise (and you're vegan) and the salad has crumbled bacon on it, do your best to act unruffled. You might consider putting some food on your plate but not eating it. Take a couple of servings of whatever you can eat and do your best to look satisfied. If your host takes notice and offers you an alternative, use your judgment about whether to accept it. The point is to keep the situation low-key for everyone's comfort.

- ✔ Eat before you go. Chances are excellent that you'll find something you can eat when you arrive. However, if you've had at least a snack before leaving home, you won't starve if it turns out that there's nothing for you to eat.

As a vegetarian, it's important not to make a fuss about your food preferences when you're a guest in someone else's home. Let them see that being a vegetarian isn't difficult and that you can easily adapt and find plenty to eat. Otherwise, you may send the message that vegetarians are antisocial refusniks — probably not the impression you want to make.

Building Consensus

Unless you live on an island, it's probably in your best interest to work at building bridges between yourself and those around you who may not share your interest in vegetarianism. Not only will it ease the way for you, but your example might even inspire others to kick the meat habit and give vegetarianism a shot.

Collaborate on a list of favorites

If you aim to include more vegetarian foods at mealtime, sit down with whomever you share your meals with and compile a list of mutually acceptable menu items that you all enjoy. You may find that you can easily modify some traditional, meat-containing recipes to make them vegetarian. For example, you can

- ✔ Substitute marinara sauce (an Italian meatless, tomato-based sauce seasoned with a variety of herbs and spices) for meat sauce on pasta dishes.

- ✔ Leave the meat out of chili and substitute a ground meatlike soy product instead, or just use beans.

- ✔ Leave the meat off pizza, or make one pizza with meat and one with vegetable toppings.

- ✔ Leave the meat out of bean burritos, nachos, and tacos. Use a ground meatlike soy product instead, or just use beans.

- ✔ Substitute vegetable broth for meat stock in soups.

- ✔ Leave the meat out of stir-fry, or let individuals add meat to their own plates after you prepare the stir-fry without it.

Invite participation

Getting others involved in meal planning, shopping, and preparing food is a masterful way of soliciting support. People who get involved in planning and preparing food are much more likely to eat the food — and like it.

Planting a garden and growing your own food — even if it's a small container garden on a patio or porch — is a good way to get others interested in your vegetarian meals. Tomatoes, basil, chives, mint, parsley, dill, and fresh greens are easy to grow and have lots of uses. Fresh, homegrown ingredients make meals seem more special and appealing.

Keep it positive

Attitude is important. You'll have more success in bringing people around to your way of looking at things if you

- ✔ **Don't push them to follow suit.** You can't force anyone to be a vegetarian. Let people decide for themselves what they will or won't eat. Resist the temptation to get up on a soapbox. If you push, people are likely to push back.

- ✔ **Show that you care by presenting meals with flair.** If you present vegetarian meals with a positive attitude and demonstrate that the food is well prepared and expected to taste good, nonvegetarians are more likely to accept it.

- ✔ **Set the example.** Eat well yourself and show people that your diet is worth emulating.

Getting a Crash Course in Veg Etiquette

If ethics or concerns about the environment motivated you to go vegetarian, it's probably safe to surmise that you'd like to see others follow your lead. Like many vegetarians, you probably wish that the semi-conscious nonvegetarian public would wake up and accept a little social responsibility. In fact, you'd like to tell them so straight to their faces. And you might do so.

The trouble is, some people don't respond well to the direct approach. In fact, *many* don't. And face it: Some people are more or less diplomatic in their approach than others. If you present your views forcefully or in a manner that puts others on the defensive, you're not likely to win people to your viewpoint, nor are you likely to make many friends.

You don't have to utter a word to send people a positive message about being vegetarian. By demonstrating that you care about your food choices, that you enjoy your food, and that eating a vegetarian diet isn't difficult or complicated, you send a silent signal and serve as a role model for others. They will notice.

If you intend to encourage people to consider a vegetarian lifestyle, think about the likely result of your actions and words. Constructive ways to promote vegetarianism include the following:

- ✔ Compiling a book of your favorite vegetarian family recipes and giving copies as gifts

- ✔ Sponsoring a vegetarian Thanksgiving dinner and inviting your family, friends, and neighbors

- ✔ Writing thoughtful letters to the editor of your local newspaper in response to relevant issues

- ✔ Establishing a vegetarian society in your town

- ✔ Thanking restaurant owners and managers for vegetarian menu choices
- ✔ Improving your food preparation skills so that you become known for your fabulous vegetarian dishes
- ✔ Preparing vegetarian dishes to take to new neighbors or friends who are ill

Keep cool, cucumber

"If you're a vegetarian, why are you wearing leather shoes?"

"I can't imagine being a vegetarian. I couldn't pass up a good steak."

"Animals are on this earth for us to use. They're raised for us to eat."

When people push your buttons, how do you react? Most vegetarians have had to entertain a few fools, and most have had to field the usual run of questions about what they eat if they don't eat meat. Sometimes the effort wears on you.

The best responses are simple and straightforward, delivered in a calm, unemotional manner. No need to engage people in lengthy discussions unless you want to. Even then, be careful not to be sucked into a debate that's going nowhere. You'll emerge a winner if you stay above the fray.

Chapter 4

Planning Vegetarian Meals

. . . .

. . . .

*N*obody wants to be a slave to a meal plan that dictates precisely what you can eat, when you can eat it, and how much you can have. Even if you tried to follow a military-strict eating pattern, life would do its best to interfere by throwing you holidays, special events, and unexpected happenings — sometimes daily!

Instead of trying to follow a precise meal plan, use this chapter as a toolbox or resource to refer to when you need guidance in making food choices. I want to help you assess those two keys to planning a health-supporting vegetarian diet: variety and adequacy. In other words, you can use the material presented here to help you determine whether you're getting enough of the right foods.

Setting Your Sights on the Big Food Picture

You want to have a general sense of the types and amounts of foods you should eat on a regular basis. The Vegetarian Food Guide Pyramid, shown in Figure 4-1, is a good place to start.

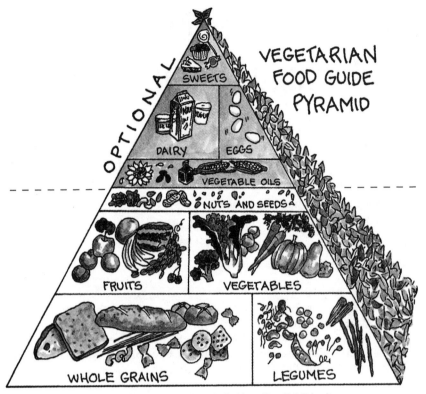

Figure 4-1:
The Vegetarian Food Guide Pyramid can help you make healthful food choices.

Notice that the broad base of the pyramid consists of whole grains and legumes. These foods should form the backbone of your meals. Notice, too, that fruits and vegetables make up the next broad band of choices that should predominate in your meals. When you're planning your meals, think in terms of dishes that are made up entirely or mostly of combinations of these four foods.

The recipes in Part IV of this book combine these foundation foods into delicious, appealing dishes that you'll want to make a regular part of your culinary repertoire.

If you look closely at the Vegetarian Food Guide Pyramid, you'll notice that vegetable oils, dairy products, eggs, and sweets are optional. These foods are not necessary for a healthful diet, and often they aren't recommended except in limited quantities.

Food isn't everything

Although food is important, it's only one of a number of lifestyle factors that you need to be aware of for good health. In addition to eating well, keep the following advice in mind:

✔ Get regular, vigorous physical activity. (See your healthcare provider before beginning a new exercise program.)

✔ Drink plenty of fluids. Though not etched in stone, 8 cups of fluid a day is a good goal. It's even better if most of the fluid is water.

✔ Get plenty of fresh air and sunshine, taking precautions to prevent excessive exposure to the sun.

✔ Get enough sleep. Most people need seven to nine hours of sleep per night.

Following this simple advice not only will contribute to your physical good health, but also will help you feel better emotionally and manage day-to-day stress.

In particular, pay close attention to the amount of junk foods and sweets that your diet contains. A treat now and then is fine, but be careful that "now and then" doesn't become "more often than not." Junk foods and sweets can displace more nutrient-dense foods from your diet and undermine your health. You'll find that the dessert recipes in this book qualify as treats in terms of taste, but they incorporate nutrient-dense ingredients and minimize fat and sugar.

Figuring Out How Much Is Enough

The amount of food you should eat from the variety shown in the Vegetarian Food Guide Pyramid depends on several factors:

✔ Your age.

✔ Your level of physical activity.

✔ The type of vegetarian diet you follow. Does it include eggs? Dairy products? To what extent?

✔ Your size. Are you tall or short? Are you overweight, underweight, or just right?

Here's a practical way to approach the question of "how much?"

1. **Lop off the optional top of the Vegetarian Food Guide Pyramid, leaving a trapezoid of foundation foods below. Make these foods the focal point of your diet.**

2. **Eat a mixture of the foods in the trapezoid, getting enough to meet your calorie needs — less if you want to lose weight and more if you want to gain weight or are growing rapidly.**

   Teens, pregnant women, breast-feeding women, and athletes, for example, may need more calories than average folks.

   If you work in foods from above the trapezoid, choose wisely, and don't permit these foods to displace too much of the foods in the trapezoid. People with higher calorie needs usually can afford more of the foods in the optional category than people who have tighter calorie budgets.

Table 4-1 shows you the number of servings that you should strive for from each area of the Vegetarian Food Guide Pyramid, whether you're a vegan, a lacto vegetarian, or a lacto-ovo vegetarian. The table also lists sample serving sizes. Following the table is a more in-depth look at the foods in each section of the pyramid, along with tips for choosing wisely.

Table 4-1		How Much of Which Foods?
Food Group	*Servings*	*Serving Size*
Whole grains	5–12	1 slice of bread
		1 ounce ready-to-eat cereal (¾ to 1 cup)
		½ cup cooked grains, cereal, rice, or pasta
Legumes	1–3	½ cup cooked dry beans, lentils, or peas
		½ cup tofu, soy products, or textured soy protein
		1 cup soymilk
Vegetables	6–9	½ cup cooked vegetables
		1 cup raw vegetables or salad
		¾ cup vegetable juice
Fruits	3–4	1 medium apple, banana, or orange
		½ cup chopped, cooked, or canned fruit
		¾ cup fruit juice
		¼ avocado
		10 olives
Nuts and seeds	1–2	1 ounce (¼ cup) almonds, walnuts, or seeds
		2 tablespoons peanut butter

Food Group	Servings	Serving Size
Vegetable oils	4–7	1 teaspoon vegetable oil
Dairy products	0–2	1 cup milk or yogurt (low-fat or nonfat)
		1½ ounces cheese (low-fat)
		½ cup ricotta cheese (part-skim)
Eggs	0–1	3 or fewer yolks per week
Sweets		1 teaspoon sugar, jam, jelly, honey, or syrup

Used with permission of the Third International Congress on Vegetarian Nutrition and Loma Linda University.

Choosing the Best Breads, Cereals, Pastas, and Other Grains

You don't have to make perfect choices all the time. An occasional piece of white bread won't necessarily help you, but it certainly won't hurt you. Over the long run, though, the types of foods you eat do make a difference in your health. When you choose breads, cereals, and other grain products, keep these general recommendations in mind:

✔ **Make it a whole grain.** Whole-grain products are less processed, so they contain more dietary fiber, vitamins, minerals, and phytochemicals than products made with processed, refined grains do.

If you have a hankering for a refined-grain product such as a baguette, Italian bread, a bagel, or French bread, don't begrudge yourself. Just be sure that you choose their whole-grain counterparts at least half the time, if not more often.

✔ **Go for variety.** Even among grains, many different types exist. Ancient grains are gaining in popularity. Try amaranth, quinoa, teff, kamut, and spelt, which you can usually find at natural foods stores. (Chapter 5 describes these grains in more detail.) Even run-of-the-mill grains come in a variety of choices, including oatmeal, wheat, rye, barley, and millet.

Commercial bread products made with white refined flour are usually enriched with added vitamins and minerals, replacing some of what is taken out during processing. Though not ideal, at least it's something. Bakery breads, however, are not enriched. So when you buy white, refined-flour breads from a bakery, their nutritional content is markedly lower than that of whole-grain breads.

Remember, grains are a foundation food. Many vegetarian dishes use grains as the basis or as a major component. Here are just a few examples of dishes that incorporate grains:

✔ Black beans with rice

✔ Couscous

✔ Barley soup

✔ Buckwheat groats (kasha) with pasta, mushrooms, and onions

✔ Pasta with beans

✔ Vegetarian chili over rice (see Chapter 13)

✔ Burritos filled with beans and rice

✔ Rice pudding (see Chapter 18)

✔ Quinoa pilaf (see Chapter 15)

✔ Whole-grain pancakes (see Chapter 11)

✔ Tabbouleh (see Chapter 16)

✔ Hot oatmeal with raisins and cinnamon

✔ Vegetable stir-fry over rice (see Chapter 15)

✔ Veggie sandwich on rye

Making Room for Legumes

Legumes — beans and peas — share the base of the Vegetarian Food Guide Pyramid with grains. Together, they're the foundation foods upon which the best diets are based. Every bean and pea is packed with nutrition. The only mistake you could make in this category would be to limit your choices.

Many people are familiar with only a few legumes. They may know pinto beans because they're used to make bean burrito filling. They may know kidney beans because they eat chili, and they may be familiar with garbanzo beans on salad bars. However, there are many more legumes than have multiple uses, so it's wise to expand your range.

Soybeans are particularly handy legumes for vegetarians. They are processed and used to make a variety of meat substitutes, such as veggie burger patties, sausages, and ground meat substitutes. These products are far healthier than their real-meat counterparts because they contain no cholesterol, little saturated fat, far less sodium, and often a substantial amount of dietary fiber.

Although you're most likely to see soybeans sold in a processed form, whole soybeans are available at natural foods stores and are the most nutritious form of this legume. You can use whole canned soybeans in every way that you use other beans. Soybeans and many soy products are uniquely rich sources of *isoflavones,* a type of phytochemical that may have substantial health benefits.

When it comes to beans, you should know that

- ✔ There's no need to feel guilty about eating canned beans. They're extremely convenient, and they're perfectly nutritious despite being canned. You can reduce the amount of sodium in canned beans by rinsing them with water in a colander and then draining them.

- ✔ Organically grown canned and dried beans are available at natural foods stores, and they're increasingly available in regular supermarkets as well. Regular canned beans are fine, but it's worth buying organic beans when you can find them and the price is reasonable. (Chapter 6 gives you more information about the advantages of organic foods.)

- ✔ Although meat substitutes such as veggie burger patties and meatless sausages are far better for you than their real-meat counterparts, comparison-shopping among meatless products still pays. Choose those that are lowest in sodium and fat and highest in fiber.

You can add more beans to your diet in an endless number of ways. Here are a few ideas to spark your imagination:

- ✔ Add a can of any kind of beans to a pot of soup, stew, or tomato sauce served over pasta.

- ✔ Add bean salads to your menus. Mix a few different kinds of beans (black beans, kidney beans, and garbanzo beans, for example) and toss them with a vinaigrette dressing. Add cherry tomato halves and diced green onions if you like.

- ✔ Create your own dips for tortilla chips, vegetable sticks, crackers, breadsticks, or toasted pita bread wedges brushed with olive oil and minced garlic. Mash cooked black beans or pinto beans. Add spices such as garlic powder, chili powder, or cumin — whatever tastes good to you. Add minced onions, grated carrots, diced tomatoes, or a scoop of salsa for extra flavor.

- ✔ Serve vegetarian chili and onions over a meatless hotdog on a bun. Add a scoop of coleslaw on top.

- ✔ Serve bean chili over rice or with a block of cornbread or pan-fried polenta.

✔ Precede a meal with navy bean, split pea, or minestrone soup, or enjoy the soup alone as the entree with a mixed green salad and a slice of bread or a roll.

✔ Add sliced vegetarian hotdogs to vegetarian baked beans for a healthier version of an old favorite.

Ramping Up Your Vegetable Consumption

It's hard to go wrong with vegetables of any sort unless they're fried beyond recognition. Whether they're fresh, frozen, or canned, all vegetables have merit. Vegetables should factor heavily into your meals, and most people should eat double the portions they usually do. If you aren't doing so already, start eating heaping helpings of vegetables, and also keep these points in mind:

✔ All vegetables are worthwhile, but some are standouts and should be eaten often. Vegetables that have exceptional nutritional merit include deep yellow, orange, and red vegetables, as well as dark green vegetables. Examples include sweet potatoes; butternut and acorn squash; red, green, and yellow bell peppers; broccoli; kale; tomatoes; Swiss chard; and carrots. These vegetables are especially rich sources of vitamins A and C, iron, and calcium.

✔ *Cruciferous* vegetables — vegetables in the cabbage family — are also particularly good choices because they're rich in phytochemicals that may protect your health. Examples include dark green vegetables such as broccoli, kale, mustard greens, and collard greens, as well as bok choy (or Chinese cabbage), kohlrabi, and cauliflower.

✔ If you cook vegetables, choose methods that expose them to high heat for as short a time as possible to help preserve their nutrient content. Nutrient-preserving cooking methods include steaming, stir-frying, and cooking in a microwave oven. (See Chapter 8 for more information about basic vegetarian cooking techniques.)

✔ If you have trouble getting enough calories on a vegetarian diet, eat more cooked vegetables — especially starchy ones like potatoes, corn, and peas — and fewer bulky raw vegetables, such as lettuce, celery, green beans, and carrots.

✔ Buy locally grown vegetables in season when you can. They're likely to be freshly picked and won't have had to travel a great distance (therefore losing nutrients) before getting to your table.

Strive for large portions of vegetables and serve them often. Make vegetables ingredients in your recipes on a regular basis. Look for creative ways to add them. For example, if your summer garden is giving you lots of tomatoes and green beans, add them to cooked pasta along with your usual toppings, or serve them alongside the rest of your meal. Combine them with a little vinegar and olive oil for a fresh summer salad.

Adding vegetables to your diet doesn't have to be difficult or time-consuming. Here are some additional ideas for making them a regular feature at meals:

✔ If it's more convenient for you, buy preprepared vegetables such as stir-fry mixes, baby carrots that have already been peeled and washed, and ready-to-eat salad mixes. You do pay more when someone else washes, peels, and chops your vegetables for you, but if it means that you'll eat more of them, it may be worth the extra cost.

✔ After grocery shopping, take ten minutes or so to wash, peel, and chop your own vegetables. Store them in an airtight container or plastic bag in the refrigerator. They'll be ready when it's time to prepare a meal, and you'll be more likely to use them if they're ready to go. This works well for such vegetables as carrots, broccoli, cauliflower, bell peppers, and onions. Potatoes, on the other hand, should be cut up just before cooking (to keep them from turning color), and tomatoes should be sliced just before serving to keep them firm and fresh tasting.

✔ Consider purchasing an electric steamer. Steamers are inexpensive and easy to use. You can use a steamer to cook potatoes, sweet potatoes, carrots, onions, corn on the cob, greens, and other vegetables. Steaming is also a good way to use up vegetables that have been sitting around for a while. Just wash the vegetables, cut them into pieces, and toss them in. Add water, set the timer, and go back to your life. There's nothing left to do until the vegetables are ready — no watching the stove or fiddling with the microwave.

✔ Serve fresh, cut-up vegetables with hummus, low-fat salad dressings, black bean dip, or salsa. Don't limit yourself to carrots, bell peppers, and broccoli, although those veggies are great choices. You can also slice yellow squash and zucchini, daikon, jicama, cauliflower, *broccoflower* (a cross between broccoli and cauliflower), and cherry tomatoes.

Note that some cut vegetables, such as carrots and celery, should be stored in water, or else they will become dry and unappetizing.

✔ Chop or grate fresh vegetables and blend them into marinara sauce for pasta, or toss them with cooked pasta and olive oil for pasta primavera. You can also add them to pasta that you have tossed with fresh *pesto* (an aromatic blend of minced fresh basil, oil, and other ingredients) or stir them into soup while it's heating on the stove.

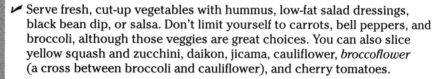

✔ Grated fresh vegetables make a fabulous sandwich filling. Grate several different vegetables (carrots, green peppers, and jicama, for example) and roll them into a flour tortilla with some refried beans, or add them to a pita pocket along with a scoop of tofu salad (see Chapter 14), hummus (see Chapter 12), or a sprinkling of grated cheese. Add a dash of balsamic vinegar and heat your sandwich briefly.

✔ Keep sweet onion on hand and use it liberally. See the broccoli and sweet onion salad recipe in Chapter 14 — you'll become addicted! You can also mince some onion and sprinkle it liberally on top of a big bowl of black bean soup.

Finding Ways to Use Fruits

Like vegetables, fruits should be included liberally in your diet. Many people think of fruit as strictly a snack or dessert food, but think about adding it to your main meals as well. You can add fresh fruit slices or chunks to mixed green salads, and a fresh fruit salad with a little mint added makes a nice accompaniment to almost any meal.

Also keep these additional thoughts about fruit in mind:

✔ All fruits have some redeeming value. Eat whichever you enjoy, but know that deeply colored fruits are packed with vitamins and minerals. In particular, deep yellow, orange, and red fruits such as papayas, mangoes, apricots, peaches, oranges, watermelon, and cantaloupe are nutrient dense. These nutritional superstars are particularly rich in vitamin A, vitamin C, and other phytochemicals.

✔ Aim for large servings of fruit. Eat at least the equivalent of two big pieces of fresh fruit every day.

✔ Canned or cooked fruit and fruit juices are fine. However, fresh fruit usually contains more dietary fiber. (See Chapter 2 for information about the benefits of fiber.)

If weight control is an issue for you, be careful not to drink too much fruit juice. Without the fiber of the fresh fruit to sate your appetite, there is the potential for you to take in a hefty number of calories from fruit juice. A half-cup of juice a day is fine, but if you're drinking it with abandon as a beverage, the calorie total may be substantial.

✔ Buy locally grown fruits in season when you can. As with vegetables, they're likely to be freshly picked and won't have had to travel a long way (therefore losing nutrients).

There are lots of ways to work more fruit into your diet — some more creative than others, but all worth considering:

✔ If you garnish a plate with fruit slices, make the garnish an edible part of the meal. Serve several apple, pear, orange, kiwi, or melon slices on the side of the plate, or add a small clump of grapes to the dish.

✔ Keep a bowl heaping full of fresh fruit on your kitchen table or counter. Cycle fruit into a fresh fruit salad if it begins to go bad before you can eat it. Peel overripe bananas and store them in an airtight plastic bag or container in the freezer. You can use them later for smoothies or in baking.

✔ Keep a supply of cut-up fresh fruit in an airtight container on the top shelf of the refrigerator. Do you remember how much more interesting fruit was when you were a kid and your mother cut it up for you? Same principle here. You're more likely to eat it if it's already cut up and in plain view.

Enjoying Nuts and Seeds

When people dispense diet advice these days, they commonly recommend avoiding nuts and seeds. They pick on nuts and seeds because of their high fat content. Nuts and seeds *are* high in fat, but they're also rich sources of phytochemicals, minerals, dietary fiber, and other important nutrients. Plus, the fat they contain isn't the harmful saturated fat found in animal products; it's monounsaturated fat, just like that in olive oil. You don't have to avoid nuts and seeds. *How* you use them is the key.

People who sit in front of the TV munching on handful after handful of salted mixed nuts are in for trouble unless they're elite athletes who can burn up the extra calories they're consuming. Because nuts and seeds are high in fat, they're also high in calories. It's hard to control your weight if you eat gobs of fatty foods.

Of course, there *are* people who have the opposite problem. If you want to gain weight, adding some nuts and seeds to your diet can be a healthful way to add calories. Here are some examples:

✔ Almonds and almond butter

✔ Cashews and cashew butter

✔ Hazelnuts

✔ Macadamia nuts

✔ Peanuts and peanut butter

✔ Pecans

✔ Pistachios

✔ Poppy seeds

✔ Pumpkin seeds

✔ Sunflower seeds

✔ Walnuts

Avocados and olives deserve a mention here as well. Both are high in monounsaturated fat, like nuts and seeds, but both can be added in small amounts to a healthful diet for the same reasons.

When you have the choice, buy nuts and seeds that have no added salt or oil. Many brands of sunflower seeds have monosodium glutamate (MSG) — a flavor enhancer — added as well. Try to avoid these brands.

Consuming Eggs and Dairy Products in Moderation, if at All

My advice is fairly straightforward here. If you eat eggs, you should

✔ Limit the number of yolks you eat — the fewer, the better.

✔ Know that two egg whites can replace one whole egg in cooking. The whites are better for you than the yolks because they contain much less fat and cholesterol. Chapter 5 describes other vegetarian and vegan egg substitutes.

If you include dairy products in your diet, use only nonfat varieties. So-called low-fat dairy products are really too high in fat for most people to use regularly.

If you enjoy yogurt, pudding, and ice cream, you may be interested in trying the dairy-free versions that are available at natural foods stores and many supermarkets. Most are made with soymilk or rice milk. They contain only a fraction of the saturated fat, if any, of the regular dairy versions. More important, they're delicious!

Controlling Other Vices

Speaking of pudding and ice cream . . . Sweets, junk foods, and added fats creep into almost every diet. Many people enjoy alcoholic beverages as well. The key is to keep the amount and frequency of consumption under control. For some people, it takes willpower and good old-fashioned horse sense. For others, it's easier not to have these foods in the house at all.

What's a reasonable approach to such foods? Here are some guidelines:

- ✔ **Sweets:** Don't let nutrient-poor sweets push the good stuff out of your diet. Limit sweets such as candy, cake, cookies, pie, and ice cream to reasonable amounts at reasonable intervals.

  What's reasonable? Aim for a small serving of something sweet each day if you can afford the calories, less often if you're trying to lose weight. A ½ cup serving of pudding, ice milk (ice cream is too high in fat to be eaten daily), frozen yogurt, or a nondairy substitute is a small serving. So is an average-sized piece of pie or cake or two or three cookies.

  If having a half-gallon of frozen yogurt in the house is too much of a temptation, vow to keep the supply out of the house. Instead, go out to a restaurant and have dessert when you really feel the need. This way, you don't feel deprived, but you'll help stave off impulsive (and compulsive!) eating.

- ✔ **Junk foods:** Treat chips and junky snack foods as you do sweets. Keeping them out of the house is the first line of defense. Limiting them to a handful once a day is next best. Choose your vice — one serving of junk food or sweets per day, if you have to have any at all.

  Remember that not all sweets and snacks qualify as junk foods. Some of the recipes in this book taste good enough to be treats. The difference is that they're made with wholesome ingredients and are lower in sugar and fat than conventional versions. You can eat these kinds of foods more liberally.

- ✔ **Fats and oils:** The best advice is to limit added fats and oils such as vegetable oils, butter, sour cream, cream cheese, and cream. When you do use fat, make it a vegetable fat. Olive oil is an excellent choice because it's monounsaturated fat and it doesn't raise your blood cholesterol level.

- ✔ **Alcoholic beverages:** Beer, wine, and liquor are vegetarian, but you should limit your intake of them. Some health organizations recommend that adults limit alcoholic beverages to the equivalent of one drink per day, but others recommend that everyone abstain.

Part II
Your Vegetarian Kitchen

The 5th Wave   By Rich Tennant

"I'm not actually buying this stuff, I'm just using it to hide the fruit, legumes, and greens until we get checked out."

In this part . . .

*V*iew your kitchen as Command Central. The kitchen is the nucleus of the vegetarian operation, where you stock supplies, plan menus, experiment with new recipes, and prepare nutritious meals. It's where you go when hunger strikes at 2:00 a.m. Your kitchen is the heart of your home.

Your kitchen is also the best place to hone your new skills. You have the most control over what you eat when you make it from scratch at home. You have more choices when you eat at home than when you eat at a restaurant or in the homes of friends and relatives.

In this part, I talk about the many ingredients that are commonly used in vegetarian cooking — some of which you're sure to be familiar with, and others of which may be new to you. I also cover how to stock your pantry, fridge, and freezer to make meal prep easy and fun.

Chapter 5

Common Vegetarian Ingredients

*V*egetarian cooking doesn't have to be exotic. Recipes don't have to include ingredients that you can't pronounce or that you can't buy at your neighborhood supermarket. Vegetarian cooking can be as all-American as corn on the cob, baked beans, and veggie burgers.

On the other hand, going vegetarian can open a window on a whole new world of flavors, textures, and aromas that derive from culinary traditions around the world. Many vegetarian cookbooks draw on these traditions, which contribute greatly to the diversity of foods that vegetarians everywhere enjoy.

This chapter highlights some of the ingredients that you'll encounter when you explore vegetarian cuisine. Some are common foods that you'll recognize and may already use; others may be unfamiliar to you. All are practical, multipurpose ingredients that are worth knowing about and keeping on hand.

Great Grains

Grains are one of the foundations of the Vegetarian Food Guide Pyramid (see Chapter 4) and a major component of all healthful diets. They're versatile because you can eat them by themselves or combine them with other ingredients to make a seemingly endless collection of dishes. Around the world, grains are familiar ingredients in soups, salads, baked goods, main dishes, side dishes, desserts, and other foods. Examples include

✔ Chinese vegetable stir-fry with steamed white rice

✔ Ethiopian *injera* (flatbread made from teff flour)

✔ Indian saffron rice with vegetables

✔ Indonesian *tempeh* (made with whole soybeans and a grain such as rice)

✔ Irish porridge (oatmeal)

✔ Italian *polenta* (typically made with cornmeal, baked or pan-fried, and often served with a sauce on top)

✔ Mexican enchiladas made with corn tortillas

✔ Middle Eastern *tabbouleh* (wheat salad)

✔ Middle Eastern couscous with cooked vegetables

✔ Russian or Eastern European *kasha* (toasted buckwheat) with bowtie pasta and cooked mushrooms

✔ Spanish rice

✔ Thai jasmine rice with curried vegetables

Grains can be categorized into two forms: whole and processed. Both forms are indispensable in vegetarian cooking.

Appreciating whole grains

Whole grains are grains that have had only the outer hull removed. This process leaves a small, round kernel, often called a *berry*. The major advantages to using whole grains in cooking are their superior nutritional value and their great taste. The major drawback is the extra time required to cook them as compared to cooking processed grains. Once you've become accustomed to the rich flavor of whole grains, though, you're likely not to be satisfied with a steady diet of processed grains ever again! You can find details about cooking grains in Chapter 8.

How many different types of whole grains do you eat regularly? Three? Four? If you're like many people, you're in the habit of eating only a small number of the many different grains that are readily available. Bran flakes for breakfast, wheat bread for sandwiches, and the occasional white rice is not an unusual pattern for the variety challenged. If you fit that pattern, you're missing out. The following list describes some of the many types of whole grains that you can find at most supermarkets and natural foods stores and how they're used.

✔ **Amaranth:** An ancient grain eaten for centuries in Central and South America. Can be cooked and eaten as a side dish or hot cereal or used to make casseroles, baked goods, crackers, pancakes, and pasta. Use it as you would use rice in recipes. Amaranth flour is also available.

✔ **Corn:** Corn kernels are actually the seeds of a cereal grass. Corn is used in cornbread, corn tortillas, and polenta.

✔ **Hulled barley:** Barley comes in two forms: hulled and pearl. Hulled barley is the more natural, more nutritious, unrefined form, having only its outermost husks removed. Not surprisingly, hulled barley is brown in color. It can be used in soups, casseroles, and stews.

✔ **Kamut:** An ancient type of wheat that has been used in Europe for centuries. Used in baked goods.

✔ **Millet:** Tiny, beadlike seeds that come from a cereal grass. Used in baked goods and as a cooked cereal.

✔ **Oats:** Oats come from cereal grasses. They're used as a hot cereal and in baked goods, veggie burger patties, and loaves.

✔ **Quinoa** ("KEEN-wah"): An ancient grain eaten for centuries in Central and South America. Can be cooked and eaten as a side dish or hot cereal or used to make casseroles, salads, a side dish with cooked vegetables, and pilaf. Use it as you would use rice in recipes.

Quinoa has to be processed in order to remove the seed coat, which contains saponin and is toxic. Before you cook quinoa, rinse it several times with water to remove any remaining saponin. The saponin is soapy; you'll know that you've rinsed the quinoa well enough when you no longer see suds.

✔ **Rice:** Rice has been grown for centuries in warm climates, where the seeds are harvested from cereal grasses that grow in wet areas called *rice paddies.* If you're a diehard white rice eater, that's fine. However, brown rice has a slightly better nutritional profile, and many people like its hearty flavor. Several quick-cooking brown rice varieties are on the market, and you can find them at regular supermarkets and natural foods stores.

Modern supermarkets also carry a wide variety of specialty rice varieties, such as aromatic jasmine rice, basmati rice, and arborio rice (a medium-grained rice used to make the Italian dish risotto). Jasmine and basmati rice are available in white or brown form, which is slightly less refined. The various forms of rice are used in casseroles, baked goods, puddings, and side dishes.

Rice is one of the least allergenic and most easily digested foods. That's why rice cereal is one of the first solid foods introduced to infants. People who are allergic to wheat and other grains can use rice flour to make baked goods such as breads and cookies.

✔ **Rye:** A form of cereal grass grown for its seeds, which are ground to make flour. Used in baked goods.

✔ **Spelt:** An ancient type of wheat that's been used in Europe for centuries. Used in baked goods.

✔ **Teff:** One of the oldest cultivated grains in the world. It's used in Ethiopia to make *injera,* a flat, spongy bread that is a staple food there. It's also used in baked goods, soups, and stews.

✔ **Wheat:** Wheat is grown around the world as a cereal grass. It's used in baked goods and pasta.

✔ **Wheat berries:** Whole wheat grains that have had only the outer hull removed. Used in baked goods and as a hot cereal.

Figure 5-1 shows you some of these grains and in which dishes they're used.

Grains often can be substituted for one another in recipes. For example, spelt, kamut, and wheat berries can be used interchangeably in casseroles and vegetable side dishes. You can substitute quinoa for rice in pilaf and casseroles — see Chapter 15 for a recipe.

Processing the facts about processed grains

Processed grains vary in the degree to which they've been processed. Technically, any grain that has been altered beyond the removal of its outer-most hull can be considered processed. However, some processed grains are nothing more than whole grains that have been cracked or broken into smaller pieces, making them quicker to cook. For example, buckwheat (kasha) is toasted and cracked into a coarse, medium, or fine-grained cereal that can be used in a variety of recipes, including baked goods. Other examples of processed grains include

✔ **Bulgur wheat:** Wheat that has been cracked, cooked, rolled, and dried. Used in tabbouleh, casseroles, chili, pilaf, stuffing, and hot cereal.

✔ **Couscous** ("KOOZ kooz"): Cracked, cooked wheat that has been pressed back together into little beads. It's fluffy like steamed rice and can be used in most of the ways that cooked rice and pasta are used. At super-markets and natural foods stores, you can find both white and whole-wheat couscous. Both are quick-cooking and can be eaten plain as a side dish or topped with raw or sautéed vegetables or sauces.

✔ **Cracked wheat:** Wheat that has been broken into pieces. Cracked wheat is used in combination with flour to make breads and other baked goods.

✔ **Pearl barley:** Barley that's processed into white kernels by removing the whole grain's outer layers. It can be used in soups, casseroles, and stews.

✔ **Wheatena:** Finely cracked wheat. Usually eaten as a hot cereal.

A VARIETY OF GRAINS

Figure 5-1:
Grains have
many, many
uses in
vegetarian
cooking.

One of the most widely used processed grain products is flour. Wheat flour —
which is the same thing as all-purpose flour — is the most commonly used
type of flour in baking. (The word *whole* distinguishes whole-wheat flour from
its less nutritious, refined, all-purpose cousin.) But virtually any grain can be
processed into flour and used in much the same way that wheat flour is used.
The flavor of the grain and its gluten content are the primary factors that
determine which type of flour is used in a recipe.

Hot beverages without the caffeine

You may be surprised to know that there are grain-based hot beverages on the market that can substitute for instant coffee. The primary advantage to these beverages is that they're caffeine free. Granted, they don't taste exactly like coffee, but many people find them appealing. Examples include Caffix and Pero.

Gluten is the protein component of a grain. It forms a weblike structure in baked goods that traps carbon dioxide and allows the foods to stretch and rise properly. The amount of gluten in a grain affects the texture of a baked good made from it. Too much can make the food tough.

Several types of flour are commonly used in baking. In addition to all-purpose flour and whole-wheat flour, you can buy bread flour, cake flour, graham flour, pastry flour, and self-rising flour. *Bread flour* is made from wheat and has a higher gluten content than cake flour and pastry flour. That makes sense, because most people want their cakes and pastries to be soft and expect their breads to be a bit tougher. *Graham flour* contains the bran and germ of the wheat. *Self-rising flour* is all-purpose flour that's mixed with baking powder and salt for *leavening* (rising power or "lift").

For simplicity's sake, most of the recipes in this book call for all-purpose flour or a mixture of all-purpose flour and whole-wheat flour. Chapter 17 contains a recipe for a rich, delicious brown bread made with graham flour if you'd like to give this type of flour a try.

Boning up on grain nutrition

Grains vary in their nutrient composition, but all are good sources of a long list of essential nutrients. As the basis of a vegetarian diet, grains supply a hefty helping of protein as well as several vitamins and minerals, including B vitamins and zinc. Whole grains are a good source of fiber, too. Grains are low in total fat, saturated fat, and sodium, and they're cholesterol free.

Table 5-1 tells you about the nutrient contents of four common grains.

Table 5-1		Nutrients in Selected Grains		
Nutrients in ½ Cup (Uncooked)	**Amaranth**	**Barley (Pearl)**	**Quinoa**	**Brown Rice Flour**
Calories	365	332	318	287
Protein	14 g	10 g	11 g	5.5 g
Total fat	6.5 g	2 g	2.5 g	2 g
Saturated fat	1.5	Trace	Trace	Trace
Cholesterol	0	0	0	0
Dietary fiber	15 g	10 g	5 g	4 g
Calcium	149 mg	26 mg	51 mg	8.5 mg
Iron	7.5 mg	2 mg	8 mg	1.5 mg
Zinc	3 mg	1 mg	3 mg	2 mg

TIP

Eating around grain allergies

Some food intolerances and allergies are easy to identify. If one person eats a big bowl of bean soup or cooked cabbage, he or she knows that gas pains will soon follow. For someone else, a glass of milk causes diarrhea. For another, a handful of peanuts or strawberries can result in congestion, wheezing, or hives.

Grain allergies are common; they cause sufferers to experience a range of symptoms, including diarrhea, abdominal pain, gas, aching, fatigue, wheezing, and runny nose. Wheat is frequently cited as the source of the problem, but a component of the gluten in the grain is more likely the culprit.

People who are allergic to wheat may also be sensitive to barley, oats, rye, spelt, kamut, and millet, because these grains share similar protein components. Some people with wheat allergies have experimented with some of these other grains, however, and found that they can tolerate them to some extent. Food allergies are tricky business, and you may need to experiment to figure out what you can and can't eat.

The safest grain for anyone with a grain allergy is rice. Rice flour is available at natural foods stores and can be used in many recipes in place of wheat flour. Natural foods stores also carry bread that has been baked with rice flour (check the store's freezer section). Check bookstores and the Internet for cookbooks and recipes designed for people with wheat and other grain allergies as well.

Cornmeal is another option for people with wheat allergies, although corn is an allergen for some people.

In case you need further convincing that grains are good for you: One cup of cooked bulgur wheat contains nearly 6 grams of protein and 8 grams of dietary fiber, and one cup of cooked buckwheat (kasha) contains nearly 7 grams of protein and 5 grams of dietary fiber. Either one, when combined with a cup of beans, would provide nearly half the protein and all the fiber that most people need in a day.

A Bounty of Beans

My mother, a longtime vegetarian, once set off a round of laughter at the dinner table when she remarked that she'd never met a bean she didn't like. A guest had just observed that the four-bean salad he'd been offered contained only one bean — green beans — that he liked. We found it hard to imagine a person having so limited a liking for beans, considering the large number to choose from and the many differences in flavor, color, and ways in which they can be used.

An almost limitless range of foods can be made from beans, as well as other legumes such as dried peas and lentils. Table 5-2 lists many popular beans and examples of foods that are commonly made with them. Figure 5-2 shows you what some of these beans look like.

Table 5-2	Beans and Their Uses
Bean Type	*Ways to Use Them*
Adzuki beans	Salads, beans and rice
Black beans	Black bean dip; bean burritos, tacos, and nachos; bean soup; beans and rice
Black-eyed peas	Hoppin' John (beans and rice)
Cannellini beans (white kidney beans)	Salads, soups, pasta with beans
Garbanzo beans (chickpeas)	Hummus, falafel, bean salads, chili
Great Northern beans	Baked beans, soups
Kidney beans	Salads, chili, casseroles, stews
Lentils	Soups, curries, stews, lentil loaf, lentils and rice
Lima beans (butter beans)	Succotash, cooked beans

Bean Type	Ways to Use Them
Navy beans	Baked beans, bean soup
Pinto beans	Refried beans for burritos and tacos, chili, stews, bean dip
Red beans	Jambalaya, beans and rice
Soybeans	Casseroles, stews
Split peas	Soups, curries

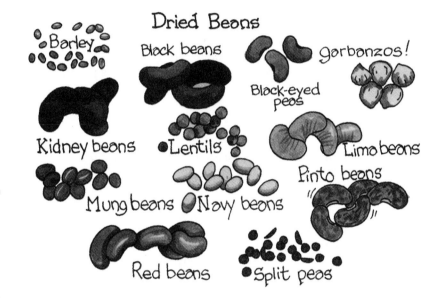

Figure 5-2:
Beans add
protein and
other
nutrients to
meals.

Beans are used in many different cultures to make a wide range of traditional foods and dishes. Examples include

- American navy bean soup
- Chinese stir-fried tofu and vegetables
- Ethiopian pureed lentil and bean dishes
- Greek lentil soup
- Indian curries and *dal* (Indian-style lentil soup)
- Indonesian tempeh
- Italian *pasta e fagioli* (pasta with beans)

✔ Mexican burritos, tacos, and nachos

✔ Middle Eastern hummus and falafel

Falafel are small, round, fried cakes made from mashed garbanzo beans and spices. They're usually served on a plate with accompaniments or in a wrap sandwich made with pita bread.

✔ Spanish black bean soup

Part IV includes many recipes that use a variety of beans.

Many beans can be substituted for others in recipes. For example, you can easily substitute black beans for pinto beans in tacos, burritos, and bean dip; the dark color often makes a striking contrast to other components of the meal, such as chopped tomatoes or greens. For a nice change of pace, use black beans in place of pinto beans in bean dips, tacos, burritos, and nachos. You can even use black beans in place of garbanzo beans to make an alternative version of *hummus* (pronounced "HUM-us"), a spicy Middle Eastern bean spread. (See Chapter 12 for a traditional hummus recipe.)

Forms of beans

Beans come in several forms, all of which are useful in vegetarian cooking. Here's a rundown on the types you'll see at the store:

✔ **Canned beans:** Canned beans are one of the most nutritious and versatile convenience foods you can buy. Conventional supermarket varieties are fine, although natural foods stores carry a wide variety of organic canned beans. Organic vegetables have the added advantage of being free of environmental contaminants.

You may want to rinse canned beans in a colander before using them. Rinsing canned beans removes the excess salt and also rinses away the fibrous outer skins of the beans that otherwise tend to flake off and look unsightly in finished dishes.

If you have leftover canned beans, add them to a can of soup or stir them into pasta sauce to use them up. You can also spoon them on top of a green salad or mash them with a little garlic and add them to a vegetable casserole.

✔ **Dried beans:** Beans were sold dried in bags long before canned beans came on the scene. Some people still prefer to buy and prepare their beans the old-fashioned way. Preparing beans from their dried form is more time-consuming and less convenient, but some people prefer the flavor and texture that result.

Dried beans are often a little firmer than canned beans. In fact, they can be too hard if you don't soak them long enough before cooking them.

Also, dried beans usually do not contain added salt; you have to season them yourself or they're bland. (The exception is bags of beans that are packaged with their own spice mixtures, which are often very salty.) See Chapter 8 for information about cooking dried beans.

✔ **Frozen beans:** You can find a few types of beans, such as lima beans (also called butter beans) and black-eyed peas, in the freezer sections of some supermarkets. They taste the same as fresh and are just as nutritious. As compared to canned beans, frozen beans have less sodium and may be slightly more nutritious — nutrients can leach out of canned beans into the water in which they're canned.

✔ **Bean flakes:** This form of dried beans is convenient and a lot of fun to use. You just shake some into a bowl, add boiling water, stir, and cover, and in five minutes you have a smooth, creamy bean paste that you can use to make nachos, burrito or taco filling, bean dip, or bean soup. The more water you add, the thinner the beans are. The bean flakes themselves will keep in the cupboard for months, just like dried and canned beans. Once you've mixed the bean flakes with water, leftovers will keep in the refrigerator for up to a week or in the freezer for up to six months.

You're more likely to find bean flakes at a natural foods store than in a supermarket. Fantastic Foods and Taste Adventure are two brands that make both dehydrated black bean flakes and pinto bean flakes.

Whether frozen, canned, or dried, beans have approximately the same nutritional value. Convenience and flavor are the major differences.

Singing the praises of bean nutrition

Most people think of beans as being high in protein because they're regularly touted as being a good meat substitute. Beans do contain protein — about 15 grams in a cup, which is approximately the amount of protein in 2 ounces of cheese or meat. Beans are also an excellent source of dietary fiber — something that meat and cheese lack — and are rich in calcium, iron, zinc, and other nutrients.

Making beans and franks vegetarian style

If you simply can't live as a vegetarian without beans with franks, add two sliced meatless vegetarian hotdogs, a handful of minced onion, and a couple tablespoons of molasses to a 15-ounce can of vegetarian baked beans (which don't contain the pork that many brands of canned baked beans do). You can also add a couple tablespoons of ketchup and dark brown sugar if you're so inclined. Stir, pour into a 1½-quart casserole dish, and bake, uncovered, at 350 degrees for 40 minutes or until hot and bubbly.

Table 5-3 gives you the details about the nutritional content of four popular types of beans.

Table 5-3	Nutrients in Four Common Beans			
Nutrients in 1 Cup (Boiled)	Black	Kidney	Garbanzo	Pinto
Calories	227	225	269	234
Protein	15 g	15 g	14.5 g	14 g
Total fat	0.9 g	0.9 g	4.0 g	0.9 g
Saturated fat	0.2 g	0.1 g	0.4 g	0.2 g
Cholesterol	0	0	0	0
Dietary fiber	15 g	13 g	12.5 g	15 g
Calcium	46 mg	50 mg	80 mg	82 mg
Iron	4.0 mg	5 mg	5.0 mg	4.0 mg
Zinc	2.0 mg	2.0 mg	3.0 mg	2.0 mg

Just 1 cup of beans gives you half the fiber you need in a day. Much of that fiber is *soluble fiber,* the kind that helps lower blood cholesterol levels and helps control blood sugar in people with diabetes.

Soy Foods

The idea that all vegetarians eat heaps of tofu may be one of the most prevalent myths about vegetarian diets. Many vegetarians never touch the stuff — although that doesn't mean that *you* shouldn't try it.

Some of the best vegetarian specialty foods are made from soybeans, a type of legume. Soybeans can be used whole (as in tempeh) or soaked (as in soymilk and tofu) or can be processed and used to make a variety of specialty foods, such as veggie burgers, soy hotdogs, and soy cold cuts.

Soy foods are associated with many health benefits. By adding soy foods to your diet, you may reduce your risk of breast, colon, and prostate cancer, and you may lower your blood cholesterol level. Soy foods can lessen your risk for coronary artery disease and osteoporosis and can help you control your blood sugar if you're diabetic.

Foods made from soybeans have been a staple in Asia for centuries, not only because they're healthful but also because they're delicious and versatile. Whether you use them a little or a lot in your own cooking, most vegetarians find that soy foods are practical and convenient ingredients to have on hand.

The various shapes and forms of soy

Soy foods come in dozens of forms. Some of them are used as ingredients in commercially produced food products, and others are sold as ready-to-eat products. Soy foods can take the place of meat, cheese, eggs, milk, and other animal products in recipes. Nutritionally, soy products are far superior to their meat counterparts because they're cholesterol-free, low in saturated fat, and usually lower in sodium. They're also free of *nitrates* and *nitrites,* preservatives that are commonly found in processed meat products and that may cause cancer.

Table 5-4 gives you an idea of types of soy products that are available and the many ways in which they can be used. If you find that you enjoy cooking with soy foods, I list recommended soy resources and soy cookbooks in Chapters 22 through 24.

Table 5-4	Soy Foods and Their Uses
Soy Product	*Description and Uses*
Meat substitutes	Meat alternatives made from soy protein, tofu, and other ingredients. They resemble meat products such as cold cuts, hotdogs, sausage, and bacon in appearance, texture, flavor, and aroma and can be used in the same ways that their meat counterparts are used.
Miso	A rich, salty East Asian condiment used to flavor soups, sauces, entrees, salad dressings, marinades, and other foods. This savory paste is made from soybeans, a grain (usually rice), and salt. It's combined with a mold culture and aged for at least one year. It doesn't have much nutritional value and is high in sodium, so, like most condiments, it should be used sparingly.
Soy cheese	A substitute for dairy cheese that comes in many different forms, such as mozzarella style, jack style, American style, and cream cheese style. It can be used to make sandwiches, pizza, casseroles, and spreads.

(continued)

Table 5-4 *(continued)*

Soy Product	*Description and Uses*
Soy mayonnaise	Several brands of soy-based mayonnaise are available at natural foods stores. They can be used in all the ways that regular mayonnaise is used.
Soymilk	A beverage made from soaked, ground, and strained soybeans. It can be used in all the ways that cow's milk is used, in recipes or as a beverage.
Soy sauce	A rich, salty, dark brown liquid condiment made from fermented soybeans.
Soy yogurt	Made from soymilk; can be used as a substitute for dairy yogurt. It often contains active cultures and is available in a variety of flavors.
Tamari	A type of soy sauce; a byproduct of the production of miso.
Tempeh	A traditional Indonesian soy food. It's made from whole soybeans that have been mixed with a grain and a mold culture, fermented, and pressed into a block or cake. It can be grilled and served as an entree and used as an ingredient in sandwich and burrito fillings, casseroles, chili, and other foods.
Textured soy protein (TSP) or textured vegetable protein (TVP)	A product made from textured soy flour. It's usually sold in chunks or granules, takes on a chewy, meatlike texture when rehydrated, and is used in such foods as vegetarian chili, vegetarian sloppy Joes, veggie burgers, and other meat substitutes.
Tofu	Soybean curd. Tofu is made in a process similar to cheese-making, using soymilk and a coagulant. It's bland tasting and is available in a variety of textures and densities. It can be used in numerous ways: cubed in stir-fry, marinated and baked, as a substitute for eggs and cheese, as a sandwich filling, and as an ingredient in dips, sauces, desserts, cream soups, and many other foods.

Like cheese, eggs, meat, and other high-protein foods, tofu and tempeh can spoil if left unrefrigerated. Don't leave foods made with tofu and tempeh out at room temperature for more than two hours. When you're finished with a meal, cover the leftovers and put them back in the refrigerator as soon as possible.

Why soy?

I've already said that soy foods are versatile and good tasting, and that's reason enough to use them. But the potential health benefits of soy are also worth knowing about. Adding soy foods to your meals makes good sense for several reasons.

Soybeans are nutritious

Whole soybeans are rich in protein, calcium, iron, zinc, B vitamins, and dietary fiber, but products made from soybeans vary in their nutrient content, depending on how much of the original soybean has been processed out. With the exception of such foods as soy sauce and tamari (which really are just salty condiments), foods made from soybeans are nutrient dense and contribute to the healthfulness of your meals.

Table 5-5 gives you the nutritional information for some popular soy foods.

Table 5-5	Nutrient Content of Common Soy Foods			
Nutrient	*Whole Soybeans (1 Cup Cooked, Enriched)*	*Tofu (4 Ounces Firm)*	*Tempeh (4 Ounces)*	*Soymilk (8 Ounces Vanilla, Fortified)*
Calories	298	183	165	150
Protein	29 g	20 g	16 g	6 g
Total fat	15 g	11 g	6 g	3 g
Saturated fat	2 g	2 g	1 g	0 g
Cholesterol	0 mg	0 mg	0 mg	0 mg
Dietary fiber	10 g	0 g	3 g	0 g
Sodium	2 mg	18 mg	5 mg	90 mg
Calcium	175 mg	258 mg	77 mg	200 mg
Iron	9 mg	13 mg	2 mg	1 mg
Zinc	2 mg	2 mg	1.5 mg	0.6 mg

Just ½ cup of tofu or tempeh supplies one-third to one-half of your protein needs for the day, not to mention several other essential vitamins and minerals. One cup of cooked, whole soybeans contains 50 percent more protein on top of *that,* plus about one-third of the recommended daily fiber intake.

Soybeans are phytochemical factories

Chapter 1 talks about phytochemicals, the substances found in plant foods that are thought to protect our health. Soybeans are a rich source of *isoflavones,* a type of phytochemical. Examples of soy isoflavones include *genistein* ("JEN is steen") and *daidzein* ("DAYD zeen"). They and other phytochemicals may be responsible for health benefits such as lowered risk of some forms of cancer.

Soy foods are good substitutes for meat

When you use soy foods in place of high-fat meats and dairy products, you substantially lower your intake of artery-clogging saturated fat and cholesterol. Doing so not only helps you minimize your intake of what you *don't* need, but also helps you work in more of what you *do* need — the vitamins, minerals, and phytochemicals found in foods of plant origin.

Table 5-6 shows you how tofu and tempeh stack up nutritionally against beef and chicken.

Table 5-6	Comparing the Nutrients in 4 Ounces of Tofu, Tempeh, Chicken, and Beef			
Nutrient	*Tofu (Firm)*	*Tempeh*	*Beef Patty (Extra Lean)*	*Chicken Breast (No Skin)*
Calories	183	165	250	142
Protein	20 g	16 g	24.5 g	27 g
Total fat	11 g	6 g	16 g	3 g
Saturated fat	2 g	1 g	6 g	1 g
Cholesterol	0 mg	0 mg	82 mg	73 mg
Dietary fiber	0 g	3 g	0 g	0 g

Soy foods have protein power

As Chapter 1 explains, vegetarians get *enough* protein without getting too much — a common problem for people who eat a typical North American diet. You may be interested to know that the *type* of protein you eat also makes a difference in your health.

Studies show that the protein found in soybeans has advantages over the protein found in meat. In contrast to animal protein, soy protein helps the body retain calcium and may help protect you against *osteoporosis,* the disease that causes weak, brittle bones. Soy protein has been found to lower blood cholesterol levels (although at the time of writing, late-breaking research suggests that it may be the isoflavones that are responsible for soy's cholesterol-lowering effects). Soy protein may help prevent kidney stones and gallstones as well.

Tofu is easy to chew and digest, so it's a good food for anyone who has trouble chewing or needs foods that are easy on the stomach. It's also a good choice as a first high-protein food for babies.

Fruit the Fabulous

Vegetarian cooking takes advantage of the variety found in foods of plant origin, and that variety isn't limited to beans and vegetables! Fruits — especially fresh fruits in season — are central to vegetarian cooking. You can use fruits in all sorts of creative ways, from cold soups and warm cobblers to pies, quick breads, and salads. Many of the recipes in Part IV of this book incorporate fruit.

Wash fresh fruits with a commercial produce wash or use a bit of hand soap and water (and rinse well) to remove pesticide residues, particularly if you're going to eat the skin of the fruit. Pay particular attention to strawberries and grapes, which often contain substantial amounts of pesticide and are frequently not washed well before being eaten. In addition, although you may not eat the peel, be sure to wash the outsides of melons, grapefruit, and other fresh fruits that are normally peeled before setting them on your cutting board to slice them. If you don't, you may contaminate your cutting board surface. You may also drag any bacteria or contaminants that are present on the surface of the fruit into the edible inner portion.

Verily Vegetables

Once you enter the realm of ethnic cuisine, you will undoubtedly find yourself face to face with vegetables that you've heard about but never tried, as well as some that sound and look as though they come from another planet. Many vegetarians know them well. You should, too.

Vegetarian cooking incorporates an unlimited number of different kinds of vegetables, but some of the more popular recipe ingredients include white potatoes, sweet potatoes, onions, bell peppers, tomatoes, greens, broccoli, and many varieties of squash. Ethnic dishes make use of such less common vegetables as bok choy (in stir-fries), kohlrabi (in stews and casseroles), and arugula (steamed or in salads). You can find recipes that incorporate these vegetables throughout Part IV.

Some vegetables are worth extra attention because of their superior nutritional value. Deep yellow and orange vegetables, for instance, are particularly rich in beta carotene, which your body converts into vitamin A. Sweet potatoes, acorn squash, tomatoes, red peppers, and pumpkin are examples. Other vegetables are potent sources of vitamin C. Examples include white potatoes, green bell peppers, broccoli, cauliflower, cabbage, and tomatoes, which are high in both beta carotene *and* vitamin C.

Cruciferous vegetables are another example of "super vegetables." They contain cancer-fighting substances as well as copious amounts of vitamins and minerals. Following are a few popular foods from this group:

- ✔ **Kale, Swiss chard,** and **bok choy** — also known as **Chinese cabbage** — are thick, green, leafy vegetables that are best when cut or torn into strips and steamed, sautéed, or stir-fried. Many vegetarians add a little olive oil and minced garlic to these cooked greens. You can eat them plain or mixed into casseroles, soups, and other dishes.

- ✔ **Kohlrabi** is a white, turnip-shaped vegetable commonly eaten in Eastern Europe. Like other cruciferous vegetables, it's full of potentially cancer-preventing phytochemicals and is very nutritious and flavorful. Kohlrabi is usually diced, boiled, and eaten cooked or added to stews.

- ✔ **Arugula** (pronounced "a ROO guh la") is a leafy green vegetable that's distinctive for its sharp, peppery flavor. It grows wild throughout southern Europe and is native to the Mediterranean. You can mix arugula with other salad greens or let it stand alone. It's eaten raw. You can find a fabulous recipe featuring arugula, Goat Cheese and Arugula Salad with Lavender-Vanilla Vinaigrette, in Chapter 14.

- ✔ **Daikon** (also known as Chinese radish) is a large, white, Asian radish. In contrast to the small red radishes that we know in North America, daikon is usually eaten cooked. However, it's sometimes used raw in salads.

Figure 5-3 shows you what these vegetables look like.

Use a commercial vegetable wash or a little hand soap to gently wash the surfaces of vegetables before eating them. Rinse them well. Doing so helps remove pesticide residues as well as protects you against potential sources of food poisoning from unclean food handlers. Pay particular attention to vegetables with a large amount of surface area, such as broccoli and cauliflower.

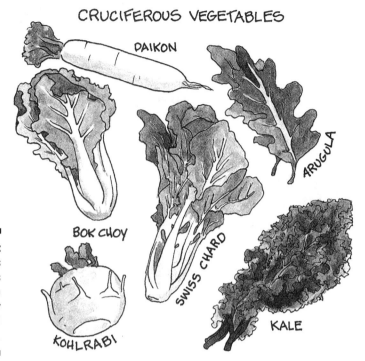

CRUCIFEROUS VEGETABLES

DAIKON

ARUGULA

BOK CHOY

SWISS CHARD

KOHLRABI

KALE

Figure 5-3:
Cruciferous
vegetables
are both
tasty
and good
for you.

Nuts and Seeds

Among the foods at the top of the Vegetarian Food Guide Pyramid (refer to Chapter 4), you find nuts, seeds, and oils. Although these foods should be used sparingly because they contain a good amount of fat and calories, they have many uses in vegetarian recipes. They also happen to be rich in protein and other nutrients, including health-supporting phytochemicals. A handful of nuts or seeds makes a nice addition to a casserole, a salad, or a plate of pasta.

Here are a couple of products made from nuts and seeds that are commonly used in vegetarian cooking:

✔ **Tahini:** *Tahini* is a smooth, rich paste made from sesame seeds. It's a traditional Middle Eastern ingredient in *hummus* — a spread made with garbanzo beans, garlic, lemon juice, and olive oil — and can be used to flavor salad dressings, sauces, dips, and other foods. Tahini is sold in cans or bottles. A layer of sesame oil generally floats at the top of the container and has to be stirred in each time you use the product.

✔ **Nut butters:** If the only nut butter you've ever eaten is peanut butter, get ready to expand your culinary horizons. Cashew butter and almond butter are equally, if not more, nutritious and just as delicious. You can use them in all the same ways that you use peanut butter — for sandwiches, cookies, and in cooking.

In case you get the bright idea to pour the oil off of natural nut butter to cut the fat, a word to the wise: Don't. You'll need a pickax to get the dry nut butter out. Another move to avoid: storing the jar upside down to keep the oil dispersed. Uh-uh. This results in oil oozing out onto the shelf. Just stir in the oil when you're ready to use the nut butter.

Dairy Products and Dairy Substitutes

Substitutes for dairy products are hugely popular with vegetarians. Lactose-intolerant nonvegetarians are also catching on — finally! — to these good-tasting and nutritious products. If you choose to include dairy products in your diet, make sure to choose wisely.

✔ **Milk:** If you use cow's milk, be sure to choose nonfat or ½% milk. Two-thirds of the fat in dairy products is the artery-clogging saturated kind. So if you use milk and other dairy products regularly, anything higher than ½% can quickly add up to too much saturated fat.

✔ **Soymilk:** *Soymilk* is a creamy beverage made from ground, cooked, soaked, and pressed soybeans. You can drink it straight or use it as an ingredient in recipes. You can pour soymilk over your breakfast cereal and dunk your cookies into it, too.

Soymilk is an excellent alternative to cow's milk for people who are lactose intolerant or are allergic to the protein in cow's milk. You can use soymilk in all the ways that you use cow's milk, and in exactly the same proportions. So if a recipe calls for 2 cups of milk, you can use 2 cups of soymilk instead.

Flavor is the major consideration in using soymilk in cooking and baking. Some people keep both plain and vanilla-flavored soymilk on hand. They use plain soymilk in *savory* recipes — those that are highly seasoned rather than sweet — and save the vanilla soymilk for desserts, smoothies, and other recipes in which a sweeter flavor would work.

Soymilk often curdles in coffee. To prevent that problem, pour the soymilk into the cup *before* adding the coffee. Add the coffee slowly, stirring constantly. If the soymilk curdles, adding a bit more soymilk and stirring again after the coffee cools sometimes does the trick. The alternative: Use rice milk. It doesn't whiten the coffee as much, but it also doesn't curdle.

✔ **Rice milk:** Rice milk is made in much the same way as soymilk and can be used in the same ways. It, too, is available in several flavors. Rice milk is whiter in color than soymilk, and some people prefer it for that reason. It's also a bit closer to cow's milk in consistency. On the other hand, rice milk isn't as nutritious as soymilk. Not surprisingly, a compromise is now available — soy and rice milk blends.

✔ **Other milk substitutes:** Almond milk, oat milk, and potato milk are also available. They're not as popular as soymilk and rice milk, but they're additional options, especially for people who are allergic to soybeans. With the exception of potato milk, which is sold as a powder under the brand name Vegelicious, the vast majority of milk substitutes are sold in aseptic cartons that are shelf-stable until opened.

✔ **Cheese:** As with cow's milk, watch out for the saturated fat content of dairy cheese. Nonfat varieties often don't melt well, but if you shred nonfat cheese and mix it into a dish such as a casserole or lasagne, it works better. If you do buy full-fat cheese, use it sparingly as you would a condiment — a sprinkling here and there for flavor.

✔ **Soy cheese:** Soy cheese comes in a variety of flavors and forms, including mozzarella style, American style, and cream cheese style. It can be used in place of regular cheese in most recipes, although, like nonfat dairy cheese, it doesn't melt as well as fattier varieties. It works best if it's used as one of many ingredients in a recipe, rather than standing alone on a cracker.

✔ **Yogurt:** Like other dairy products, you should buy nonfat or reduced-fat yogurt. Any variety can be used in baked goods and other recipes, and plain yogurt can substitute for sour cream in dips. You can even put a dollop on a burrito or a bowl of fruit.

✔ **Soy yogurt:** Soy yogurt is just like its cow's milk counterpart — a creamy, pudding-like food that's a favorite snack and also can be used in baked goods and other recipes. It can substitute for sour cream as a topping and in dips. Soy yogurt is widely available at natural foods stores and comes in a variety of flavors as well as plain. Like regular yogurt, it is available with active cultures.

✔ **Butter:** Yes, butter is nearly all saturated fat. Many people feel that the flavor of butter is unsurpassed and prefer to use butter over margarine on bread and toast and in baking. If you do use butter, use it sparingly for health reasons — and use olive oil instead whenever possible.

It's also worth noting that in terms of your health, butter is a better choice than most brands of margarine. Margarine contains trans fatty acids, which research has shown raise blood cholesterol levels even higher than butter does.

Sweet endings

Vegetarians — and even vegans — have nothing to lose when it comes to enjoying rich, decadent desserts. In fact, some of the most superb cheesecakes, chocolates, chocolate cakes, brownies, pies, cookies, and other sweets contain no animal products whatsoever. Chapter 18 provides some good examples, and you can buy excellent ready-made vegetarian specialty products and ingredients at natural foods stores. Here are some examples:

✔ **Vegan chocolate:** Milk chocolate contains milk and milk byproducts, so it's not vegan. Instead, vegans can use carob chips, which are free of animal products, as well as many brands of semi-sweet and dark chocolate. Read labels to verify that animal ingredients have not been used. Many specialty, gourmet, and natural foods stores carry better-quality chocolates that are less likely than other brands to contain animal ingredients. Two brands available at natural foods stores are Cloud Nine and Tropical Source. A vegan brand found in some specialty shops is Sharffen Berger.

✔ **Frozen nondairy desserts:** Natural foods stores carry several brands of ice cream substitutes that are made from soy or rice milks. They're delicious. Fruit sorbets are another option. You can even find ice cream bars, ice cream sandwiches, and other traditional frozen novelty products made from the same nondairy ingredients.

✔ **Sugar substitutes:** Many vegans don't like to use granulated table sugar because about half of it sold in the U.S. and Canada is made by using a whitening process that utilizes animal bone char. Instead, they prefer to use alternate sweeteners, including raw sugar (also called turbinado sugar), rice syrup, and maple syrup. There are even fruit juice concentrates on the market that can take the place of sugar in recipes. Instructions for making substitutions vary and are usually listed on the label.

Eggs and Egg Substitutes

You may have seen ads touting the fact that eggs are now lower in cholesterol than previously thought. Doesn't matter — eggs are still one of the most concentrated sources of cholesterol that you could possibly eat. If you use eggs in cooking or eat them for breakfast, make them a once-in-a-while food, or use the whites and pitch the yolks.

Mainstream egg substitutes such as Eggbeaters and Scramblers have been around for years. Essentially, they're egg whites with yellow food coloring added. These substitutes have one advantage over plain old egg whites: color. The yellow color of eggs doesn't make much difference if you're baking cupcakes; however, French toast made with egg whites alone is a little, well, white.

Vegetarians have a secret that's far more convenient and even better for you than conventional egg substitutes. It's a commercial powdered product called Ener-G Egg Replacer, a mixture of vegetable starches sold in a 1-pound box that lasts a long, long time. Blend a little in a cup with a couple tablespoons of water, and — voilà! — you have a replacement equal to one egg in most recipes. Just store it in your cupboard. No need to refrigerate; it's there when you need it. It contains no saturated fat or cholesterol, and there's no risk of salmonella poisoning, either!

You can use powdered egg replacer in virtually any recipe that calls for eggs. You can even make meringue with it. The only thing it doesn't do is replace real eggs eaten fried or as an omelet. For that, you can use tofu scrambled with spices (see Chapter 11). I give you some other tricks for replacing eggs in recipes in Chapter 9.

Chapter 6

Stocking Your Vegetarian Pantry

*"I*f I'm a vegetarian, do I have to shop at a health food store?"

"What should I have on hand for quick meals?"

A well-stocked kitchen makes planning and preparing vegetarian meals a pleasure — and you don't have to shop at a health food store if you don't want to (but try it; you might like it!). In this chapter, I discuss where you can go to stock your vegetarian kitchen, as well as what to put on your shopping lists to ensure that you'll have a complete range of ingredients on hand for any occasion.

For the lowdown on common vegetarian ingredients and how they function within vegetarian meals, see Chapter 5.

So Many Stores, So Many Choices: Deciding Where to Go

Vegetarian kitchens are among the most interesting because vegetarian cuisine draws from many different cultures. A kitchen stocked with wholesome ingredients for meatless meals means cupboards, fridge, and freezer full of delicious, varied foods and specialty products from around the world.

Vegetarian foods are also among the highest-quality foods. Vegetarian kitchens are brimming with whole-grain breads and cereals, fresh seasonal fruits and vegetables, beans and peas the colors of the rainbow, and a wide range of herbs, spices, and flavorful condiments.

Shopping for these foods is half the fun of vegetarian cooking. Where you shop is up to you: It depends on what's available in your area, the kinds of foods you like best, and the shopping environment you prefer. The choices are extensive.

- ✔ **Plain-vanilla supermarkets:** The supermarket merits mention because some people think that you have to shop at a natural foods store (see the following entry) to maintain a vegetarian diet. Not so. You can get everything you need to make delicious vegetarian meals at your neighborhood supermarket. Plain-vanilla shopping will do just fine — just steer clear of the meat.

  Regular supermarkets are dramatically increasing the number of natural brands and specialty foods they carry. If your neighborhood supermarket doesn't carry a product that you'd like to be able to buy there, speak with the store manager. He or she may be able to begin stocking it or special-order it for you.

- ✔ **Natural foods stores:** Those odd little health food stores of yesteryear have morphed into colossal natural foods superstores that are modern and bright and rival the most mainstream of supermarkets in the range of products they carry and the level of customer service they provide. Natural foods, which you can read much more about in the section "Shopping Vegetarian Style: Naturally" later in this chapter, represent the fastest-growing segment of the food industry.

  Natural foods stores typically carry a wide range of nonfood products as well. Many are available as vegetarian or vegan choices, and most — if not all — have not been tested on animals.

- ✔ **Food co-ops:** *Food cooperatives* or *co-ops* are similar to natural foods stores but are usually smaller and are managed and run cooperatively by a group of people or members. Food co-ops usually buy natural foods, locally grown seasonal produce, and other foods in volume and pass the price breaks along to their members.

  Food co-ops can be especially useful in small or rural towns where people don't have access to large natural foods stores. The rules vary among co-ops, but members usually have the option of working a certain number of hours per week or month unloading the truck; stocking, bagging, or delivering foods; or running the store in exchange for discounts on purchases.

  To find a food co-op in your area, ask among your friends or check with your local vegetarian society.

✔ **Ethnic food markets:** A trip to an ethnic food mart is an education. You may feel as though you've been spirited halfway across the globe. Ethnic food markets thrive in cities of all sizes where there are pockets of — or even large numbers of — people from other cultures who have dietary traditions that U.S. and Canadian supermarkets don't readily accommodate. In ethnic markets, they can buy the spices, canned goods, dry goods, and fresh produce that they can't find elsewhere. Some foods, such as exotic fresh fruits and vegetables, are flown in from overseas. Some stores stock specific preferred brand names and even specialty household goods.

✔ **Gourmet and specialty shops:** Gourmet and specialty shops carry lots of foods that vegetarians enjoy. You often can find interesting products here that you aren't likely to find at either a natural foods store or a regular supermarket. For example, gourmet shops carry a variety of flavored vegetable oils, salad dressings, richly seasoned soup bases and marinades, syrups, jams, preserves, gourmet mustards, pesto and other pasta sauces, and interesting varieties of crackers, breads, pasta, and baked goods.

✔ **Mail order and online catalogs:** A convenient way to buy vegetarian specialty foods as well as organic produce is to order it online (see Chapter 24 for recommended sites) or through a catalog. The upside is time saved and accessibility to foods that you may not be able to find locally. The downside is that you can't see what you're getting until it arrives.

Starting a kitchen garden

You can buy fresh herbs at the supermarket; in the winter months, doing so may be a necessity. In the growing season, however, nothing compares to raising your own herbs.

Even if you have no backyard to speak of, you can grow your own herbs and a few fresh vegetables on your patio or deck. Some of the quaintest kitchen gardens make use of a small patch of soil or several terra cotta pots set outside the kitchen door or on a windowsill. A small trellis or topiary form can guide vines and upright plants, and you can group several different kinds of herbs and compact vegetable plants in a relatively small space.

Herbs such as basil, dill, parsley, rosemary, and chives and vegetables such as bell peppers,

lettuce, and tomatoes need full to part sun to thrive. Plant seedlings in rich soil augmented with mushroom compost. A layer of hardwood mulch helps keep weeds to a minimum, and those that appear will be easier to pull out.

You'll want to individualize your kitchen garden according to your own preferences, but plants that are easy to grow and have lots of uses in vegetarian cooking include arugula, leaf lettuce, bell peppers, cherry tomatoes, chives, dill, parsley, rosemary, and sweet basil.

For much more information about herb gardening, check out *Herb Gardening For Dummies* (Hungry Minds, Inc.).

Shopping Vegetarian Style: Naturally

Being vegetarian doesn't necessarily mean that you must buy and eat natural foods. If you *are* a vegetarian, though, or if you're just interested in eating healthfully, you probably want to know something about natural foods.

Although the term *natural* has no legal definition, the general understanding is that natural foods are minimally processed and as close to their natural state as possible. They don't contain artificial flavoring, artificial coloring, synthetic preservatives, or other additives that don't occur naturally in foods.

Natural breakfast cereals and cookies, for example, are usually made with whole-grain flours and are sweetened with unrefined sweeteners such as maple syrup, fruit juice, rice syrup, and raw sugar. Boxed mixes are typically made with unrefined ingredients and are lower in sodium than regular boxed mixes. Natural pancake mix, for instance, is usually made with whole-grain flour and is free of artificial preservatives. Many natural products are made with organically grown ingredients, too.

Other reasons to make it natural

Vegetarians can find unique food products and specialty items geared for their needs at natural foods stores, but they're not the only people who benefit from the range of products available. Natural foods stores stock a large number of products specifically designed for people with special needs, such as food allergies. Examples include

- ✔ Wheat-free breads and cereal products for people with allergies to wheat

- ✔ Gluten-free breads and cereal products for people with certain medical conditions or intolerance to *gluten,* the protein component in certain grains

- ✔ Milk alternatives for people who are lactose intolerant

- ✔ Egg substitutes for people who are allergic to egg whites

- ✔ Caffeine-free hot beverages

Natural foods stores also carry a greater number of cholesterol-free and low-sodium specialty products than regular supermarkets do. People who need to monitor their blood cholesterol levels or blood pressure can buy

- ✔ Egg-free mayonnaise

- ✔ Low-sodium condiments, soups, and snack foods

- ✔ Cholesterol-free ice cream substitutes

- ✔ Carob chips that are free of the cocoa butter found in regular chocolate

- ✔ Eggless noodles and baked goods

- ✔ Frozen entrees that are low in sodium and saturated fat and free of cholesterol

Overall, natural foods tend to be more healthful than regular supermarket brands. Even natural "junk foods" tend to be less junky than their conventional counterparts.

What gives natural foods their edge is what *hasn't* been stripped off. When foods undergo processing, something is usually taken away, and other substances are often added. Unfortunately, more often than not, good stuff is taken out and bad stuff is added. Because natural foods are made from ingredients that are as close to their natural state as possible, they undergo minimal processing — the maximum amounts of vitamins, minerals, dietary fiber, and beneficial phytochemicals remain intact. At the same time, natural foods have less of what most people *don't* need: added fats, sugar, and salt.

Some natural cakes and cookies do have redeeming nutritional values. However, many natural sweets and snack foods are low in nutritional value, just like their mainstream counterparts. Even though they're natural, you should limit your consumption of them. Don't let these foods displace more nutrient-dense foods from your diet.

Understanding Organics

Natural isn't necessarily organic, although natural foods are often made with organic ingredients. There's a difference.

The term *organic* usually applies to foods that have been grown without synthetic fertilizers and pesticides, using farming methods that are ecologically sound and Earth friendly. For a food to be certified as organic, the soil it was grown in must have been free of prohibited substances for at least three years.

At natural foods stores, you find a wide range of organically grown fruits and vegetables. Many come from local farmers, especially when the produce is in season. Buying locally supports small farmers in the community and helps ensure the freshness of the products being sold.

Organically grown fruits and vegetables have the same nutritional value as conventionally grown produce, but they're often not as pretty as those grown with chemical fertilizers and pesticides. They may have small blemishes, and they won't be glossy like their non-organic counterparts, which often have a waxy coating added. But don't let the appearance of organically grown foods deter you from buying them. To understand the advantages of organic, you have to go beyond both appearance and vitamin and mineral content.

Organics and the law

For many years, industry standards for organically grown foods have been voluntary, and rules for certifying foods as organic have varied from state to state. Recently, however, the federal government has been working to establish rules for defining foods as organic. Those inside and outside the natural foods industry have hotly debated the terms. Both natural and organic foods have become big business. Longtime advocates of natural and organic foods are battling large, mainstream industries that are trying to break into the market by watering down the criteria for defining a food as organic. Those within the natural foods industry support proposed rules that say the following:

✔ The label *organic* can be carried only by raw produce that is 100 percent organic or processed foods that contain 95 percent organic ingredients. Organic foods must be grown without the use of added hormones, pesticides, or synthetic fertilizers, and the soil must have been free of these prohibited substances for at least three years.

✔ Processed foods that contain 50 to 95 percent organic ingredients may be labeled "made with certain organic ingredients."

✔ If a product contains less than 50 percent organic ingredients, the word *organic* may be used only in the ingredient list on the product label.

The primary advantage to eating organically grown foods is that they are lower in environmental contaminants. By buying organically grown food, you also support farmers who use Earth-friendly farming methods. And finally, organics may taste better because they're not bred for beauty, which often takes away from flavor. The more demand there is for organic foods, the more widespread the practice of organic farming will become.

If you don't have access to a big natural foods store with a good supply of organic produce, your best bet may be to seek out local farmers at roadside stands or at farmers markets where you can buy locally grown fruits and vegetables in season. Ask the farmer about his or her use of synthetic fertilizers and pesticides, and avoid them when possible.

In smaller stores that carry only a limited supply of organically grown produce, the stock may not turn over quickly. What's in the bin may be getting old and close to spoiling. Little blemishes are one thing, but if the fruits or vegetables are shriveling up or rotting, don't buy them.

If you don't have access to organic produce or can't afford it (organic foods typically cost more than conventional ones), cheer up. If you're eating a diet that's high in fruits, vegetables, and whole grains, the fiber content of your diet will help remove environmental contaminants from your body. Roughage binds with contaminants and helps move waste through your system faster, leaving contaminants less time to be in contact with the lining of your intestines.

Knowing Where Animal Ingredients Hide

When you shop for groceries, it's important to read the labels on food packages so you can be sure you're getting what you want. It's also important to know that you're avoiding what you *don't* want.

Sometimes that's easier said than done. Animal products are not always explicitly stated on package labels. Sometimes they're disguised in unfamiliar terms, such as scientific or chemical names. That's less of a problem at natural foods stores, where packages often clearly label vegetarian and vegan products and ingredient lists tend to be short and simple. However, in regular supermarkets and in gourmet and specialty shops, you want to have the information that Table 6-1 provides.

Table 6-1	Hidden Animal Ingredients	
Ingredient	*What It Is*	*How It's Used*
Albumin	The protein component of egg whites	To thicken or add texture to processed foods
Anchovies	Small, silvery fish	In Worcestershire sauce, Caesar salad dressing, as a pizza topping, and in Greek salads
Animal shortening	Butter, suet, lard	In packaged cookies and crackers, refried beans, flour tortillas, and ready-made piecrusts
Carmine (carmine cochineal or carminic acid)	Red coloring made from ground-up insects	In bottled juices, colored pasta, candies, frozen pops, and "natural" cosmetics
Casein (caseinate)	A milk protein	As an additive in dairy products such as cheese, cream cheese, cottage cheese, and sour cream
Gelatin	Protein from the bones, cartilage, tendons, and skin of animals	In marshmallows, yogurt, frosted cereals, gelatin desserts, and Beano
Glucose (dextrose)	Fruits or animal tissues and fluids	In baked goods, soft drinks, candies, and frosting

(continued)

Table 6-1 *(continued)*

Ingredient	What It Is	How It's Used
Glycerides (mono-, di-, and triglycerides)	Glycerol from animal fats or plants	In processed foods, cosmetics, perfumes, lotions, inks, glues, and automobile antifreeze
Isinglass	Gelatin from air bladder of sturgeon and other freshwater fish	To clarify alcoholic beverages and in some jellied desserts
Lactic acid	Acid formed by bacteria acting on the milk sugar lactose	In cheese, yogurt, pickles, olives, sauerkraut, candy, frozen desserts, chewing gum, fruit preserves, and dyeing and textile printing
Lactose (saccharum lactin, D-lactose)	Milk sugar	As a culture medium for souring milk, in processed foods such as baby formulas and sweets, and in medicinal diuretics and laxatives
Lactylic stearate	Salt of stearic acid (see stearic acid)	As a dough conditioner
Lanolin	Waxy fat from sheep's wool	In chewing gum, ointments, cosmetics, and waterproof coatings
Lard	Fat from the abdomens of pigs	Baked goods
Lecithin	Phospholipids from animal tissues, plants, and egg yolks	In cereal, candy, chocolate, baked goods, margarine, vegetable oil sprays, cosmetics, and ink
Lutein	Deep yellow coloring from marigolds or egg yolks	As a commercial food coloring
Natural flavorings	Unspecified; could be from meat or other animal products	Processed and packaged foods
Oleic acid (oleinic acid)	Animal tallow (see tallow), vegetable fats and oils	In synthetic butter, cheese, and spice flavoring for baked goods, candy, ice cream, beverages, condiments, soaps, and cosmetics

Ingredient	What It Is	How It's Used
Pepsin	Enzyme from pigs' stomachs	With rennet to make cheese
Propolis	Resinous cement collected by bees	As a food supplement and in "natural" toothpaste
Stearic acid (octadecenoic acid)	Tallow, other animal fats and oils	In vanilla flavoring, chewing gum, baked goods, beverages, candy, soaps, ointments, candles, cosmetics, and suppository and pill coatings
Suet	Hard white fat around kidneys and loins of animals	In margarine, mincemeat, pastries, and bird feed
Tallow	Solid fat of sheep and cattle separated from the membranous tissues	In waxed paper, margarine, soaps, crayons, candles, rubber, and cosmetics
Vitamin A (vitamin A1, Retinol)	Vitamin obtained from vegetables, egg yolks, or fish liver oil	In vitamin supplements, for the fortification of foods, and in "natural" cosmetics
Vitamin B12	Vitamin produced by microorganisms and found in all animal products; synthetic form (cyanocobalamin or cobalamin on labels) is vegan	In supplements and fortified foods
Vitamin D (D1, D2, D3)	D1 is produced by humans upon exposure to sunlight; D2 (ergocalciferol) is made from plants or yeast; D3 (cholecalciferol) comes from fish liver oils or lanolin	In supplements and fortified foods
Whey	Watery liquid that separates from the solids in cheese-making	In crackers, breads, cakes, and processed foods

Labels sometimes indicate that a product may or may not contain a specific animal ingredient. For example, a label might read that a package of cookies contains "animal and/or vegetable shortening." The manufacturer will use whichever ingredient is available or least expensive at the time of production. You have to take your chances if you buy such a product.

Alternatively, an ingredient listed may have the potential of being derived from a plant or an animal source. Vegans likewise have to take their chances if they choose to buy such products. An example is candy labeled as containing lecithin, which may come from a plant or an animal source.

Shopping Strategically

Grocery shopping isn't rocket science, but if you've never given your approach any thought, this may be the time to do so. Your shopping habits influence what you buy, and what you buy ultimately dictates what you eat. If you're trying to eat more healthfully, or you want to ensure that you have what you need on hand to fix the kinds of meals you want, you may want to think about the manner in which you shop.

Smart shopping habits can help ensure that you have the right foods on hand when you need them, and that you shop efficiently and waste minimal time at the grocery store. With that goal in mind, consider the following advice:

- Shopping at the same store each week can become boring and make you dread the task. Instead, rotate your shopping trips among several supermarkets and natural foods stores. On occasion, stop at a specialty store, a gourmet store, or an ethnic market to introduce fresh ideas and interesting new products to your kitchen.

- In season, make it a habit to go out of your way to shop at a farmers market or a roadside produce stand once in a while.

- Keep a running grocery list on the kitchen counter or refrigerator door. Take the list with you when you go to the store. It'll keep you from forgetting the ketchup, and many people find that focusing on a list helps minimize impulsive purchases of foods they should avoid.

- Spend extra time in the produce section and experiment with new fruits and vegetables often.

- If you have trouble resisting junk foods and sweets — or any other food that you tend to eat in excess — go to the store *after* you've eaten. Going to the store hungry increases the chances that you'll make impulsive purchases and decreases your resistance to temptation.

  On the other hand, if you're in a rut and want to introduce some new foods into your routine, going to the store hungry can make you notice foods that you hadn't noticed before. Going shopping when you're full but not feeling rushed is another possibly less dangerous strategy.

Making Your Lists and Checking Them Twice

How often you go grocery shopping depends in part on how quickly you run through groceries, how much time you have to shop, and how much (or little) you enjoy shopping. It also depends on the kinds of foods you like to keep on hand.

If you plan to stock a good supply of fresh fruits and vegetables, you'll probably need to shop weekly or every ten days, even if it's just a mini-stop to pick up fresh produce. You can purchase foods that keep in the freezer or cupboard much less often — every other week or monthly.

Also keep the following points in mind:

✔ The lists that follow contain suggestions of what you may want to keep on hand for a well-stocked vegetarian kitchen. Adapt them to suit your own tastes and preferences.

✔ If you'd like, photocopy these lists and keep a copy taped to your refrigerator door. Mark off items as you need them, and then take the lists to the store when you shop.

✔ The lists include vegan options where dairy products or eggs are listed. Additional vegan products, such as frozen entrees and baked goods, are available throughout the store, but you'll have to read product labels to identify them.

It's time to go shopping!

Weekly

The foods on this list have to be purchased frequently — every week or so — because they are perishable and will not keep long without spoiling.

Fresh fruit (especially locally grown, in season)

❑ Apples

❑ Apricots

❑ Bananas

❑ Blueberries

❑ Cantaloupe

❑ Cranberries

❑ Grapefruit

❑ Grapes

❑ Guavas

❑ Honeydew

❑ Kiwi

❑ Lemons

❑ Limes

❑ Mangoes

❑ Nectarines

❑ Oranges

❑ Peaches

❑ Pears

❑ Pineapples

❑ Plums

❑ Strawberries

❑ Watermelon

Prepared fresh fruit

❑ Fresh juices: orange, grapefruit, apple cider

❑ Chilled, bottled mango or papaya slices, pineapple chunks, fruit salad

❑ Packaged cut fruits

Fresh vegetables (especially locally grown, in season)

❑ Asparagus

❑ Beets

❑ Bell peppers

❑ Bok choy

❑ Broccoli

❑ Brussels sprouts

❑ Cabbage

❑ Carrots

❑ Celery

❑ Collard greens

❑ Corn

❑ Cucumbers

❑ Kale

❑ Leeks

❑ Lettuce and other greens

❑ Mung bean sprouts

❑ Onions

❑ Potatoes

❑ Tomatoes

Prepared fresh vegetables

❑ Fresh vegetable juices: carrot, carrot/spinach, beet

❑ Packaged cut vegetables and mixed greens

❑ Fresh herbs: basil, dill, mint, rosemary, sage, thyme, others

Fresh deli and refrigerated items

❑ Eggs (use whites only, or use commercial vegetarian egg replacer)

❑ Fresh salad dressings (olive oil–based or fat-free)

❑ Fresh marinara sauce

❑ Fresh pasta (made without eggs for vegans and lacto vegetarians)

❑ Fresh pizza (with tomato sauce and veggie toppings; try cheeseless)

❑ Fresh salsa

❑ Hummus

❑ Nonfat milk or soymilk

❑ Nonfat yogurt or soy yogurt

❑ Nonfat cheese or soy cheese

❑ Three-bean salad

❑ Tofu

Breads (especially whole-grain)

❑ Breadsticks

❑ Bagels (any kind except egg for vegans and lacto vegetarians)

❑ English muffins

❑ French bread

❑ German whole-grain bread

❑ Hard rolls

❑ Hoagie rolls

❑ Italian bread

❑ Kaiser rolls

❑ Low-fat whole-grain muffins

❑ Oat bread

❑ Onion bread

❑ Pita pockets

❑ Pumpernickel bread

❑ Rye bread

❑ Sourdough bread

❑ Tortillas (corn or flour, not fried, especially whole-wheat)

❑ Whole-wheat (especially whole-grain) bread

❑ Whole-wheat pizza crust

Dairy products (for non-vegans)

❑ Milk (nonfat)

❑ Eggs (free-range)

❑ Cheese (Parmesan, cottage, reduced-fat ricotta, American, others)

Also need: _____

_____

Monthly

You can shop for these foods less often because they'll keep in your refrigerator, freezer, or cupboard for months.

Canned and jar goods

❑ Applesauce

❑ Artichoke hearts

❑ Beans (canned or dried): vegetarian baked beans, garbanzo beans, black beans, pinto beans, kidney beans, navy beans, split peas, vegetarian refried beans, lentils, black-eyed peas, bean salad

❏ Fruits: apricots, pineapple, peaches, pears, mandarin oranges, grapefruit, cranberry sauce (without gelatin), fruit cocktail

❏ Soups: lentil, vegetarian, vegetarian split pea, tomato

❏ Spaghetti sauce

❏ Tomato sauce and paste

❏ Vegetables: green beans, peas, carrots, asparagus, corn, tomatoes

Snacks and treats

❏ Bean dip

❏ Canned pumpkin and fruit pie fillings

❏ Flat breads (including matzo) and breadsticks

❏ Fruit toppings: prune, cherry, apricot

❏ Popcorn (bag kernels or microwave)

❏ Granola bars

❏ Rice cakes and popcorn cakes

❏ Tapioca and flan

❏ Tortilla chips

❏ Whole-grain cookies

❏ Whole-grain crackers

❏ Whole-grain toaster pastries

Herbs and spices

❏ Basil

❏ Bay leaves

❏ Cinnamon

❏ Cumin

❏ Curry powder

❏ Dill

❏ Vegetable bouillon

❏ Garlic

❏ Ginger

❏ Paprika

❏ Pepper

Beverages

❑ Bottled water

❑ Club soda

❑ Fruit and vegetable juices and blends

❑ Herbal teas

❑ Plain or flavored mineral waters

❑ Plain or flavored seltzer waters

❑ Sparkling cider, sparkling grape juice

Dry items

❑ Couscous (whole-grain if available)

❑ Dried bean flakes

❑ Dry cereals (whole-grain): raisin bran, shredded wheat, bran flakes, others

❑ Grains: barley, millet, bulgur wheat, kasha, amaranth, spelt, teff, quinoa

❑ Hot cereals (whole-grain): oatmeal, whole wheat, mixed-grain

❑ Pasta (made without egg yolks for vegans and lacto vegetarians)

❑ Rice: basmati, jasmine, brown, wild, Arborio

❑ Soup mixes or cups

❑ Soymilk (aseptically packaged)

❑ Textured vegetable protein (TVP)

❑ Tofu (aseptically packaged)

❑ Vegetable oil spray

❑ Vegetarian egg replacer

❑ Whole-grain bread, pancake mixes, and all-purpose mixes

❑ Whole-wheat flour, other flours

Condiments

❑ BBQ sauce

❑ Chutney

❑ Fruit preserves, jams, jellies

❑ Hoisin sauce

❑ Honey (for non-vegans)

❑ Horseradish mustard

❑ Ketchup

❑ Marinades

❑ Mayonnaise (fat-free or soy)

❑ Mustard

❑ Natural butter-flavored sprinkles

❑ Pickles and pickle relish

❑ Salad dressings (fat-free)

❑ Salsa

❑ Stir-fry sauce

❑ Sun-dried tomatoes

❑ Sweet-and-sour sauce

❑ Syrups, molasses

❑ Vinegar: balsamic, herbed, fruited, malt, rice

Dried fruits

❑ Apples

❑ Apricots

❑ Blueberries

❑ Cherries

❑ Currants

❑ Dates

❑ Figs

❑ Prunes

❑ Raisins

Freezer staples

❑ Frozen bagels (eggless for vegans and lacto vegetarians)

❑ Frozen waffles and pancakes

❑ Frozen pasta (without eggs for vegans and lacto vegetarians)

Frozen juices

- ❑ Apple
- ❑ Cranberry-raspberry
- ❑ Orange
- ❑ Grape
- ❑ Grapefruit
- ❑ Lemonade
- ❑ Limeade
- ❑ Pineapple-orange
- ❑ Tangerine-orange

Frozen meat substitutes

- ❑ Meatless burger crumbles
- ❑ Meatless "bacon"
- ❑ Meatless "sausage" links and patties
- ❑ Vegetarian burger patties
- ❑ Vegetarian hotdogs

Frozen novelties

- ❑ Frozen egg substitute (for lacto-ovo vegetarians; vegans and lacto vegetarians can use commercial vegetarian egg replacer)
- ❑ Frozen juice bars or Popsicles
- ❑ Frozen yogurt
- ❑ Sorbet and yogurt bars (for non-vegans)
- ❑ Tofu or rice-based ice cream

Frozen fruits

- ❑ Blueberries
- ❑ Cherries
- ❑ Mixed fruit
- ❑ Peaches
- ❑ Pineapple
- ❑ Raspberries
- ❑ Strawberries

Frozen vegetables

❑ Broccoli

❑ Carrots

❑ Cauliflower

❑ Corn

❑ Green beans

❑ Lima beans

❑ Mixed vegetables

❑ Peas

❑ Spinach

❑ Stir-fry mixes

Also need: _____

_____

Part III

Tools and Techniques

The 5th Wave   By Rich Tennant

"I'm pretty sure it's pizza dough that gets tossed, not pasta dough."

In this part . . .

Certain cooking skills are basic to every cuisine. A good chef is likely to be able to work magic whether the dish contains meat, cheese, eggs, milk, butter, or no animal products whatsoever.

If you have a limited range of cooking skills, what you do best is probably the thing you've had the most experience doing. It's not surprising, then, that for anyone who's new to vegetarian cuisine, working with tofu, tempeh, vegetarian egg replacer, and other common vegetarian ingredients may require a bit of practice.

The chapters in this part familiarize you with the tools you need to prepare vegetarian dishes and the ins and outs of cooking with several common vegetarian ingredients. You also get a primer on modifying recipes to replace animal products such as milk and eggs if you want to do so.

Chapter 7

Tools of the Trade

* *

In This Chapter

▶ Choosing pots, pans, and baking supplies

▶ Having other essentials on hand

▶ Collecting fun little extras that can make your meals more appealing to the eye

* *

*T*o some extent, the kitchen equipment you choose to have on hand is a reflection of your lifestyle and preferences. Some people go all their lives with little more than a couple of pots and a wooden spoon, while others have every kitchen gizmo under the sun. For example, not everyone needs a large countertop mixer. A handheld electric mixer might do, or you may even prefer an old-fashioned hand beater.

This chapter presents a balanced, realistic view of what you need to equip a basic vegetarian kitchen. Use the lists in this chapter to inventory your own supplies — see what's missing and decide whether you'd like to add those pieces to your own collection. If you're the type who likes to supplement the basics with some of those fun little extras that are available, I also talk about which gizmos you might find helpful to have.

Paying full price for pots, pans, baking supplies, appliances, and other kitchen tools is virtually never necessary. Unless you want a very high-end brand of pans or bakeware that rarely, if ever, goes on sale, high-quality products are available at many discount and outlet stores. Keep your eyes open for special sales and promotions, too.

Pots and Pans

Most vegetarian cooks need several pots and pans in assorted sizes. A non-stick skillet is also useful because it's easy to clean and enables you to cook with less fat, which may be one of your goals as a vegetarian.

The following are the pots and pans you want to have on hand:

- ✔ 1-quart saucepan
- ✔ 2-quart saucepan
- ✔ 3-quart saucepan
- ✔ 9-inch skillet
- ✔ 4½-quart pot

Do you cook for crowds? If so, you may want to consider having one or two jumbo-sized pots for cooking large batches of soup, stew, chili, or marinara sauce — a 6-quart pot or larger — and possibly a larger skillet as well.

In addition, some specialty pots and pans may be useful, depending on the type of cooking you like to do:

- ✔ Small, deep saucepans with pour spouts can be convenient for heating sauces, melting chocolate or butter, and warming maple syrup on the stovetop.
- ✔ Some people like to use a steamer or double boiler insert for cooking easy-to-scorch foods over a pot of boiling water and for steaming vegetables and other foods.

Baking Pans, Sheets, Molds, and Other Supplies

Most cooks need a few bare-minimum baking essentials:

- ✔ Two cookie sheets
- ✔ A muffin tin (for baking cupcakes and muffins)
- ✔ An 8-inch square baking pan
- ✔ A 9-x-13-inch baking pan
- ✔ At least one loaf pan
- ✔ One or two pie tins
- ✔ Two round cake pans
- ✔ A set of two or three stainless steel mixing bowls
- ✔ At least one set of measuring spoons

✔ At least one set of dry measuring cups

✔ A liquid measuring cup

Even if you don't bake cookies or cakes, you'll find lots of uses for these items.

Whether you choose nonstick, stainless steel, glass, or other types of bakeware is up to you. Each has advantages and disadvantages, so it's a matter of personal preference. Note that stainless steel mixing bowls are easy to keep clean and don't break and chip like glass, and that inexpensive aluminum bakeware tends to rust.

Depending on the types of dishes you like to prepare, you may also want to have

✔ A variety of cookie cutters

✔ A deep, straight-sided ring pan or angel food pan (for making sponge cakes or angel food cakes and other ring cakes)

✔ A Bundt pan (also for making ring-style molded cakes — see Figure 7-1)

Figure 7-1:
You use a Bundt pan to make ring-style molded cakes.

BUNDT PAN

✔ Some cookie molds

✔ A variety of casserole dishes and ramekins (for baking custards, soufflés, and other dishes)

✔ A soufflé dish

Appliances

Only you know which appliances are truly time-savers and work-relievers for you. Preferences for appliances are a personal thing. For example, I know people who don't use a dishwasher because they rarely dirty more than a few dishes each day and prefer to wash them in the sink.

Blending your way to bliss

You can make the creamiest, richest ice cream imaginable with nothing but frozen bananas and a heavy-duty blender (such as a Vita Mix) or juicer (such as Champion). Just whirl frozen chunks of banana in the blender or run them through the juicer. Out comes banana soft-serve ice cream that rivals premium brands in richness and texture. You can also add strawberries, blueberries, other bits of frozen fruit — even chocolate or carob chips — for a change of pace.

That said, here's a list of the appliances that many people find particularly helpful. They may or may not be appropriate for you.

- ✔ A blender
- ✔ A coffee grinder

    You can also buy a second grinder and reserve it for spices and nuts. Keep the coffee out of this one, or the flavors will blend in unpleasant ways.

- ✔ A countertop mixer or electric hand mixer
- ✔ An electric can opener
- ✔ An electric griddle
- ✔ An electric steamer
- ✔ A food processor
- ✔ A heavy-duty juicer or blender
- ✔ A microwave oven
- ✔ A mini food processor (for chopping nuts, spices, and herbs and small quantities of foods)
- ✔ A pressure cooker (for cooking dried beans and grains rapidly — see Chapter 8)
- ✔ A rice cooker
- ✔ A slow cooker
- ✔ A waffle iron
- ✔ A wide-slot toaster

Utensils

A fork can sometimes double as a whisk, and you can use a knife as a spatula in a pinch, but most people find that having a range of specialty utensils really does make life in the kitchen easier. You may not need every one of these utensils, but many people find the following to be particularly useful:

- A hand-held potato masher
- A large slotted spoon
- One or two stainless steel whisks
- A pasta fork (wooden with prongs)
- A pastry blender
- A pastry brush
- A pizza cutter
- A small strainer (like a small colander with a handle)
- A colander (for draining pasta and washed fruits and vegetables)
- A soup ladle
- A stainless steel spatula (for turning veggie burger patties or removing cookies from a cookie sheet)
- Two or three rubber or silicon spatulas
- Wooden spoons of various shapes and sizes

Knives

There are really just a few basic knives that most vegetarians find especially useful to have on hand. You can buy other, fancy specialty knives, and many are quite nice. However, at the least, you should have the following:

- A 6-inch serrated knife for cutting tomatoes, fruit, and so on
- A paring knife
- An 8- to 10-inch serrated knife for cutting breads
- An 8- to 10-inch chef's knife for cutting vegetables

Figure 7-2 shows you what these knives look like.

Figure 7-2:
The basic
knives that
you need for
vegetarian
cooking.

chef's knife

paring knife

serrated knife

Dishes

Everyday dishes are purely a matter of personal preference and what your budget will allow. Some people like to have two or three sets so that they can change off depending on the season or their moods. Some people like to mix dishes from one set with another, and some people prefer not to have sets at all but to collect interesting odd pieces.

If inexpensive utilitarian dishes are all you require, that's fine. But if you really enjoy setting a pretty table and collecting fine dishes, you might enjoy having a range of types, such as pottery, fine china, and antique pieces.

No matter what type of dishes you have, you need a few serving bowls. Having at least one pitcher and a serving platter is also convenient. A soup tureen can be a fun item to own, and even a vegetarian can find a use for a gravy boat: Use it to serve hot maple syrup, fruit toppings, and sauces and gravies for savory entrees and desserts. (A small pitcher can serve the same purpose.)

Bone china is a type of fine, translucent white china that's traditionally made of bone ash from animals. It may also be made with calcium phosphate. Check the label on the underside of your fine dishes to see whether they are bone china. If you have vegan guests over for dinner, they probably won't want to eat from them. And if you've become a vegan yourself, you may want to think about whether you want to keep them.

Extras

If you're strictly the eat-to-survive type and you don't particularly enjoy spending a lot of time making your meals look pretty, you can skip this section. On the other hand, if you appreciate attractively set tables and foods presented with flair, this section is for you.

Appearances do count, and a table that's set attractively and food that's presented beautifully can add immeasurably to the enjoyment of a meal. If you're introducing vegetarian foods to someone who is skeptical (at best) about a meal without meat, why not dazzle your guest with food that looks as good as it tastes?

Although not essential to a well-equipped vegetarian kitchen, lots of extras can make a meal look special and enhance your enjoyment of it. Here are some of my favorites:

- ✔ Special serving dishes, such as a two-tiered plate or an interesting pottery bowl

- ✔ Paper doilies in different shapes, sizes, and colors for lining plates of cookies or desserts

- ✔ Interesting chargers to place under dinner plates

   A *charger* looks like an extra-large dinner plate. It's used as a liner to be placed underneath the dinner plate. Chargers can be festive in silver or gold, or they may be made of painted wood, wicker, or other materials.

- ✔ Decorative trivets to place under hot dishes

- ✔ Decorative spreaders and condiment forks

- ✔ Placemats made of rich fabrics, straw or bamboo, or oilcloth

- ✔ Cloth napkins

- ✔ Tablecloths or table runners made of interesting and beautiful fabrics

Other little extras that you may also want to consider include tools and appliances that, although not absolutely necessary, can be a lot of fun to use. Here are some examples:

- ✔ **A bread machine:** Fill your house with the aroma of freshly baked bread. Experiment with various mixes available in supermarkets, or use a cookbook designed for use with bread machines to make your own breads from scratch. (*Bread Machines For Dummies,* also published by Hungry Minds, Inc., is a great reference for bread machine users and includes a host of yummy recipes.)

- ✔ **A pizza stone and a flat wooden paddle:** Cooking on a pizza stone helps produce an evenly baked, golden crust. Removing the pizza by using the big, flat paddle helps a saucy pizza stay intact and prevents mishaps in transferring the pizza to a plate.

Chapter 8

Vegetarian Cooking Basics

. . . .

In This Chapter

▶ Working with various vegetarian ingredients

▶ Mastering basic cooking techniques

▶ Maintaining control of your kitchen

▶ Getting a jump on the week ahead

. . . .

*M*ost of the recipes in this book require only basic cooking skills — no need for talent on the level of Julia Child or Wolfgang Puck. A few of the recipes are somewhat more advanced and include several more steps than the others, but you can tackle those recipes if you are confident and have intermediate cooking skills. If you don't, you can save them for a time when you've acquired a bit more experience.

The purpose of this chapter is to provide you with instructions and tips to pave the way if you have limited cooking experience. Even if you're a pro, you may want to scan this material on the chance that you'll pick up a stray tidbit of information that may prove useful. Few of us are so experienced that we can't learn a thing or two from someone else.

Preparing Ingredients: Essential Tips

In this section, I talk about how to prepare dried beans, peas, grains, and soy products — a few of the ingredients that figure prominently in many vegetarian recipes. I also give you some additional tips for working with common vegetarian ingredients.

Cooking beans

Canned beans and bean flakes are by far the most convenient forms of beans because they take so little time to prepare. Canned beans really only need to be reheated to serving temperature, which can take as little as ten minutes on the stovetop or one minute in a microwave oven. Rehydrating bean flakes with hot water takes only five minutes.

Split peas and lentils also take a relatively short time to cook and don't necessarily have to be soaked first, as dried beans do. Cooking dried beans takes more preparation and time, but many people find that the texture, flavor, and lack of added sodium are worth the effort.

On the stovetop

Follow these steps (illustrated in Figure 8-1) to cook dried beans on the stovetop:

1. **Place the dried beans in a colander, rinse them well with cold water, and pick out anything that doesn't belong.**

   Dried beans are about as close to their natural state as any food you can find in the supermarket. For that reason, they're sometimes bagged with tiny pebbles and bits of sticks or dirt that need to be picked out or rinsed away before you cook the beans. Run your fingers over and through the beans as you rinse.

2. **Drain the clean beans and dump them into a pot.**

   You will add 3 cups of water for every 1 cup of dried beans, so use a pot that's large enough for the amount of beans and water you'll be using.

3. **Add cold water to the pot.**

   For every cup of dried beans, add 3 cups of water.

4. **(Optional) Bring the pot of beans and water to a rolling boil. Boil for a minute or two and then remove the pot from the heat and cover it with a tight-fitting lid.**

   This step is recommended because it helps soften the beans faster, reducing the soaking time.

   In cooking terms, *rolling boil* means that water is bubbling up rapidly and breaking the surface. The bubbles seem to roll on the surface. A rolling boil is also called a *rapid boil*.

5. **Let the beans soak.**

   The longer you soak them, the softer they'll become. If you let them set too long, however, you run the risk of having them spoil and get moldy. At a minimum, let the beans set for two hours. At most, let them set for several hours or overnight.

   If you plan to soak beans for longer than two hours, put the pot in the refrigerator to retard the growth of mold.

   Note that black-eyed peas, lentils, and split peas do not need to be soaked because they soften so quickly when cooked.

COOKING DRIED BEANS

1. PLACE BEANS IN A COLANDER. RINSE WELL WITH COLD WATER.
HEY!
PICK OUT ANYTHING THAT DOESN'T BELONG!

2. AFTER YOU CLEAN AND DRAIN THE BEANS, DUMP THEM INTO A POT.

3. ADD WATER TO THE POT (3 CUPS OF WATER TO 1 CUP OF BEANS).
1CUP

4. BRING BEANS TO A ROLLING BOIL. BOIL FOR A MINUTE OR 2.
REMOVE THE POT FROM HEAT. COVER WITH A TIGHT FITTING LID.

5. SOAK THE BEANS.
FOR AT LEAST 2 HOURS. AT MOST FOR SEVERAL HOURS OR OVERNIGHT.

6. RINSE AND DRAIN ONCE MORE.
HERE WE GO AGAIN
☆ OPTIONAL

7. COOK THE BEANS! ON THE STOVETOP....
....BRING TO A GENTLE BOIL AND COOK UNTIL TENDER.

☆ TIP:
IF YOU KEEP A LID ON THE POT, LEAVE IT SLIGHTLY ASKEW SO THE STEAM CAN ESCAPE, SO THE WATER DOESN'T BOIL OVER THE TOP.

OR YOU CAN COOK THE BEANS IN A PRESSURE COOKER.

8. WHEN THE BEANS ARE FINISHED COOKING, REMOVE FROM HEAT AND DRAIN.

Figure 8-1:
Although canned beans are fine, you may want to try cooking dried beans so that you can control the amount of sodium and achieve better flavor and texture.

6. (Optional) Rinse and drain the beans once more.

After the beans have finished soaking, many people like to rinse them in a colander once more before cooking them. If you give them a second rinse, you may find that the beans cause less flatulence when you eat them. The downside to rinsing a second time is that some nutrients from the beans leach into the soaking water. If you skip the second rinse and instead cook the beans in the water in which they soaked, you may save some nutrients.

After rinsing the beans a second time, drain them and then add them back to the pot. Fill the pot again with fresh, cold water (3 cups of water per cup of dried beans).

7. **Cook the beans.**

Bring the pot of beans to a gentle boil and let them cook until they're tender. (See Table 8-1 for the cooking times for various types of beans.) If you keep a lid on the pot, leave it askew a bit so that steam can escape. Doing so helps prevent the water from boiling over the top of the pot.

A *gentle boil* is less frantic than a rolling boil. When water is gently boiling, bubbles break the surface but are smaller than the bubbles you see in a rolling boil.

Beans vary greatly in the amount of time they need to cook. Lentils and split peas don't need to be soaked and take only 30 minutes or so to cook. Dried kidney beans or pinto beans may take an hour and a half to cook, while garbanzo beans may take up to two hours. The cooking time also depends on how soft you want the beans to be. If you're going to mash or puree the beans for dips, spreads, or soup, you want them to be softer. If you plan to use them in chili or on a salad, you may want them to be firmer. From time to time, lift a bean out of the pot with a spoon, let it cool for a moment, and then bite it to see how soft it is.

Beans that are old and have been stored for a year or more may take longer to cook than beans that are fresher.

8. **After the beans have finished cooking, remove them from the heat and drain them.**

Table 8-1	Timetable for Cooking Soaked Beans	
Bean (1 Cup Dry, or about ½ Pound)	**Approximate Cooking Time (Hours)***	**Yield (Cups)**
Adzuki beans	1–1½	2
Black beans	1½	2
Black-eyed peas	1	2
Cannellini beans	1–1½	2
Garbanzo beans (chickpeas)	2–3	3
Great Northern beans	1½–2	2
Kidney beans	1½–2	2
Lima beans (butter beans)	1–1½	1½
Navy beans	1½–2	2
Pinto beans	2–2½	2

Bean (1 Cup Dry, or about ½ Pound)	Approximate Cooking Time (Hours)*	Yield (Cups)
Red beans	1½–2	2
Soybeans	2–3	2

* Cooking time depends on degree of softness desired

In a pressure cooker

Soaking and cooking dried beans is the tried-and-true method. Many people prefer the flavor of beans cooked the old-fashioned way, and they like that no salt has been added, as it is to canned beans. Still, a much faster way to cook beans may appeal to purists: pressure-cooking.

Advocates of pressure cookers swear by them. But many of us are tempted to beat a path in the opposite direction when the words *pressure cooker* are uttered. That's because we have vivid memories of the old jiggle-top pressure cookers that our mothers used. Those old pressure cookers were temperamental and always seemed to be threatening to blow the roof off the house. Nowadays, special safety valves make pressure cookers easy to use.

Pressure cookers come in various sizes; a 6- to 8-quart size is practical for most people. Pressure cookers may seem large, but when you use one, you don't fill it all the way up with food. Instead, you fill it only one-half to three-quarters of the way full, depending on what you're cooking. The remaining space is needed for the steam that builds up and increases the temperature in the pot. Figure 8-2 shows a couple of different types of pressure cookers.

Figure 8-2:
Pressure
cookers
make
cooking
dried beans
much faster.

If you're the adventurous type and would like to give the new-generation pressure cookers a try, the rewards are high. Pressure cookers are easy to learn to use, and they cut way down on the time it takes to prepare dried beans and other legumes, as well as whole grains. Soaked beans take only minutes to cook in a pressure cooker, and even unsoaked beans cook in a fraction of the time it takes to cook soaked beans on the stovetop.

Follow these steps to cook dried beans in a pressure cooker:

1. **Put the beans in the pressure cooker and add the appropriate amount of water.**

   Use about 3 cups water for every cup of soaked beans or 4 cups water for every cup of unsoaked beans (or follow the instructions that come with your pressure cooker).

   If you're using an old jiggle-top pressure cooker (the kind with a removable pressure regulator), add 1 tablespoon of oil for each cup of beans to help reduce foaming.

2. **Lock the lid in place.**

   Put the lid on the pot and lock it. Pressure cookers are designed to lock securely into place and create an airtight seal that permits the pressure inside to rise.

3. **Heat it up.**

   Turn the heat on the stove to high and bring the pressure cooker up to high pressure. Cook at high pressure for the necessary length of time, depending on the type and amount of beans you're cooking (see Table 8-2).

4. **Cool it off.**

   After the beans have finished cooking, release the pressure by removing the pot from the stove and letting it sit until the pressure comes down naturally. A quicker option is to set the pot in the sink and run cold water over it until the pressure drops.

Table 8-2	Timetable for Pressure-Cooking Beans		
Bean (1 Cup Dry, or about ½ Pound)	**Cooking Time (Minutes) Under High Pressure***		**Yield (Cups)**
	Soaked Beans	**Unsoaked Beans**	
Adzuki beans	5–9	14–20	2½
Black beans	5–9	18–25	2
Black-eyed peas	Not soaked	10–11	2¼
Cannellini beans	9–12	22–25	2
Garbanzo beans (chickpeas)	13–18	30–40	2½
Great Northern beans	8–12	25–30	2¼

Bean (1 Cup Dry, or about ½ Pound)	Cooking Time (Minutes) Under High Pressure*		Yield (Cups)
	Soaked Beans	Unsoaked Beans	
Kidney beans	10–12	20–25	2
Lentils	Not soaked	4–6	2
Lima beans (butter beans)	4–7	12–16	2
Navy beans	6–8	16–25	2
Pinto beans	4–6	22–25	2¼
Red beans	4–6	22–25	2¼
Soybeans (beige)	9–12	28–35	2¼
Split peas	Not soaked	6–10	2

* Assumes that pressure is released quickly by using cold water
Source: Great Vegetarian Cooking Under Pressure, *by Lorna Sass*

An excellent guide to preparing quick vegetarian meals by using a pressure cooker is *Great Vegetarian Cooking Under Pressure,* by Lorna Sass.

Cooking grains

As Chapter 4 explains, grains are one of the foundation foods of vegetarian cooking. Chapter 5 tells you about the many, many types of grains that you can work into your meals — make it a point to go beyond plain old white quick-cooking rice!

Here are a few points to consider when using grains in vegetarian cooking:

✔ **Cooking times vary — often considerably.** Quick-cooking rice has its fans, but many people feel that they sacrifice flavor when they buy *parboiled grains* — grains that have been boiled for a few minutes and then dehydrated prior to packaging. Parboiled grains take less time to rehydrate and cook than grains that have not been cooked previously.

Most processed grains, such as couscous, regular white rice, bulgur wheat, kasha, and pearl barley, cook relatively quickly as compared to their whole or intact counterparts. That's because the hardest outer layers of the grain have been removed, and there may be more surface area due to the grain being cracked (as with bulgur wheat) or broken (as with couscous). Processed grains may take from 2 minutes to 45 minutes to cook on the stovetop. Whole grains, such as wheat berries, millet, and brown rice, take much longer because they still have their hard hulls. Whole grains can take from 30 minutes to more than 2 hours to cook. (Table 8-3, later in this chapter, provides cooking times for a long list of grains.)

✔ **Consider a rice cooker.** Many people swear by their rice cookers, which resemble slow cookers but are specially made to make perfectly steamed, fluffy rice without stovetop supervision. Add water and rice, set the timer, and walk away. The appliance keeps the rice warm and fluffy until you're ready for it.

✔ **Quinoa needs special handling.** Quinoa has to be processed in order to remove the seed coat, which contains saponin and is toxic. Before you cook quinoa, rinse it several times with water to remove any remaining saponin. The saponin is soapy; you'll know that you've rinsed the quinoa well enough when the suds disappear.

✔ **Make more than you need.** When you cook whole grains, go ahead and make a pot full. Leftovers will keep for at least a week in the refrigerator (cover tightly to prevent the grains from drying out) or for months in the freezer. Leftover grains are good reheated or used as an ingredient in another dish, and you'll save time because they've been precooked.

On the stovetop

You prepare all grains on the stovetop by following the same three basic steps. The only thing that varies from grain to grain is the length of cooking time. The one exception: quinoa. Remember to rinse it thoroughly — three or four times — to remove the bitter coating before cooking it.

1. **Bring 2 or more quarts of water to a boil.**

   See Table 8-3 for the correct amount of water to use. For most grains, you need about 2 cups of water per cup of uncooked grain.

2. **Add the grain to the water.**

   See Table 8-3 to determine the proper amount of grain to use to get the cooked amount you want. Note that 1 cup of uncooked grain expands to approximately 3 cups when cooked.

3. **Reduce the heat and let the grain simmer, keeping the pot covered with a tight-fitting lid.**

   If you have problems with the water boiling over, turn the heat down further or tip the lid slightly to the side, letting just a crack of steam escape (and leave the lid in that position). Simmer for the amount of time shown in Table 8-3 or until all the water has been absorbed.

   If you find that a little extra water remains in the pan after you take the pot off the stove, you can either drain off the water or let the grains sit for ten minutes to allow them to absorb more water. Either way, use a fork to fluff the cooked grains after a few minutes.

TIP

Keeping leftover grains moist

Although leftover grains keep well in the refrigerator or freezer, they still tend to dry out. To restore their moisture content when you reheat them, try steaming them over boiling water by using a steamer basket, a double boiler insert, or an electric steamer. Doing so makes them fluffier and improves their texture.

Table 8-3	Timetable for Cooking Grains on the Stovetop		
Grain (1 Cup)	*Water Needed for Cooking (Cups)*	*Cooking Time (Minutes)*	*Yield (Cups)*
Amaranth	2½	25	3½
Barley: pearl	2½	40	3½
Barley: hulled	2½	90	3½
Bulgur	2	20	3
Couscous	2	5	3
Kamut	2	60	2½
Kasha	2	10	3
Millet	2	25	3
Oats (whole)	2	60	2½
Quinoa	2½	20	3
Rice (brown)	2	50	3
Spelt	2	90	3
Teff	3½	20	3
Wheat berries	2½	120	3

In a pressure cooker

If you simply can't wait an hour for whole grains to cook, but you don't want to resort to using parboiled grains, a pressure cooker may be the way to go. A pressure cooker seals tightly and traps steam inside, permitting the temperature inside the pot to rise higher than that of boiling water. This makes food inside the pot cook much faster than it ordinarily would.

Cooking grains in a pressure cooker requires approximately the same proportions of water to grain that the stovetop cooking method requires. The cooking time is far shorter in a pressure cooker, however. And if you soak whole grains for several hours before pressure-cooking them, you can cut the cooking time almost in half.

Table 8-4 gives you the approximate proportions of water and grains to use for pressure-cooking, as well as cooking times.

Table 8-4	Timetable for Pressure-Cooking Grains		
Grain (1 Cup)	*Water Needed for Cooking (Cups)*	*Pressure-Cooking Time (Minutes)*	*Yield (Cups)*
Amaranth	1¾	4	2
Barley: pearl	3	20	3½
Barley: hulled	3	40	3½
Buckwheat	1¾	3	2
Bulgur	1½	5	3
Kamut	3	40	2½
Millet	2	10	3½
Oats (whole)	3	30	2½
Quinoa	1½	1	3
Rice (brown)	1¾	20	3
Spelt	3	40	2½
Teff	1½	1	3
Wheat berries	3	25	2

When you cook pearl or hulled barley, buckwheat (kasha), kamut, or whole oats in a pressure cooker, add 2 or 3 teaspoons of vegetable oil to the pot to help control the foaming inside the pressure cooker.

Taming the tofu

If you're using tofu that's packed in water, remove the tofu from the container and pat it dry with a paper towel before you begin working with it. To press out even more water, place a flat object on top and let the tofu drain for at least 30 minutes. This step isn't necessary for all recipes, but it isn't a bad idea, especially if you're making a salad filling or a marinated dish or you're grating the tofu and using it in pasta filling. Some recipes that include lots of ingredients with a high water content, such as fresh vegetables (vegetarian lasagne, for example), tend to become watery. Waterlogged tofu only adds to the problem.

If you're using frozen tofu, thaw it by setting it in a colander or strainer and running warm water over it for several minutes. Let the tofu drain for at least 10 to 15 minutes, and then press the excess water out with your hands, as you would a sponge. Blot the tofu dry with paper towels before proceeding with the recipe.

For food safety reasons, treat tofu as you would dairy products, meat, or eggs and don't leave it standing at room temperature for more than two hours. To thaw frozen tofu overnight, set it in a covered bowl in the refrigerator; don't leave it out on the counter. Leftover tofu should be put back in the refrigerator as soon as possible.

The tofu that you see packaged in plastic tubs of water generally contains one or two blocks of tofu totaling 16 ounces. Tofu packaged in an aseptic brick pack comes in one 10.5- to 12-ounce piece. When recipes call for 4 ounces of tofu, you can estimate the amount based on the original package weight. Weighing the tofu on a scale isn't necessary. You don't have to be exact when it comes to the amount of tofu you use in most recipes; just get as close as you reasonably can.

When a recipe calls for tofu in cup measurements (for example, ½ cup tofu), you have two choices: You can chop the tofu into little cubes and measure it in a dry measuring cup (press it down tightly with a fork or the back of a spoon), or you can estimate the number of ounces you need and measure accordingly. For example, there are 8 ounces in 1 cup of tofu, so if a recipe calls for ½ cup, you can figure that you need about 4 ounces. Rather than cubing the tofu or smashing it into a measuring cup, you can estimate a 4-ounce chunk based on the original amount in the package.

Tips for tempeh

Unlike tofu, tempeh has no excess water to be pressed out. Tempeh isn't as malleable as tofu is, either, because it's made from whole soybeans rather than soymilk. In recipes in which you need to crumble the tempeh, you can soften it and make it easier to crumble by steaming it for a few minutes first. Let the block of tempeh set in a steamer basket over a pot of boiling water for two or three minutes. Be sure to let it cool before you handle it with your bare hands. In most recipes, you use chunks or slabs of tempeh that don't require special handling or preparation.

Like tofu, frozen tempeh should be thawed overnight in the refrigerator. Alternatively, you can set it in a colander and run warm water over it for several minutes. Never leave tempeh out on the kitchen counter overnight. Leftover tempeh should be refrigerated.

Most recipes list the amount of tempeh needed in ounces rather than cups. Estimate the portion you need for your recipe based on the number of ounces in the original package. On occasion, a recipe may call for tempeh by the cup. For example, a recipe for mock chicken salad may call for 1 cup of crumbled tempeh. In that case, you crumble the tempeh into a measuring cup.

As with tofu, there's no need to be persnickety about precise measurements of tempeh. A little more or less usually makes no difference in a recipe.

Prepping fruits and vegetables

You have two areas to focus on when preparing fresh fruits and vegetables: washing them and cutting them.

Washing

You need to wash fruits and vegetables before you do anything else with them, regardless of whether you're going to eat the peel or skin. If you like to use a commercial vegetable and fruit rinse, spray the food liberally with the solution and rinse well. If you don't use a commercial rinse, you can use a small amount of dish soap or hand soap. Just lather the fruit or vegetable and rinse well. Either way, rinse twice to be sure that all the soap or cleaner residue has been removed.

Fruits and vegetables that have lots of crevices and surface area — broccoli, cauliflower, grapes, and strawberries, for example — should be doused in a pan or sink full of water. Rinse especially well to ensure that as much pesticide residue (if they aren't organically grown), dirt, and debris as possible have been removed.

If fruits or vegetables have a waxy coating, no amount of washing will take the coating off, and chemicals will be sealed inside. Peel any produce that has been coated with wax before you use it.

Even though you won't be eating the rind, wash the outsides of melons, oranges, and other fruits and vegetables before setting them on a cutting board or cutting them with a knife. Setting unwashed food on a cutting board can contaminate the surface and introduce potentially dangerous bacteria to foods that are subsequently placed on that surface. Cutting into unwashed foods can drag bacteria into the edible portion of the food.

Cutting

Use a paring knife to peel and cut apples, pears, peaches, bell peppers, and other small fruits and vegetables. A French chef's knife is useful for cutting larger foods such as melons and squash, and a serrated knife is best for cutting soft fruits or vegetables such as tomatoes and kiwi fruit. (Chapter 7 contains more information about these knives, as well as an illustration of them.)

A French chef's knife is best for dicing sliced fruits and vegetables into smaller pieces. This particular knife is wide at the base near the handle and tapers to a point at the far end. To use the knife, you set the point on the cutting board, hold the food item carefully with one hand, raise the back of the knife with your other hand, and rock the knife up and down, leaving the tip on the cutting board as you cut. This technique dices or minces foods quickly and efficiently.

CUT FRUITS AND VEGETABLES WITH A FRENCH CHEF'S KNIFE

TIP STAYS ON THE BOARD

TO USE THE KNIFE, SET THE POINT ON A CUTTING BOARD. HOLD THE FOOD CAREFULLY WITH ONE HAND AND RAISE THE CHEFS KNIFE, WITH YOUR OTHER HAND. ROCK THE KNIFE UP AND DOWN. LEAVE TIP ON BOARD AS YOU CUT.

Figure 8-3:
The quick and efficient way to dice fruits and vegetables.

To cut down on the time it takes to prepare a meal, you may want to wash and chop vegetables and fruits ahead of time. Store precut produce in an airtight container in the refrigerator and take it out again when you're ready to begin preparing the meal.

Tussling with tahini

A few of the recipes in this book call for *tahini* — sesame paste. The tahini that you buy in cans or jars at natural foods stores has a layer of oil floating on top. When a recipe calls for a tablespoon or two of tahini, stir the oil into the tahini before scooping out the amount you need. Another option is to store the tahini in the refrigerator, where it won't separate at all.

Mastering Simple Cooking Techniques

Because the recipes in this book are meant to be used by people of all skill levels, the cooking methods are relatively simple and straightforward. The pointers that follow are tricks of the trade and gentle reminders for novices.

Most people who are comfortable in the kitchen have had years of experience. Like becoming fluent in a foreign language, cooking skills become second nature with time. If you have little experience in preparing meals, begin with small projects and simple recipes. Over time, your confidence will build, you'll have more successes and fewer flops, and you'll be ready to move on to more complicated recipes.

For information about the tools you use to perform these cooking techniques, see Chapter 7.

Baking

Baking is an essential technique for preparing desserts and breads, such as cookies, pies, cakes, rolls, and quick breads. A few entrees are baked as well. Keep the following tips in mind when you bake:

- ✔ **Preheat the oven.** Set it to the temperature the recipe calls for, and turn on the oven at least ten minutes before putting the dish in.

- ✔ **Set a timer.** Some people are reminded to check on their food when they notice a wonderful aroma coming from the kitchen. Unless you trust your nose, it's better to set a small freestanding timer, set the timer on the oven or microwave, or watch a clock to be sure that you take the food out before it's overdone. Otherwise, by the time you smell it, it may be overdone already.

- ✔ **Invest in nonstick bakeware to cut down on the amount of fat you add to pans to prevent sticking.** Nonstick pans tend to burn foods more readily, though, so reduce the oven temperature by 25 degrees or so if you use them.

If you use regular shiny bakeware (loaf pans, baking pans, casseroles, and so on), grease the pan by rubbing vegetable oil around the inside with a paper towel or your clean hands. Olive oil works well for most entrees and savory dishes, but it has too strong a flavor if you're making something sweet. For cookies, pies, muffins, and the like, grease the pan with corn oil instead.

✔ **Measure accurately.** Take the time to measure dry ingredients such as flour, baking soda, and baking powder accurately, or the dish may not turn out right. Scoop the ingredient into a dry measuring cup or measuring spoon and use a knife to neatly remove the excess from the top.

✔ **Check for doneness.** Insert a toothpick or knife into the center of the baked good to see if it's cooked well enough. If the toothpick or knife comes out clean, the food is ready. If not, leave it in the oven for a few more minutes and then check it again.

Boiling

Earlier in this chapter, I covered the methods for cooking grains and dried beans, which call for boiling a pot of water, adding the food, and then turning down the heat, covering the pot, and letting the food simmer until it's done. The same technique holds true for cooking pasta. However, after you add pasta to a pot of boiling water and reduce the temperature, you should keep the lid *off* the pot. Pasta tends to boil over, and keeping the lid off while it simmers helps prevent too much heat from building up inside the pot.

When a food is done cooking, remove the pot from the burner and set it elsewhere — on a cool burner or a trivet on the kitchen counter, for example. This is especially true if you use an electric range. The coils stay hot for several minutes after you turn off the heat, and leaving a pot on the burner may cause the food to continue cooking. Overcooking turns many foods — including pasta — into mush.

When you're preparing a food such as pasta that can overcook if it's left in a pot of hot water, drain it immediately after removing it from the stove. Pour it *slowly* into a colander in the kitchen sink so that you don't get splashed.

Steaming

Cooking foods for the minimum amount of time necessary helps them retain their nutrients. Steaming foods is one of the best ways to conserve nutrients in such foods as broccoli, cabbage, potatoes, and cauliflower.

You can steam vegetables, tofu, and other foods in several ways. One of the handiest ways is to add several tablespoons of water to a bowl, set the food in the bowl, cover the bowl with a paper towel or piece of plastic wrap, and then microwave it. An ear of corn may need only 2 minutes, whereas a medium-sized baked potato may need 7 or 8 minutes.

Another method of steaming food is to add several tablespoons of water or vegetable broth to a pot, heat it to boiling, and then add the food. Cover and let the food steam for as long as necessary. When the food is done, remove the pot from the stove and drain it in the kitchen sink.

Use caution when draining pots of steamed food. If the pot has been covered with a lid, open it carefully by lifting the side of the lid that's farthest from you. Doing so prevents a shot of hot steam from hitting you in the face.

You can also use a stainless steel or bamboo vegetable steamer insert to steam foods. These inserts look like small baskets that sit inside a pot and hold the food above the water at the bottom of the pot. Yet another alternative is an electric steamer — an appliance that can steam several cups of food at one time. Electric steamers are convenient and relatively inexpensive. You can find them at most stores that carry small kitchen appliances.

Sautéing and stir-steaming

Sauté means to fry food in a small amount of fat over high heat. Some recipes call for onions, garlic, or bell peppers to be sautéed in a skillet before other ingredients are added. If you use a nonstick skillet, you can forgo the oil. If not, you need to add a drop or two of olive oil or another vegetable oil to the skillet to keep the food from sticking. Get the skillet hot and then add the vegetables. Move them around frequently with a spatula or wooden spoon to keep them from sticking and burning.

You can usually tell when onions are done because they become translucent. Garlic may turn slightly brown when done, and bell peppers become soft.

A variation on pan-frying is *stir-steaming,* which makes use of a little water to steam the food at the same time it's being cooked in the skillet. Either use a nonstick skillet or add a drop or two of oil to a regular pan. Also add a few tablespoons of water. Get the water very hot and then add the food. Cover the skillet and let the food steam, lifting the lid to stir the food occasionally. Stir and steam until the food is cooked.

Stewing

Soups, chilis, and stews differ from many other recipes in that you usually leave them to cook on the stove for a longer period — up to an hour or more in some cases. You usually turn the heat down to low, and the food simmers for most of the cooking time. Occasionally, you need to stir the food with a long-handled wooden spoon to keep it from sticking to the bottom of the pan and burning.

When you make soups, chilis, stews, and tomato-based sauces, it's best to use a deep pot. Foods are not as likely to stick to the bottom of a deep pot, and controlling the heat is easier. Using a deep, narrow pot also helps minimize splashes and splatters. Keeping a lid on the pot, cracked a little to one side to let the steam escape, helps control splattering and keeps your stove-top and burners cleaner as well.

CAUTION!

Sanitation sense

Taking care to attend to some basic sanitation precautions can save you, your family, and anyone else who eats your food from all-too-common sicknesses caused by *food-borne pathogens* — bacteria or viruses that contaminate food and cause the people who eat that food to get sick.

You know the ol' 24-hour flu that seems to afflict people outside of flu season (and often around Thanksgiving, when nonvegetarians eat turkey)? Well, guess what? It's not the flu. It was probably caused by something they ate. For that reason, keep the following pointers in mind while you cook:

✔ Wash your hands before you handle dishes, silverware, and food. If you stop what you're doing to answer the telephone, let the dog out, or take out the trash, wash them again when you're through.

✔ Wash your hands after touching your hair, face, or mouth and after blowing your nose or using the bathroom.

✔ If you sneeze or cough, cover your mouth with your hand or a tissue. Then wash your hands.

✔ The best type of trashcan for your kitchen is one with a lid that you can open and close

with a foot pedal. That way, when you're busy working with food in the kitchen and need to toss something, you won't have to use your hands to lift the lid.

✔ Keep cold foods cold and hot foods hot. Don't let foods sit out unless you're about to serve a meal. After meals, put leftovers away immediately or as soon as it's practical. Never let leftovers sit out for more than two hours.

✔ Using a dishwasher isn't just convenient; it's also sanitary. Dishwashers heat the water to a much higher temperature than you'd use if you were washing dishes by hand. Dishwashers sanitize dishes and kill bacteria that may be present.

✔ Avoid unpasteurized or raw milk and cheeses made from raw milk. They can carry *Listerium,* a type of bacteria can that be especially dangerous to pregnant women and their unborn babies.

✔ Eating raw eggs can give you salmonella poisoning. If you use eggs in cookie and cake batters, don't lick the spoons or beaters. Switching to a pasteurized egg substitute or vegetarian egg replacer can reduce or eliminate the risk of salmonella poisoning.

Being the Master of Your Domain

One of the tricks to making food prep enjoyable is to keep the kitchen under control. This task may sound simpler than it is, especially if you don't consider organization your strong suit. However, a certain level of kitchen control helps you save time and maximizes your efficiency.

Here are some tips for keeping your kitchen under control:

✔ **Clear out the clutter.** When you're ready to begin fixing a meal or preparing a recipe, the first step is to clear the counters of anything that may get in the way: foods that should go back into the refrigerator or cupboard, dirty dishes (put them in the dishwasher to get them out of the way), and anything else that belongs elsewhere.

✔ **Bring out the supplies.** After you've cleared off the counters, set out all the utensils, ingredients, and other supplies that you need to prepare the recipe you want to make. If you're going to make more than one dish, take out the supplies for the one you'll tackle first. Once that dish is well underway or finished, you can take out the supplies for the next recipe.

✔ **Use and re-use.** Try to minimize the number of utensils, mixing bowls, measuring spoons, and measuring cups you use. If you use a measuring cup to scoop flour for a recipe, shake it out and reuse the cup to measure sugar or other ingredients. Likewise, if you use a teaspoon to measure vanilla, rinse it out, dry it with a towel, and re-use it to measure baking soda. You'll create less clutter this way, and you won't have as much to wash when you're finished.

✔ **Clean as you go.** Once you have used a bowl or utensil and won't need it again, rinse it and put it in the dishwasher (or off to one side in the sink if you don't use a dishwasher). Similarly, if you've used an ingredient and won't need any more, put it where it belongs in the cupboard or fridge. Putting things away as you go gives you a sense of progress, makes your final cleanup a breeze, and helps keep you organized as you work.

Periodically, pick up a wet sponge and wipe up spills or crumbs on the counter and stovetop. Keeping your workspace from getting too messy makes your job easier and much more pleasant.

Being a Weekend Warrior in the Kitchen

For most people, weekends are the time to catch up and — if you're really productive — to work ahead. You can use the extra time to get a head start on your meals in two ways: prepare ingredients that you'll use later to fix meals, and make batches of foods that will keep for several days in the refrigerator or for weeks in the freezer.

Get the components ready

How often have you walked into the kitchen and been too famished to take the time to toss a salad or heat some rice to go with the leftover chili in the refrigerator? I thought so. Doing the prep work ahead of time so all that's left to do is assemble the meal can make the difference between eating well and getting by.

What can you prepare ahead of time? Try any of the following for starters (most of these foods need to be stored in an airtight container in the refrigerator until you use them).

- Cook a pot of rice.
- Peel carrots, snap green beans, wash salad greens, and slice bell peppers and cucumbers.
- Wash clumps of grapes, blueberries, and strawberries.
- Slice melons into chunks.

    If you have fresh mint from the garden, toss a sprig into a container of melon chunks or berries. The fruit will pick up the minty flavor.

- Wash and cut up zucchini, yellow squash, onions, cauliflower, and broccoli.
- Soak beans and grains.
- Chop or mince vegetables that you may need later for recipes, including onions and bell peppers.

Take advantage of the time you have to do these things now, because you may not be willing to wait during the week.

Make it now, enjoy it later

Coming home to a refrigerator full of fresh, homemade foods is sure to put a smile on your face after a long day. What better way to feel nurtured and content, even if you're cooking only for yourself? Busy people are much more likely to eat well if they make the effort to prepare at least *some* foods ahead of time. Here are some ideas to get you started.

These foods will keep for two or three days in the refrigerator:

- Mixed green salads (without dressing)
- Coleslaw
- Melon chunks mixed with blueberries and strawberries

- ✔ Fresh peach slices with blueberries (sprinkle with a little granulated sugar)
- ✔ Freshly squeezed orange juice and grapefruit juice
- ✔ Tomato, cucumber, and onion salad
- ✔ Winter salad with apples, pears, chopped figs, chopped walnuts, and cinnamon
- ✔ Tofu salad (see the recipe in Chapter 14)
- ✔ Pancake batter

These foods will keep for several days to a week in the refrigerator:

- ✔ Vegetarian chili (see Chapter 13)
- ✔ Three-bean salad (see Chapter 14)
- ✔ Marinated vegetable salad
- ✔ Carrot, pineapple, and raisin salad
- ✔ Tabbouleh (see Chapter 16)
- ✔ Hummus (see Chapter 12)
- ✔ Rice pilaf
- ✔ Black bean spread (keep tightly covered)
- ✔ Refried bean filling for burritos, tacos, and nachos (keep tightly covered)
- ✔ Potato salad
- ✔ Vegetarian lasagne, stuffed shells, and manicotti (see Chapter 15)
- ✔ Puddings
- ✔ Cobblers and crisps
- ✔ Muffins
- ✔ Quick breads

It's also nice to have foods stored in the freezer for times when you don't feel like cooking, have unexpected guests, or are running short on time. When you fix lasagne or pot of chili or you bake a batch of cookies or muffins, consider doubling the recipe and storing half in the freezer. Doing so takes little extra time, and you'll have a meal, snack, or dessert ready to pull out of the freezer and reheat when you need it.

Foods that freeze well include the following:

- Muffins, cookies, quick breads, and pancakes

  If you freeze pancakes, place sheets of waxed paper between them so that they don't stick together.

- Fruit cobblers, crisps, and pies (but not meringue or cream pies)

- Lasagne, manicotti, and stuffed shells

- Grain and vegetable casseroles

- Soups (expect for those that contain potatoes)

- Vegetarian chili

- Berries, melon chunks, and peach slices

- Grapes and bananas (great for snacks, or use the frozen bananas to make smoothies — be sure to peel them before freezing!)

- Leftover rice

Chapter 9

Adapting Recipes

* *

In This Chapter

▶ Understanding cookbook logic

▶ Replacing meat in nonvegetarian recipes

▶ Removing eggs from baked goods, casseroles, main-dish loaves, quiches, and other foods

▶ Substituting for milk, cheese, butter, sour cream, and yogurt

* *

*W*hen the topic turns to finding replacements for meat, eggs, and dairy products in traditional recipes, my thoughts drift to *Gilligan's Island,* the old television sitcom about a deserted tropical island and a ship full of castaways. Mostly, I remember the coconut cream pies and banana cream pies that the characters were somehow able to make, despite the fact that no eggs, no butter, and not a drop of milk was to be found on the island (unless you count the coconut milk). Those mouth-watering pies mesmerized me, but I couldn't figure out how they could have made them.

It wasn't until years later that I realized that many of the ingredients that most people take for granted as being vital to recipes can be replaced by a wide range of other foods that serve essentially the same functions. So *that's* how they did it!

Many vegetarians don't mind using eggs and/or dairy products in their recipes, but lacto vegetarians avoid eggs, and vegans avoid both eggs and dairy products. Even many nonvegetarians want to cut back on animal products of all types, if only to decrease their intake of saturated fat and cholesterol.

The recipes in this book have been modified to be vegetarian or were vegetarian from the start. In this chapter, however, I show you how to work with your favorite *non*vegetarian recipes, replacing the meat, eggs, and dairy products if you want to do so. In many cases, you can use these substitutions to further alter vegetarian recipes as well — for example, to turn a lacto-ovo vegetarian recipe into a vegan one.

You don't have to buy vegetarian cookbooks to find good meatless recipes. Page through traditional cookbooks and flag your favorite recipes. By making simple substitutions for the meat, eggs, and/or dairy products they contain, you can make many of these recipes vegetarian.

What You Didn't Know about Traditional Cookbooks

Because you may not have known that you don't need eggs, milk, or butter to make your favorite recipes, you probably never realized that most standard cookbooks don't give you other choices.

Think about it. Pick up a copy of *Better Homes and Gardens New Cookbook, Betty Crocker's Cookbook,* or *The Joy of Cooking* and peruse the sections for baked goods and desserts. Virtually every recipe calls for animal products. Whether it's a pie, cookies, a cake, or a quick bread, it's nearly guaranteed to be made with eggs, milk, butter, or all three.

Using animal products in recipes is a Western cultural tradition — something that most people don't question. We're so accustomed to using these ingredients in recipes that our expectations about how certain foods should taste, look, and feel in the mouth depend on their use.

For example, say your favorite muffin recipe was being judged at the state fair. Instead of using eggs in the recipe, though, you used soft tofu. The muffins may taste wonderful, but the texture may be a bit different than the texture of muffins made with eggs. The judges would be likely to count this difference in texture against you because the "standard" for muffins includes the texture imparted by eggs.

Here's another example: French toast is traditionally made with bread dipped in a mixture of milk, eggs, and spices and cooked on a griddle. The egg yolk gives the French toast its characteristic color, and the milk-and-egg batter gives the food a particular texture and appearance. Instead, you can make French toast by using a batter made with soymilk and mashed bananas rather than milk and eggs (a recipe included in this book in Chapter 11). The result is delicious, but the vegan version of this recipe has a lighter color and a less-crispy texture than its traditional counterpart.

Remember, when you substitute non-animal ingredients for animal ingredients in recipes, the finished products often differ from those made the traditional way. They're not necessarily better or worse. Judge the new recipe on its own merits rather than on how it compares to the nonvegetarian (or nonvegan) version. You may even want to give the recipe a new name to distinguish it from the old one. For instance, egg salad made with tofu and soy mayonnaise rather than eggs and regular mayonnaise might become Sunshine Salad or Julie's Secret Sandwich Filling.

Determining the amount of a non-animal ingredient to use in place of an animal ingredient in a recipe is often a matter of trial and error. Take your best guess and go from there. You'll frequently find that precise measures aren't all that important anyway. A little more or less mashed banana in a quick bread recipe, for example, isn't likely to hurt the final product.

Pencil in notes of the amounts you used to give you a place to start the next time you try the recipe, and erase and update your notes as needed. You can also experiment with different ingredients to see which one is best in a recipe for which more than one substitution may work. For example, you may be able to use both tofu and mashed banana as an egg substitute in a cake recipe, but one may give you a better result than the other.

Where's the Beef? Weeding the Meat Out of Recipes

Replacing meat in even the most traditional meat-based recipes has become surprisingly easy. A wide range of versatile and great-tasting products are now available at natural foods stores and neighborhood supermarkets. Use these products in place of meat in recipes, and you'll not only get excellent results in flavor and texture, but you'll also radically reduce the foods' saturated fat and cholesterol contents. In some cases, you'll even boost the dietary fiber content. It's a no-brainer. Go for the meat substitutes.

Tofu and tempeh

Both tofu and tempeh are soy products, but after that commonality, they part company. They're very different in appearance and texture, and they function differently in recipes.

- ✔ **Tofu** is a smooth, creamy food that has little flavor or odor. It picks up the flavor of whatever you cook it with. Because it blends well, it can be used to replace dairy products in sauces, dips, puddings, and fillings. It can also stand in for eggs in many recipes. You can read more about tofu in Chapter 5.

  To replace meat with tofu in recipes, cut up firm or extra-firm tofu into cubes and stir-fry it. You can also cut tofu into chunks or slabs, marinate it, and cook it.

Some people like to freeze tofu before using it. After frozen tofu thaws, it has a chewier, more meatlike texture.

✔ **Tempeh** is made with whole soybeans, so it has a chunkier texture than tofu. It works well crumbled and used in place of meat in such recipes as sloppy Joes, chicken salad, and chili. You can also grill it, barbecue it, bake it, broil it, or use it in chunks in stews and casseroles.

Seitan

Seitan ("SAY tan") is a delicious, chewy food made from wheat gluten, the protein component of wheat. You can make it at home from scratch or by using mixes that you find at natural foods stores, but most people find preparing it to be a challenge. It's much easier and more convenient to buy seitan ready-made at a natural foods store. Look for it in the refrigerated section.

If you've never tasted seitan before, I recommend that you seek out a Chinese restaurant in a big city, where you're likely to find it on the menu. Seitan is used in a variety of dishes, typically in strips or chunks. You owe it to your-self to try it. It's not a bad idea to try seitan in a restaurant before attempting to make it yourself at home. That way, you're apt to sample well-prepared seitan and know what it should look and taste like when you make it yourself.

Textured vegetable protein

Textured vegetable protein, or TVP, has been used widely throughout Western Europe for many years. It's only recently caught on in the U.S. and Canada. TVP is a soy product that can take the place of ground meat in such foods as taco and burrito filling, chili, sloppy Joe filling, and spaghetti sauce. It's sold as vegetable crumbles in the frozen foods sections of supermarkets or dried in small bits or chunks in boxes, bags, or bulk bins at natural foods stores. You can also buy TVP via mail order — see Chapter 24 for sources.

Bulgur wheat

Bulgur wheat is rolled, cracked wheat. It has a nutty flavor and can be used to add texture to soups, stews, sauces, and chili in much the same way that TVP functions in recipes. It absorbs the liquid in whatever it's cooked with, so it thickens foods. Toss a handful into a pot of chili, and the leftovers will be even thicker the next day. Like TVP, cooked bulgur wheat can be used in place of ground meat in foods.

The origin of meat substitutes

The first meat substitute sold in the United States was called Soy Bean Meat. The Seventh-Day Adventist Church was responsible for most of the early development of meat substitute products in the U.S. as a service to its members. The Adventist Church advocates a vegetarian diet, and church stores all over the country still sell specialty vegetarian products, such as replacements for chicken, beef, tuna, and processed meats.

Veggie burgers, franks, cold cuts, and breakfast "meats"

You can now find a vegetarian version of just about every processed meat. Hankering for some old-fashioned bologna or a hotdog? You can find a soy version that tastes and looks very much like the real thing. From burger patties and bacon to sausage and corndogs, manufacturers now make a complete array of meatless products. On the whole, these products taste great, but you'll want to experiment to see which brands you like best.

Use these healthy imposters in all the same ways you used to use their real-meat counterparts. Just swap the old for the new. For example:

- Use soy-based "bacon" to make a BLT.
- Serve pancakes and waffles with soy-based "bacon" or "sausage" patties or links.
- Slice tofu hotdogs into baked beans for beans and franks.
- Top a tofu hotdog with vegetarian chili and chopped onions or slaw for a chilidog.
- Add crumbled soy "bacon" to spinach salad or German-style potato salad.
- Make a club sandwich or sub sandwich with veggie cold cuts.
- Top pizza with soy "pepperoni" or crumbled soy-based "sausage."

Nutritionists often consider meatless convenience products to be *transition foods* — vegetarian products that simulate the look, flavor, and texture of meat and can stand in for meat in recipes. They serve as a crutch for people who are making the move from a meat-centered diet to a vegetarian one. These products can help you make the switch, or they can simply be a fun way to make over an old favorite food.

Substitutes for gelatin

Many people are surprised to learn that the gelatin they've eaten since childhood is a rendered byproduct of various animal parts, including bones and cartilage. Needless to say, vegetarians do not eat gelatin or foods made with it.

Vegetarian forms of gelatin are available and are usually made from sea vegetables. Agar is one example, made from red algae. Natural foods stores carry plain and fruit-flavored powdered vegetarian gelatin. You can use these products in most of the same ways that commercial nonvegetarian gelatin is used.

In traditional recipes that call for gelatin to be liquefied and then added to cold water, you may need to change the process a bit if you want to substitute vegetarian gelatin. You may need to blend the vegetarian gelatin into cold liquid before bringing the liquid to a boil. Vegetarian gelatin sets quickly, so you may also need to add additional ingredients right away rather than waiting for the liquid to thicken, as you may have done when using nonvegetarian gelatin.

Substituting for Eggs

The next time you feel the need to run to your neighbor's house to borrow an egg, think again. Chances are you have a number of ingredients in your refrigerator or cupboard that would substitute nicely for the egg in that recipe.

Eggs serve a variety of functions in recipes. They often work as binders, holding the other ingredients together, as in a casserole or cake. Eggs also can act as leavening agents, providing lift and affecting texture. The purpose of the egg in a recipe determines what you can use as a substitute. In some cases, you can omit the egg altogether, and the recipe isn't noticeably affected.

In this section, I look at some of the foods that you can use to replace eggs in recipes.

Ousting eggs from baked goods

Eggs are used in baked goods for *leavening,* or lightness. They also may serve as a binder. The purpose the egg serves in the original recipe — as well as the amount of egg the recipe calls for — determines whether you need a substitute and, if so, which alternate ingredient will best serve the function of the egg in the recipe.

Replacing eggs for color

Sometimes, removing the eggs from a recipe also removes the characteristic color. Sponge cake and French toast, for example, wouldn't be golden yellow if it weren't for the eggs they contain. Egg salad made with tofu instead of eggs would be white. Of course, a lack of yellow color doesn't necessarily diminish flavor. On the other hand, if yellow is what you want, you may find that a dash of turmeric, yellow mustard, saffron, or — if need be — a couple drops of yellow food coloring does the trick.

Flat foods such as pancakes and cookies don't rely on eggs for lift. In fact, in many cases, you can eliminate the egg without noticeably affecting the final product. That's especially true if the recipe calls for only one egg. If you do omit the egg, however, it's a good idea to add a tablespoon or two of additional liquid — soymilk, fruit juice, or water, for example — for each egg omitted to restore the recipe to its original moisture content.

When a recipe calls for three or more eggs — as many cakes do — the eggs perform a vital function and need to be replaced with an ingredient that can deliver a similar effect.

In recipes for baked goods that have a light, airy texture, replace eggs with an ingredient that provides lift. Any of the following ingredients can replace one whole egg in a recipe:

- Half a small, ripe, mashed banana. This substitution gives the food a mild banana flavor, which can be nice in recipes for muffins, cookies, pancakes, and quick breads.

- ¼ cup of any kind of tofu blended with the liquid ingredients in the recipe. Light or reduced-fat tofu cuts down on the fat and calories in the finished product.

- 1½ teaspoons of a commercial vegetarian egg replacer, such as Ener-G Egg Replacer, mixed with 2 tablespoons of water. This product is a combination of vegetable starches and works wonderfully in virtually any recipe that calls for eggs. Natural foods stores sell it in 1-pound boxes.

- ¼ cup of applesauce, canned pumpkin or squash, or pureed prunes. If you use these foods, know that, depending on the recipe, they may add a hint of flavor. If you want to give the food a lighter texture, add an extra ½ teaspoon of baking powder, because using fruit purees to replace eggs can make the finished product somewhat denser than the original recipe.

- A heaping tablespoon of soy flour or bean flour mixed with a tablespoon of water. This mixture works similarly to vegetarian egg replacer.

✔ 2 tablespoons of cornstarch beaten with 2 tablespoons of water. This, too, works much like vegetarian egg replacer.

✔ 1 tablespoon of finely ground flaxseeds whipped with ¼ cup of water. The flaxseeds gel and bind with the other ingredients.

Replacing eggs in casseroles, loaves, burger patties, and main dishes

Some recipes need an ingredient that binds all the other ingredients together. Eggs are famous for acting as the glue that holds meatballs, meatloaf, and casseroles together. Lacto vegetarian and vegan versions of these traditional foods need something to serve the same purpose. Fortunately, you have lots of options.

As you might suspect, your choice of ingredients to replace eggs in these types of foods depends on the degree of "stick" you need, as well as how the ingredient will blend with the other flavors in the recipe. Cooked oatmeal may work fine as a binder in a veggie burger patty, for example, but may not be a welcome addition to a vegetable casserole if you don't care for the flavor or texture that it brings to the dish.

As always, if you're altering a traditional recipe, you have to experiment a bit to determine just the right amount of an ingredient to serve the purpose. A good starting point with most recipes in which egg acts as a binder is to use 2 to 3 tablespoons of any of the following ingredients (or a combination of them) to replace one whole egg. If the original recipe calls for two eggs, start with 4 to 6 tablespoons of egg substitute.

✔ Tomato paste

✔ Arrowroot starch

✔ Potato starch

✔ Cornstarch

✔ Whole-wheat, unbleached, oat, or bean flour

✔ Finely crushed breadcrumbs, cracker meal, or matzo meal

✔ Quick-cooking rolled oats or cooked oatmeal

✔ Mashed potatoes, mashed sweet potatoes, or instant potato flakes

You can also try ¼ cup of any kind of tofu blended with 1 tablespoon of flour or 1½ teaspoons vegetarian egg replacer mixed with 2 tablespoons of water.

Replacing eggs in sandwich fillings, salads, and scrambled eggs

Finding substitutes for eggs that are hidden in recipes is one thing; finding suitable substitutes for eggs that are more visible in foods is quite another. Fortunately, tofu looks remarkably like cooked egg whites and functions in much the same way in several popular recipes.

✔ You can use chopped firm or extra-firm tofu in place of egg whites in egg salad. Use your favorite egg salad recipe, but substitute tofu for the hard-boiled eggs. You can even replace regular mayonnaise with soy mayonnaise for a vegan version. Try the recipe in Chapter 14.

✔ Cubes of chopped firm tofu are a nice addition to a mixed green salad or spinach salad, standing in for the customary chopped hard-boiled eggs. You can also add chopped or minced tofu to a bowl of Chinese hot and sour soup.

✔ Try scrambled tofu instead of scrambled eggs at breakfast. Natural foods stores stock "tofu scrambler" seasoning packets, which you may also find in the produce section of your regular supermarket, near the tofu. Many vegetarian cookbooks (including this one — see Chapter 11) give recipes for scrambled tofu. The recipes usually include turmeric to give the tofu a yellow color similar to that of scrambled eggs. You can also use scrambled tofu to fill pita pockets or as a sandwich filling on hoagie rolls.

Replacing Milk and Milk Products in Recipes

If you're vegan — or even if you're just looking to reduce your reliance on dairy products, which contribute saturated fat and cholesterol — replacing dairy products in recipes is a breeze. The most common dairy products used in traditional recipes are milk, yogurt, sour cream, butter, and cheese. You can find good nondairy alternatives for all these products, and they work beautifully in virtually every recipe.

Milk substitutes

In place of cow's milk in recipes, use soymilk, rice milk, potato milk, nut milk, oat milk, or any combination of these. It's so easy. You can use any of these milk alternatives cup for cup in place of cow's milk. That's all there is to it.

In general, soymilk is more nutritious than rice milk, almond milk, and soy/rice milk blends. Fortified soymilk is even more nutritious because it contains extra calcium, vitamins A and D, and vitamin B12. If you use substantial amounts of a milk alternative in cooking, consider using a fortified variety for the extra nutrients.

You'll find that plain and vanilla-flavored soymilks and other milk substitutes are the most versatile varieties. I like to keep plain or vanilla on hand because the mild flavors blend into just about any recipe. Use plain soymilk in savory recipes such as main dish sauces and soups. Use vanilla soymilk in sweeter dishes, such as puddings and custards, and on cereal, in baked goods, and in smoothies. Chocolate or carob soymilk is available, too, and can be used in recipes in which you want a chocolate flavor, as in pudding or a smoothie.

Substitutes for yogurt and sour cream

Natural foods stores stock soy-based plain and flavored yogurts that make excellent replacements for dairy yogurt. They're made with active cultures, and they're delicious. You can also buy soy-based sour cream alternatives at natural foods stores. The big nutritional advantage to these products is that they're cholesterol-free and contain far less saturated fat than their dairy counterparts.

You can use soy yogurt and sour cream in most of the same ways that you use the dairy-based versions. A potential drawback in cooking, however, is separation. The soy products tend to separate when they're heated in a pan on the stove, so they may not work in certain sauce recipes. In cold recipes, you won't have any problems substituting them for dairy yogurt and sour cream. You can use them cup for cup as replacements.

When a recipe calls for buttermilk, you can make a nondairy version by adding 2 teaspoons of lemon juice or vinegar to 1 cup of soymilk or other milk replacer.

Cheese substitutes

The cheese alternatives on the market vary widely in flavor and meltability. Although they have the distinct advantage of being much lower in saturated fat and free of cholesterol as compared to most dairy-based cheeses, the nondairy varieties are often accused of being short on flavor and function, particularly in cooked foods in which the creaminess of melted cheese is an important feature. You need to shop around and experiment with various brands to find a cheese substitute that works well in your recipes and has a good flavor. Where cheese substitutes are concerned, it's "to each his own." Your own taste preference may not be the same as others'.

If you're a lacto or lacto-ovo vegetarian, full-fat and even low-fat dairy-based cheeses can contribute substantial amounts of saturated fat and cholesterol to your diet. Consider using soy- or nut-based cheeses instead, at least some of the time.

You're likely to find the best range of cheese alternatives at natural foods stores. The products they stock are typically soy- or nut-based and come in such flavors and styles as mozzarella, jack, cheddar, Parmesan, and cream cheese. On the whole, these cheese alternatives taste better than you might expect, and they're free of cholesterol and much lower in saturated fat than their dairy counterparts.

Soy- and nut-based cheese substitutes tend not to melt as well as regular, full-fat dairy cheeses, but they usually melt better than nonfat *dairy* cheeses. One reason is that where nonfat dairy cheeses tend to be low in overall fat, soy- and nut-based cheeses tend to be fairly high in vegetable fat. The vegetable fat improves meltability and even makes up somewhat for the difference in flavor.

If you want to use cheese substitutes, think about the type of recipes you plan to make in order to achieve the best results. For example, most cheese substitutes do well as an ingredient in a mixed dish, such as a casserole, in which the cheese doesn't have to stand alone but is mixed with other ingredients throughout the dish. Reviews are often not as favorable when soy cheese is used to make grilled cheese sandwiches or when it has to hold its own as an appetizer with crackers.

Cheese alternatives also vary in sodium content. Some are higher, some are lower, and some are about the same as their dairy counterparts. If you're concerned about your sodium intake, check the labels on the products you find.

You can make a nondairy substitute for ricotta cheese or cottage cheese by mashing a block of tofu with a fork, adding a few teaspoons of lemon juice, and mixing well. In place of Parmesan cheese, try nutritional yeast, which has a savory, cheesy flavor. It works well as a substitute for Parmesan cheese on casseroles, salads, baked potatoes, popcorn, and pasta. You can find it at natural foods stores.

Butter substitutes

Vegans can go to natural foods stores for soy-based butter and margarine substitutes that are free of dairy products and byproducts such as casein. However, even these vegan versions are not optimal for good health. Vegetable oils used to make all forms of margarine, including soy margarine, have been chemically altered, resulting in a form of fat called *trans fatty acids*. They're firm at room temperature, just like animal fats such as butter and lard. Trans fatty acids increase your risk for coronary artery disease even more than saturated animal fats do.

If health is a concern, you're better off using liquid olive oil whenever you can. Use a pastry brush to apply olive oil to breads and vegetables, for example. For recipes in which olive oil would not be appropriate due to flavor (as in most desserts, muffins, and quick breads), use canola oil or corn oil. As a general rule, you can substitute $\frac{7}{8}$ cup of vegetable oil for 1 cup of butter in recipes.

The great butter versus margarine debate

You should know that butter is better than margarine, even though it's high in saturated fat. Margarine contains trans fatty acids, which raise blood cholesterol levels even higher than the saturated fat in butter and other animal fats does. If you want to use margarine anyway, choose the brand that's lowest in saturated fat. Check the product label, and choose a product that contains no more than 1 gram of saturated fat per serving.

Part IV
The Recipes

The 5th Wave   By Rich Tennant

"I'LL HAVE A PIECE OF THE DEATH-BY-SKIM-TOFU."

In this part . . .

This is the heftiest portion of the book, containing 100 meat-free gems that I have carefully selected to offer you a range of satisfying, delicious vegetarian dishes. Some are earthy. Some are sophisticated. None is difficult or time-consuming to prepare. You'll also find sample menus for breakfast, lunch, dinner, and snacks, as well as helpful information about planning vegetarian meals for holidays and other special occasions.

Bon appétit!

Chapter 10

Beverage Basics

In This Chapter

▶ Enjoying beverages as snacks or thirst quenchers
▶ Giving your imagination a license to roam

*O*ne surefire way to put a smile on someone's face is to surprise him or her with a distinctive drink served with a meal, coupled with a light snack, or just as a between-meal pick-me-up. Sure, you can always open a container of fruit juice or brew a pot of coffee or tea. But just one or two simple steps more can put a spin on an otherwise ordinary drink and transform a meal into a special occasion.

In this chapter, I include recipes for a variety of beverages, from fruity smoothies to warm cocoa.

Smoothie Snacks

Smoothies are a modern-day twist on the milkshake. Instead of being laden with saturated fat from ice cream, however, smoothies are usually more healthful blends of such ingredients as fresh fruit, fruit juice, soymilk, and frozen yogurt or nondairy alternatives. Best of all, they take mere minutes to make, as these recipes illustrate.

Caramel Apple Smoothie

This smoothie has a creamy light brown color. All that's missing is the stick.

Preparation time: *Less than 10 minutes*

Yield: *Two 12-ounce servings*

1 cup apple juice (use fresh apple cider or tart, freshly squeezed apple juice, if available)

2 cups nonfat vanilla frozen yogurt

½ cup diced apple (use a tart variety, such as Granny Smith)

2 tablespoons caramel sauce or topping

5 or 6 ice cubes

1 Place all the ingredients in a blender.

2 Blend on high speed for about 1 minute or until smooth, stopping every 15 seconds to scrape the sides of the blender with a spatula and to push the solid ingredients down to the bottom of the blender.

3 Pour into two tall (16-ounce) tumblers and serve immediately with iced tea spoons and straws.

Per serving: *Calories 352 (From Fat 0); Fat 0g (Saturated 0g); Cholesterol 0mg; Sodium 183mg; Carbohydrate 78g (Dietary Fiber 1g); Protein 9g.*

Ice cubes, crushed in blending, improve the mouth feel or texture of smoothies, making them frostier. Vegans can replace frozen yogurt with a nondairy alternative available in natural foods stores.

☺ *Winter Berry Smoothie*

Rich purple jewel tones dotted with tiny black flecks create a stunning, light refreshment — turn to the color section of this book for a photo. Serve this smoothie in a clear glass because the color is so spectacular. This one's a crowd-pleaser, so if you have company, plan to multiply the recipe. Fortunately, this recipe is so easy that it takes only minutes to make.

Preparation time: *5 minutes*

Yield: *One large serving (2 cups) or two smaller servings*

1 cup vanilla soymilk

½ ripe banana

1 cup frozen mixed berries (strawberries, blackberries, blueberries, and raspberries)

2 tablespoons pure maple syrup

1 Place all the ingredients in a blender.

2 Blend on high speed for about 1 minute or until smooth, stopping every 15 seconds to scrape the sides of the blender with a spatula and to push the solid ingredients down to the bottom of the blender.

3 Pour into a tall (16-ounce) tumbler or two smaller (8-ounce) glasses and serve immediately with an iced tea spoon and a straw.

Per serving: *Calories 190 (From Fat 27); Fat 3g (Saturated 0g); Cholesterol 0mg; Sodium 63mg; Carbohydrate 39g (Dietary Fiber 3g); Protein 4g.*

Orange Crème Smoothie

Known as an Orange Julius in some circles, this drink is reminiscent of the orange creamsicle you may have enjoyed in summers past.

Preparation time: *10 minutes*

Yield: *Two 12-ounce servings*

1 cup orange juice

2 cups frozen nonfat vanilla yogurt

½ cup fresh orange sections (remove every bit of peel and white membrane — see Figure 10-1 for instructions)

1 teaspoon pure vanilla extract

5 or 6 ice cubes

1 Place all the ingredients in a blender.

2 Blend on high speed for about 1 minute or until smooth, stopping every 15 seconds to scrape the sides of the blender with a spatula and to push the solid ingredients down to the bottom of the blender. Thin the mixture as needed with a little more orange juice until it reaches the desired consistency.

3 Pour into two tall (16-ounce) tumblers and serve immediately with iced tea spoons and straws.

Vary It! *The fresh orange tastes great in this recipe, but you can leave it out if it's too much work or if you happen to be out of oranges.*

Per serving: *Calories 304 (From Fat 0); Fat 0g (Saturated 0g); Cholesterol 0mg; Sodium 132mg; Carbohydrate 65g (Dietary Fiber 1g); Protein 9g.*

Sectioning an Orange to Eliminate Membranes

Figure 10-1:
The easy way to remove the white membranes of an orange.

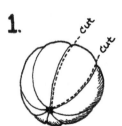

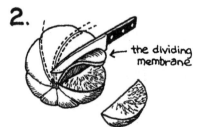

← the dividing membrane

Thirst Quenchers, Tummy Warmers, and New Twists on Old Favorites

Freshly squeezed orange or grapefruit juice in the morning is always sublime, just as a tall, ice-cold glass of lemonade refreshes from head to toe in the summertime. You'll want to keep these tried-and-true favorites on the menu, but let your imagination guide you in creating new ones as well, such as those that follow.

Beverages can be as simple as a combination of two or more fruit and/or vegetable juices or a more elaborate concoction of your own design. Ingredients might include

- Fruit and/or vegetable juices

- Milk (soy, rice, or cow's)

- Frozen yogurt or nondairy alternative

- Herbs such as fresh mint or basil

- Spices such as cloves or cinnamon

- Orange or lemon peel

- Coffee (hot or iced)

- Tea (herbal or regular, hot or iced)

- Lemonade (regular or pink)

The benefits of a juicer

Consider splurging on a juicer so that you can make your own fresh fruit and vegetable juices at home. The options range from a simple vise for squeezing citrus fruits to more expensive machines that can liquefy carrots, spinach, celery, and other foods. Freshly squeezed juice has the maximum amount of vitamins and an undeniably delicious flavor.

If your juicer removes the pulp from the fruits and vegetables, don't throw this healthful fiber away. Find a way to use it, such as by adding it to soups or baked goods.

☺ Sunshine in a Cup

This simple mixture is a striking bright orange and is gorgeous served from a glass pitcher in stemmed glasses. Packed with vitamins C and A, it's also a nutrition power-house. Adjust the proportion of orange juice to carrot juice to suit your preference.

Preparation time: *3 minutes*

Yield: *Six 1-cup servings*

4 cups freshly squeezed orange juice (about 5 medium oranges)

2 cups fresh carrot juice (about 4 carrots if you're juicing them yourself)

6 sprigs parsley

1 Combine the orange juice and carrot juice in a glass pitcher and stir gently to mix the two juices thoroughly.

2 Chill for an hour or two before serving, if desired.

3 Pour into serving glasses and garnish each glass with a sprig of parsley.

Per serving: *Calories 98 (From Fat 9); Fat 1g (Saturated 0g); Cholesterol 0mg; Sodium 45mg; Carbohydrate 23g (Dietary Fiber 0g); Protein 2g.*

⏾ *Jasper*

Jasper is a combination of two summertime staples: iced tea and lemonade. This version is made with regular brewed tea, but you can make endless variations by blending lemonade with any number of varieties of herbal tea.

Preparation time: *3 minutes*

Yield: *6 servings*

3 cups pink lemonade	6 lemon wedges
3 cups cold brewed tea	6 mint leaves
Crushed ice	

1 Combine the lemonade and tea in a pitcher.

2 Stir gently to mix the two ingredients thoroughly.

3 Pour over crushed ice in tall glasses and garnish each glass with a lemon wedge and a mint leaf.

Vary It! *Make Apple Jasper by substituting apple juice for the lemonade.*

Per serving: *Calories 51 (From Fat 0); Fat 0g (Saturated 0g); Cholesterol 0mg; Sodium 7mg; Carbohydrate 13g (Dietary Fiber 0g); Protein 0g.*

☕ Brown Bear Cocoa

For cold-weather comfort, nothing compares to a mug of hot cocoa. This version, made with soymilk, is creamy but free of saturated fat.

Preparation time: *10 minutes*

Yield: *Six 1-cup servings*

⅓ cup unsweetened cocoa	4½ cups plain or vanilla soymilk
⅓ cup sugar	½ teaspoon pure vanilla extract (optional if using vanilla soymilk)
1½ cups water	

1 Combine the cocoa, sugar, and water in a 3-quart saucepan.

2 Heat until boiling, stirring frequently, and then boil for 2 minutes, stirring constantly.

3 Add the soymilk, stir, and continue to heat and stir until steaming hot.

4 Remove from the heat. Add the vanilla and stir briskly with a whisk before serving.

Per serving: Calories 179 (From Fat 45); Fat 5g (Saturated 0g); Cholesterol 0g; Sodium 146mg; Carbohydrate 28g (Dietary Fiber 0g); Protein 7g.

☕ Steamy Spiced Soymilk

Cardamom seed is a member of the ginger family. It's traditionally used in Indian and Indonesian curries and pastries, as well as for medicinal purposes. Hot milk with cardamom is a relaxing bedtime treat or a soothing solution for a sore throat or cold. If your neighborhood supermarket doesn't stock cardamom seed, you can find it at gourmet or specialty stores as well as in ethnic markets.

Preparation time: *10 minutes*

Yield: *Four 1-cup servings*

4 cups plain or vanilla soymilk	3 tablespoons light brown sugar
2 teaspoons ground cardamom	1 teaspoon pure vanilla extract (optional if using vanilla soymilk)

1 Combine all the ingredients in a 2-quart saucepan.

2 Heat on low until very hot but not boiling, stirring frequently. Serve immediately.

Per serving: Calories 182 (From Fat 45); Fat 5g (Saturated 0g); Cholesterol 0mg; Sodium 123mg; Carbohydrate 27g (Dietary Fiber 0g); Protein 6g.

Chapter 11

Rise and Shine, It's Breakfast Time!

* *

In This Chapter

▶ Replacing eggs with tofu

▶ Making the healthiest and most delicious pancakes ever

▶ Starting the day the oatmeal way

▶ Waking up to a miso morning

* *

*Y*ou may grab a bagel as you dash out the door. You may prefer cold cereal and a glass of juice. All vegetarian. All quick and easy. But what about those occasions when you have more time and you'd like to serve something special?

Most people don't have much trouble thinking of vegetarian options for breakfast. For egg eaters, the all-American standards — poached, sunny-side-up, over-easy, soft-boiled, scrambled, and omelets — are still on the menu. Even for vegans and those looking for more healthful choices, lots of options remain. Muffins and other breakfast breads, hot cereals, pancakes and waffles, fresh fruit, and fruit juices are all vegetarian and can be made vegan as well.

A big surprise to many people who are new to vegetarianism is that tofu works wonderfully as a stand-in for eggs in certain recipes. In some recipes, it's subtle and disguised. In others, such as the first two recipes in this chapter, it's right out there in plain view. Another recipe uses tofu to replace cream cheese in a delicious bagel spread. Tofu is a superfood!

Using Tofu as a Replacement for Eggs

Although tofu can't quite take the place of an egg fried sunny-side-up, it can hold its own as an egg substitute in many other ways. You can mix tofu with spices and pan-fry it in a skillet, along with sliced onions and bell peppers, to make a variation of scrambled eggs "scrambled tofu" style. This dish may taste somewhat bland if you're new to it, but it's a classic among vegetarians, who have grown to appreciate it. With toast and hash brown potatoes, it makes a hearty and healthful breakfast alternative. Tofu also works wonderfully as an egg substitute in quiche. I include both a tofu quiche and a traditional egg quiche here so that you can compare nutrient composition and flavor.

You can also substitute ¼ cup (about 3 ounces) of any type of tofu for one whole egg in virtually any baked good. So, for example, if a recipe for muffins calls for one egg, you can use ¼ cup tofu instead. It's best to add the tofu by blending it with the liquid ingredient(s) in the recipe to ensure that you incorporate it smoothly, without lumps.

☜ Peppers and Tofu Scrambler

Because tofu picks up the flavors with which it's cooked, this dish tastes very much like its egg counterpart — a savory blend of onions, bell peppers, and spices. Turmeric gives the dish its yellow hue and helps the tofu stand in for eggs. If you've never eaten tofu served this way, give it a couple of tries. It grows on you! Serve this dish hot with toast and juice. You can also serve it hot or cold as a sandwich filling in a pita pocket, Kaiser roll, or hoagie roll.

Preparation time: *10 minutes*

Cooking time: *10 minutes*

Yield: *4 servings*

2 tablespoons olive oil

1 medium onion, chopped

2 teaspoons minced garlic

2 cups bell pepper strips (green, red, yellow, or mixed)

Two 12-ounce bricks firm tofu

½ teaspoon black pepper

1 teaspoon turmeric

1 tablespoon soy sauce

Salt to taste

1 Heat the olive oil in a large skillet. Over medium heat, cook the onion, garlic, and bell peppers in the oil, stirring occasionally, until the onions are translucent and the peppers are soft, about 8 minutes.

2 Crumble the tofu into the onion-bell peppers mixture. Add the black pepper, turmeric, and soy sauce and mix everything together with a wooden spoon or spatula. Heat thoroughly, mixing and scrambling the ingredients continuously, about 2 minutes.

Per serving: Calories 149 (From Fat 90); Fat 10g (Saturated 1g); Cholesterol 0mg; Sodium 547mg; Carbohydrate 11g (Dietary Fiber 3g); Protein 8g.

If you've used a partial package of tofu for a recipe, cube the leftover tofu and save it in the refrigerator. You can add it to a soup or salad, or use the remainder in place of eggs in a recipe.

☽ Savory Mushroom Tofu Quiche

The base of this quiche is tofu, but the texture and consistency are very similar to those of a traditional quiche made with eggs. This dish is delicious served with home-fried potatoes (see the recipe for Seasoned Home Fries in Chapter 16) or a muffin and a seasonal fresh fruit salad. You might even add a side of soy-based link sausages or sausage patties. For brunch or lunch, consider serving this quiche with potatoes and steamed greens, such as kale or spinach.

Preparation time: *45 minutes (including 30 minutes to press the tofu)*

Cooking time: *60 to 70 minutes*

Yield: *6 servings*

Two 12-ounce bricks firm tofu

2 tablespoons soy sauce

1 teaspoon dry mustard

½ teaspoon salt

¼ teaspoon black pepper

2 teaspoons minced garlic

2 tablespoons flour

2 tablespoons lemon juice

3 tablespoons olive oil

1 medium onion, chopped

½ cup canned mushrooms or 2 cups sliced fresh mushrooms

9-inch pie shell, unbaked

Paprika

1 Slice the tofu and place it between two clean towels. Set a heavy cutting board or similar weight on top and press the tofu for 30 minutes.

2 Preheat the oven to 350 degrees. In a medium mixing bowl, combine the tofu, soy sauce, dry mustard, salt, black pepper, garlic, flour, and lemon juice. Mash with a pastry blender or fork and mix the ingredients together well. Set aside.

3 In a small skillet, heat the olive oil. Add the onion and cook over medium heat until the onion is translucent. If you're using fresh mushrooms, sauté them with the onion.

4 Add the onion and mushrooms to the tofu mixture. Stir until the ingredients are well blended.

5 Pour the mixture into the unbaked pie shell and spread the filling evenly. Sprinkle the top lightly with paprika.

6 Bake for 60 to 70 minutes or until the crust is lightly browned and the quiche is set and looks firm in the middle when you jiggle the pan. Serve immediately.

Per serving: *Calories 257 (From Fat 162); Fat 18g (Saturated 2g); Cholesterol 0mg; Sodium 769mg; Carbohydrate 17g (Dietary Fiber 2g); Protein 10g.*

Traditional Savory Mushroom Quiche

This traditional, egg-based quiche is more flavorful than its tofu counterpart, but it's also higher in saturated fat and cholesterol. Reserve it for a special occasion, or serve it with fresh fruit or steamed vegetables and whole-grain toast or muffins to help balance this dish nutritionally.

Preparation time: *25 minutes*

Cooking time: *35 minutes*

Yield: *6 servings*

3 tablespoons olive oil	*¼ teaspoon black pepper*
2 tablespoons chopped green onions	*¼ teaspoon nutmeg*
1 pound fresh mushrooms, thinly sliced	*9-inch pie shell, unbaked*
½ teaspoon salt	*2 ounces Swiss cheese, grated*
1 teaspoon lemon juice	*Paprika*
4 eggs	*Tomato slices and parsley for garnish (optional)*
1 cup 1% milk	

1 In a medium skillet, heat the olive oil. Add the green onions and cook for about 1 minute.

2 Add the mushrooms, salt, and lemon juice. Cover the skillet and cook over low heat for 10 minutes.

3 Remove the cover, increase the heat, and bring the mixture to a boil. Cook for another 10 minutes or until the liquid in the pan has evaporated. Continue cooking, stirring constantly, for an additional 3 minutes. Remove from the heat.

4 Preheat the oven to 350 degrees.

5 Break the eggs into a medium bowl and beat them lightly with a fork or whisk. Stir in the milk, black pepper, and nutmeg, and then add the mushroom mixture. Stir to combine.

6 Set the pie shell on a cookie sheet. Pour the filling mixture into the pie shell. Sprinkle the Swiss cheese evenly across the top. Add a few shakes of paprika for color.

7 Place the quiche in the oven and bake for 35 minutes or until browned on top. Test for doneness by inserting a toothpick or knife in the center. When it comes out clean, the quiche is done.

8 Remove from the oven and let stand for 10 minutes. Garnish with tomato slices and parsley sprigs if desired and serve hot.

Vary It! *Add ¼ cup minced red bell pepper in Step 2.*

Per serving: *Calories 344 (From Fat 225); Fat 25g (Saturated 7g); Cholesterol 153mg; Sodium 436mg; Carbohydrate 19g (Dietary Fiber 1g); Protein 13g.*

Concocting a Cream Cheese Stand-In

Anyone who loves cream cheese but bemoans its saturated fat content will appreciate the following recipe. You can use tofu in a baked dish that's quick and easy to make and results in a spread that's similar in texture and consistency to whipped cream cheese.

Maple Nut Spread

This recipe makes a dense, smooth, creamy, not-too-sweet spread for French toast, bagels, English muffins, or toast.

Preparation time: *15 minutes*

Cooking time: *40 minutes*

Yield: *8 servings (2 cups)*

⅓ *cup raisins or currants*	½ *cup pure maple syrup*
½ *cup very hot water*	½ *teaspoon cinnamon*
½ *pound firm tofu*	*1 tablespoon tahini*
¼ *cup plain soy yogurt (vanilla is fine if that's what you have on hand) or regular lowfat yogurt*	*2 teaspoons pure vanilla extract*
	2 teaspoons flour
	⅓ *cup chopped walnuts*

1 Preheat the oven to 350 degrees. Lightly grease a 1-quart baking dish or casserole.

2 Place the raisins or currants in a small bowl or cup and pour the hot water over them. Set them aside to soak.

3 Place the tofu, yogurt, maple syrup, cinnamon, tahini, vanilla, and flour in a food processor or blender. Blend well, stopping frequently to scrape the sides. Turn the ingredients with a spatula if necessary to facilitate thorough blending.

4 Drain the raisins and chop them into small pieces or give them a whirl in a food processor. Add the raisins and walnuts to the tofu mixture and stir well.

5 Pour the tofu mixture into the baking dish and bake, uncovered, for 40 minutes or until set. Cool completely before serving.

Vary It! *For a stronger maple flavor, add* ½ *teaspoon maple extract in Step 3.*

Per serving: *Calories 172 (From Fat 54); Fat 6g (Saturated 1g); Cholesterol 0mg; Sodium 42mg; Carbohydrate 23g (Dietary Fiber 1g); Protein 7g.*

Making Vegetarian Versions of Breakfast Favorites

Pancakes, waffles, French toast, and hot cereal have always been vegetarian, but vegetarians often give these everyday foods a twist that nonvegetarians don't. The difference: Vegetarians tend to be more health conscious. When it comes to foods like these, vegetarians often prefer to use whole grains, add such extras as dried fruit and nuts, and substitute nondairy alternatives for fatty dairy products to cut down on saturated fat, cholesterol, and animal protein. Try these three recipes and see for yourself.

The wonders of wheat germ

Wheat germ is the nutrient-dense embryo of the whole-wheat kernel. When wheat is processed into flour, the germ is removed and sold separately. Wheat germ has a rich, nutty flavor that lends itself well to a variety of recipes and uses, including pancakes, breads, cookies, muffins, and cooked cereal; you can sprinkle it on top of casseroles, loaves, and even yogurt, too. After you open a jar of wheat germ, store it in the refrigerator to keep the oil in it from turning rancid.

Healthy Pancakes

These pancakes, pictured in the color section of this book, are fluffy yet hearty. As kids, my brother and sisters and I simply called them "Healthies," and we'd beg Mom to make a batch on weekend mornings. Make these pancakes as soon as possible after mixing the batter, because the leavening action of the baking powder begins as soon as it mixes with the liquid ingredients. Batter left too long will begin to lose its leavening power and could result in flat, dense pancakes. Leftover pancakes keep well in the refrigerator or freezer and can be reheated in the microwave.

Preparation time: *10 minutes*

Cooking time: *5 minutes*

Yield: *6 servings (about twelve 5-inch pancakes)*

1 cup whole-wheat flour	*½ teaspoon salt*
½ cup white flour	*1¾ cups skim milk or soymilk*
⅓ cup wheat germ	*¼ cup vegetable oil*
1 teaspoon baking soda	*1 egg*
1 teaspoon cinnamon	*2 egg whites, beaten stiff (see note)*
1 tablespoon baking powder	

1 Measure the dry ingredients into a medium-sized bowl.

2 Add the milk or soymilk, oil, and whole egg and stir well using a whisk. Break up any remaining chunks of flour by using the back of a spoon.

3 Fold in the beaten egg whites with a wooden spoon or rubber spatula. The batter will be thick but light and somewhat foamy.

4 Pour the batter by ⅓ cup measures onto a hot, oiled skillet. When the pancakes are bubbly all over and the edges are browned, turn them over and cook on the remaining sides for about 30 seconds, or until the undersides are browned. Serve immediately.

Egg whites are beaten stiff when they have thickened enough to form a peak when you pull the beaters out of the bowl. If you keep beating egg whites past this point, they can collapse and become thin again. The key is to stop beating when you notice that the whites are forming soft peaks that can stand up on their own.

Per serving: *Calories 253 (From Fat 99); Fat 11g (Saturated 2g); Cholesterol 37mg; Sodium 461mg; Carbohydrate 30g (Dietary Fiber 4g); Protein 10g.*

○ *French Toasties*

Bananas and soymilk take the place of eggs in this version of a traditional recipe for French toast. This is not your mom's French toast, but it's an interesting, tasty adaptation that's flavorful and nutritious.

Preparation time: *10 minutes*

Cooking time: *5 minutes*

Yield: *4 servings*

2 large ripe bananas	*8 slices multigrain or whole-wheat bread*
1 cup plain or vanilla soymilk	*Powdered sugar*
¼ teaspoon nutmeg	*Maple syrup*
½ teaspoon vanilla (go ahead and use it even if you're using vanilla soymilk)	*Sliced kiwi fruit and strawberry halves for garnish (optional)*

1 In a blender or food processor, puree the bananas, soymilk, nutmeg, and vanilla. Pour the mixture into a shallow pan such as a pie tin, cake pan, or 8-x-8-inch baking pan.

2 Generously oil a griddle and heat it until a drop of water spatters when flicked onto the pan.

3 Dip both sides of each slice of bread into the soymilk mixture and transfer each slice to the griddle. The first side will take about 2 minutes to brown. Turn gently and carefully, as the bread tends to stick to the griddle. Cook the second side for about 3 minutes.

4 Carefully remove the French toast from the griddle and turn it so that the brown side is face up. Dust each slice of French toast with powdered sugar and serve with a pitcher of warm maple syrup. If desired, garnish with thin slices of kiwi fruit and strawberry halves.

Per serving: Calories 245 (From Fat 27); Fat 3g (Saturated 0g); Cholesterol 0mg; Sodium 229mg; Carbohydrate 48g (Dietary Fiber 5g); Protein 7g.

☉ Oats and Apples

This recipe is very simple, but the tartness of the Granny Smith apples makes it special. Expect an oatmeal-like texture with a bit of crunch from the nuts and some sweetness added by the apples and brown sugar. This cereal can be eaten as is but is delicious served with vanilla soymilk on top.

Preparation time: *5 minutes*

Cooking time: *5 minutes*

Yield: *Two 1-cup servings*

1¾ cup water	2 tablespoons chopped walnuts or pecans
1 cup quick-cooking rolled oats	1 teaspoon cinnamon, plus extra for dusting
½ Granny Smith apple, peeled and finely diced	2 tablespoons brown sugar

1 Bring the water to a boil in a medium-sized saucepan.

2 Add the oats and boil for 1 minute, stirring constantly.

3 Add the apples, nuts, and cinnamon and cook on low heat for an additional 2 to 3 minutes or until heated through. The mixture will be thick and creamy.

4 Remove from the heat and ladle into serving bowls. Top each serving with a dusting of cinnamon and 1 tablespoon brown sugar.

Vary It! *For softer apples, add the apples with the water in Step 1. Then add the oats and the remaining ingredients and cook as directed.*

Per serving: *Calories 273 (From Fat 72); Fat 8g (Saturated 1g); Cholesterol 0mg; Sodium 13mg; Carbohydrate 48g (Dietary Fiber 6g); Protein 6g.*

Starting the Day the Miso Way

Miso is a fermented soy condiment — a rich, salty, savory paste — that's a key ingredient in many East Asian dishes, including soups, sauces, gravies, and salad dressings. Although you may not think of using miso at breakfast time, it's a common sight on breakfast tables in Japan, where miso soup is the traditional way to start the day.

☺ *Morning Miso Soup*

This simple recipe for miso soup takes only minutes to make — quick enough for even the most harried of mornings. A big mug full is comforting at breakfast, but you can eat this soup as a snack or part of a meal anytime. See the photo in the color section of this book.

Preparation time: *Less than 10 minutes*

Cooking time: *5 minutes*

Yield: *4 servings*

2 cups vegetable broth

2 cups hot water

4 tablespoons miso

1 teaspoon fresh ginger root, grated (optional)

½ cup diced firm tofu

3 tablespoons thinly sliced scallion greens

½ cup thinly sliced mushrooms (see Figure 11-1)

1 Pour the vegetable broth and 1 cup of the hot water into a medium saucepan.

2 In a separate bowl, dissolve the miso in the remaining 1 cup hot water. Mix well, and then add to the contents of the saucepan.

3 Add the ginger root (if desired) and mushrooms and heat until simmering, about 5 minutes.

4 Remove from the heat and stir in the tofu and scallion greens. Serve in a mug or bowl.

Per serving: *Calories 76 (From Fat 27); Fat 3g (Saturated 0g); Cholesterol 0mg; Sodium 1217mg; Carbohydrate 9g (Dietary Fiber 2g); Protein 6g.*

How to Trim and Slice Mushrooms

Figure 11-1:
Sliced mushrooms are a key ingredient in Morning Miso Soup.

1. wipe away dirt using a paper towel or a dish towel

2.

Cut off stem

3. slice

Chapter 12

Delicious Dips and Spreads

In This Chapter

▶ Favorite Middle Eastern dips and spreads

▶ Recipes with a Tex-Mex flair

▶ Just plain garlic

Dips and spreads make wonderful appetizers or simple snacks, and leftovers can double as sandwich fillings. Those that I've included in this chapter are quick and easy to make and keep in the refrigerator for several days to a week.

Making Middle Eastern Dips and Spreads

The recipes in this section are of Middle Eastern origin, where vegetarian foods abound. The first is perhaps the most popular vegetarian dip. You find it on the menu at every Middle Eastern restaurant and most vegetarian restaurants as well. Many variations exist, but the basic dip is made with garbanzo beans and olive oil.

Beans, a staple in most vegetarian diets, make great dips because you can puree them to a creamy texture and flavor them with a variety of ingredients. For more information about beans as ingredients in vegetarian cuisine, see Chapter 5.

Hummus

Hummus is a smooth, creamy, and garlicky dip or spread that's made primarily from garbanzo beans, or chickpeas. This healthful dish is enjoyed throughout the Middle East and typically is served in a shallow bowl with warm wedges of pita bread for dipping. You can also serve hummus as a dip for raw vegetables and as a pita pocket filling.

Preparation time: *10 minutes*

Yield: *Eight ¼-cup servings*

15-ounce can garbanzo beans, rinsed (about 1¾ cups)	¼ teaspoon cumin
¼ cup water	2 teaspoons olive oil
1 large clove garlic, minced	½ fresh lemon
¼ cup tahini	Paprika
¼ cup lemon juice	

1 Place the garbanzo beans, water, garlic, tahini, lemon juice, and cumin in a blender or food processor and process until smooth and creamy. Pour into a shallow bowl.

2 Drizzle the olive oil over the hummus, followed by a squeeze of fresh lemon juice and a dusting of paprika. Chill and then serve.

Vary It! *Add 1 roasted red bell pepper or 1 tablespoon chopped fresh dill in Step 1.*

Per serving: *Calories 115 (From Fat 54); Fat 6g (Saturated 1g); Cholesterol 0mg; Sodium 12mg; Carbohydrate 12g (Dietary Fiber 4g); Protein 5g.*

Tahini

Tahini is a paste made from ground sesame seeds. It has a mild sesame flavor and is used as an ingredient in some dips and salad dressings. You can find tahini at natural foods stores, Middle Eastern and specialty stores, and some supermarkets. It's often sold in a can with a plastic lid or in a jar, like natural peanut butter, with a layer of oil floating on top. Stir in the oil before scooping out the tahini.

Winter Berry Smoothie (Chapter 10); Healthy Pancakes (Chapter 11)

Old-Fashioned Cinnamon Rolls (Chapter 17)

Morning Miso Soup (Chapter 11)

Vegetarian Chili with Cashews (Chapter 13);
Whole-Wheat Crescent Rolls (Chapter 17)

Easy Gazpacho (Chapter 13);
Goat Cheese and Arugula Salad with
Lavender-Vanilla Vinaigrette (Chapter 14)

Tabbouleh; Green Beans and Walnuts (both in Chapter 16)

**Cuban Black Beans (Chapter 15) over rice;
Fried Plantains (Chapter 16)**

Tomato and Garbanzo Bean Salad (Chapter 14);
Quinoa Pilaf (Chapter 15)

Pasta Primavera (Chapter 15)

Chinese Vegetable Stir-Fry (Chapter 15)

Honey Wheat Beer Bread; Zucchini Bread (both in Chapter 17)

Vegetarian Feast: Clockwise, from top center: Rosemary-Roasted Red Potatoes (Chapter 16); Cheese and Nut Loaf (Chapter 19); Stuffed Squash (Chapter 19); Wilted Spinach with Garlic and Pine Nuts (Chapter 19); Chocolate Bourbon Pecan Pie (Chapter 19)

Bottom: Charleston Benne Wafers; center: Date Squares;
top right: Oatmeal-Cherry Cookies (all in Chapter 18)

Summertime Strawberry Shortcake (Chapter 18)

Decadent Chocolate Tofu Cheesecake (Chapter 18)

⟲ *Baba Ghanouj*

Like hummus, baba ghanouj is a traditional Middle Eastern recipe. Prepared in a food processor or blender, it is smooth and creamy. It has a mild garlicky flavor that can hold its own as a dip and works well as a sandwich spread or filling for pita pocket sandwiches with sliced tomatoes and cheese. You can also layer it with hummus to combine their flavors.

Preparation time: *30 minutes (including time for the eggplant to cool after baking)*

Cooking time: *60 minutes (to cook the eggplant)*

Yield: *6 ¼-cup servings*

1 medium eggplant (about 1 pound)	*3 tablespoons lemon juice*
3 tablespoons tahini	*¼ cup finely chopped parsley*
2 teaspoons minced garlic (see Figure 12-1)	

1 Preheat the oven to 350 degrees. Lightly grease a 9-x-13-inch baking pan.

2 Slice the eggplant in half lengthwise and place both halves in the baking pan, insides facing down, and cover it with foil.

3 Bake the eggplant for about 1 hour, or until soft. Remove it from the oven and allow it to cool enough to be handled.

4 Scoop out the eggplant seeds with a spoon, and use a paring knife to gently peel off the outer dark skin. (It will be easy to remove.)

5 Place the eggplant in a blender or food processor. Add the remaining ingredients and blend until smooth. Using a spatula, transfer the mixture into a serving bowl and chill for 1 hour before serving with warm pita wedges for dipping.

Per serving: *Calories 70 (From Fat 36); Fat 4g (Saturated 1g); Cholesterol 0mg; Sodium 13mg; Carbohydrate 8g (Dietary Fiber 3g); Protein 2g.*

Mincing Garlic

HEY! Crush the garlic clove under the blade of a knife.

Pull away the paper-like skin.

Put the clove on the cutting board. Make slices through the clove in one direction, then slice crosswise, to mince!

Figure 12-1:
Minced garlic lends flavor to baba ghanouj.

Creating Tex-Mex Specialties

Tortilla chips are to Tex-Mex cooking as pita bread is to Middle Eastern fare. Serve the recipes that follow alongside a big bowl of yellow, white, or blue corn tortilla chips or a plate of fresh vegetable sticks, or layer these dips on sandwiches.

☞ *Black Bean Dip*

This dip has a mild flavor and a smooth, creamy texture. With the salsa added, it works well as a dip for tortilla chips and for raw vegetable pieces such as broccoli and cauliflower florets, baby carrot sticks, and bell pepper strips. Depending on what you have on hand, you can garnish the dip with parsley sprigs, minced green onions or tomatoes, grated cheddar or Jack cheese, a dollop of sour cream or mashed avocado, or any combination of these ingredients. If the dip sets for about 30 minutes, it thickens enough to be used as a filling for burritos or tacos. If you plan to use this as a filling or spread, the salsa is optional.

Preparation time: *10 minutes*

Cooking time: *10 minutes*

Yield: *Eight ¼-cup servings*

15-ounce can black beans, rinsed	*2 teaspoons minced garlic*
½ cup warm water	*¼ cup mild salsa (optional)*
½ small onion, minced	

1 Combine the beans and water in a 2-quart saucepan. Cook over medium heat for 2 to 3 minutes or until the beans are hot.

2 Remove from the heat and mash the beans well with a potato masher or fork. Add the onion and garlic and stir well.

3 Return the mixture to the stovetop and heat on low for 5 minutes, stirring constantly.

4 Stir in the salsa, if desired, and heat until the beans are hot and bubbly. Add more water by the tablespoon, if necessary, until the dip reaches the desired consistency.

5 Remove from the heat and serve.

Vary It! *In this recipe, the onions remain crunchy. If you prefer the onions cooked, sauté them for a few minutes in a teaspoon of olive oil before adding them to the beans in Step 1.*

Per serving: *Calories 55 (From Fat 9); Fat 1g (Saturated 0g); Cholesterol 0mg; Sodium 218mg; Carbohydrate 10g (Dietary Fiber 4g); Protein 4g.*

⟳ Fresh Avocado and Lime Dip

Enjoy this rich, mildly flavored dip with tortilla chips, spread a layer on a sandwich, or fold some into a burrito. Avocado has a buttery consistency whether you mix the dip by hand or make it smooth in a blender or food processor. Note that this recipe is best used soon after preparation; the dip will turn dark on the surface. You can delay the discoloration by covering the surface of the dip with plastic wrap and keeping it chilled.

Preparation time: *10 minutes*

Yield: *4 ¼-cup servings*

1 medium avocado	*1 teaspoon minced garlic*
¼ cup finely diced sweet onion (such as Vidalia)	*2 tablespoons lime juice*
	2 tablespoons salsa (optional)

1 Cut the avocado in half, remove the seed and peel, and place the meat in a small bowl. (See Figure 13-3 for peeling and seeding instructions.) Mash the avocado with a potato masher or fork until it's fairly smooth.

2 Add the remaining ingredients and mix well by hand. For a much smoother result, you can puree everything in a blender or food processor. If you do so, however, stir in the salsa by hand after processing.

Per serving: *Calories 94 (From Fat 63); Fat 7g (Saturated 1g); Cholesterol 0mg; Sodium 66mg; Carbohydrate 9g (Dietary Fiber 4g); Protein 2g.*

How to Pit and Peel an Avocado

Figure 12-2:
Extracting the meat of an avocado for blending into Fresh Avocado and Lime Dip.

And Now for Something Completely Different

Some of the best-tasting foods are the simplest to fix. The recipes in this section are good examples. They're quick and easy to prepare and feature a short list of fresh ingredients.

 **Roasted Garlic**

This dish is fun to serve — it makes the house smell so good, and it seems fancy. Pop a garlic bulb into the oven for an aromatic and nutritious spread on French bread rounds or homemade rolls.

Preparation time: *1 minute*

Cooking time: *60 minutes*

Yield: *4 servings*

1 large garlic bulb

2 teaspoons olive oil

1 Preheat the oven to 350 degrees.

2 Pull the outer, loose layers of tissue off the garlic bulb, leaving enough so that the cloves remain intact.

3 With a sharp knife, cut off the top of the bulb (about ¼ inch of the top — see Figure 13-3) to expose the tops of the cloves inside. Drizzle the tops of the cloves with the olive oil.

4 Wrap the bulb loosely in aluminum foil, seal the foil completely, and place in the hot oven.

5 Bake for about 1 hour, or until the cloves are soft. Remove from the oven.

6 Place the garlic bulb on a small serving dish. Lift the cloves out of the bulb with a dinner knife and smear the softened garlic on bread. If the cloves are hard to spread, squeeze the bulb to loosen them.

Per serving: Calories 20 (From Fat 9); Fat 1g (Saturated 0g); Cholesterol 0mg; Sodium 1mg; Carbohydrate 2g (Dietary Fiber 0g); Protein 0g.

PREPARING ROASTED GARLIC

1. PREHEAT THE OVEN TO 350°.

2. PULL THE OUTER, LOOSE LAYERS OF TISSUE OFF THE BULB. LEAVE ENOUGH TISSUE SO THE CLOVES REMAIN INTACT!

3.

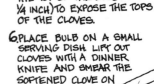

DRIZZLE THE TOPS WITH OLIVE OIL.

USE A SHARP KNIFE TO CUT OFF THE TOP OF THE BULB (ABOUT ¼ INCH) TO EXPOSE THE TOPS OF THE CLOVES.

4. WRAP THE BULB LOOSELY WITH FOIL, COMPLETELY AND PLACE IN THE HOT OVEN.

5. BAKE FOR ABOUT 1 HOUR UNTIL CLOVES ARE SOFT. REMOVE FROM OVEN.

6. PLACE BULB ON A SMALL SERVING DISH. LIFT OUT CLOVES WITH A DINNER KNIFE AND SMEAR THE SOFTENED CLOVE ON BREAD.

Figure 12-3: Roasted Garlic is easy to prepare and fun to serve.

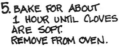

Creamy Pumpkin Spread

Slightly sweet with a rich pumpkin flavor, this spread is good served on toasted English muffins, bagels, or toasted French bread rounds. It also works as a dip for apple and pear slices.

Preparation time: *3 minutes*

Yield: *12 servings (about 1½ cups)*

1 cup pureed pumpkin (about half a 15-ounce can)

½ cup light cream cheese

2 tablespoons honey

½ teaspoon cinnamon (optional)

Combine all the ingredients in a blender or food processor and whip until smooth and creamy.

Vary It! *For a savory dip, omit the honey and cinnamon and substitute ½ teaspoon white pepper and a dash of hot sauce. Serve on toast or with sliced fresh vegetables.*

Per serving: *Calories 41 (From Fat 18); Fat 2g (Saturated 1g); Cholesterol 5mg; Sodium 51mg; Carbohydrate 5g (Dietary Fiber 1g); Protein 1g.*

Chapter 13

Soups for All Seasons

In This Chapter

▶ Incorporating beans and lentils into savory soups

▶ Enjoying cold soups in hot weather

▶ Adapting traditional soup recipes to make them vegetarian

Soups are welcome anywhere, anytime. In Chapter 11, soup is on the menu for breakfast. In this chapter, cold and hot soups vie for top billing at lunch and dinner, too. Soups work well as side dishes, appetizers, and light meals or snacks.

Beans and lentils are the foundation for many favorite vegetarian soups. They give soups a hearty, stick-to-your-ribs quality. Soups made with beans or lentils are flavorful and filling, so they're especially well suited to standing in as the main course. I include two taste-worthy examples in this chapter, with instructions for cooking beans, whether canned, flaked, or dried. Other soup recipes in this chapter feature seasonal vegetables and fruits.

Making Bean Soups

Whether you use canned beans for convenience or cook them the old-fashioned way — soaked and cooked from the dried form or quick-cooked in a pressure cooker (see Chapter 8 for instructions) — the recipes that follow taste great and are packed with nutrients. In the first recipe, dry lentils are used because they cook quickly and don't need presoaking.

⏲ *Lentil Soup*

This soup has a rich, savory flavor, and the lentils cook quickly because of their small size and flat shape. If you have leftover cooked spinach, stir it into this soup to add color and a healthful nutrition boost.

Preparation time: *10 minutes*

Cooking time: *About 60 minutes*

Yield: *8 servings*

1¼ cups dried lentils (½ pound)	½ teaspoon black pepper
5 cups water	2 tablespoons olive oil
1 medium onion, chopped	16-ounce can stewed or crushed tomatoes
1 teaspoon minced garlic	1 bay leaf
½ teaspoon salt	

1 Rinse the lentils in a colander or strainer.

2 Combine the lentils, water, onion, garlic, salt, black pepper, and olive oil in a large saucepan. Cover and cook on medium-high heat until boiling, about 14 minutes.

3 Stir in the tomatoes and bay leaf.

4 Reduce the heat to low, cover, and let simmer for 45 minutes or until the lentils are tender.

Vary It! *In place of regular crushed tomatoes, try fire-roasted crushed tomatoes if you can find them at your grocery store.*

Per serving: *Calories 144 (From Fat 36); Fat 4g (Saturated 1g); Cholesterol 0mg; Sodium 325mg; Carbohydrate 22g (Dietary Fiber 3g); Protein 6g.*

☙ *Vegetarian Chili with Cashews*

Raisins add a touch of sweetness to this chili, and cashews add a rich, nutty flavor. Serve it over steamed rice with cornbread and a green salad on the side. This chili is thick and thickens considerably more if left overnight. You can find a photo in the color section of this book.

Preparation time: *20 minutes*

Cooking time: *45 minutes*

Yield: *6 large servings*

2 tablespoons olive oil	*1 teaspoon black pepper*
4 medium onions, chopped	*16-ounce can stewed tomatoes or whole peeled tomatoes*
2 large green bell peppers, seeded and chopped	*2 tablespoons red wine vinegar*
2 stalks celery, minced	*1 bay leaf*
4 teaspoons minced garlic	*1 cup cashew pieces*
1 teaspoon dried basil	*⅓ cup raisins*
1 teaspoon oregano	*3 cups cooked dark red kidney beans (two 15-ounce cans)*
½ teaspoon chili powder	
1 teaspoon ground cumin	

1 In a large pot, heat the olive oil. Add the onions, green bell peppers, and celery and cook over medium heat until the onions are translucent, about 10 minutes.

2 Stir in the garlic, basil, oregano, chili powder, cumin, and black pepper.

3 Add the tomatoes (with their juice), vinegar, and bay leaf. Reduce the heat to low and continue cooking for 2 to 3 minutes.

4 Stir in the cashews and raisins and cook over low heat for another 16 to 17 minutes.

5 Add the beans and cook for an additional 25 minutes, stirring frequently. The chili is done when all the ingredients are well blended and soft and the chili is thick and bubbly.

Vary It! *In place of dark red kidney beans, a mixture of garbanzo beans, pinto beans, and red kidney beans is nice. A handful of fresh or frozen corn kernels adds color.*

Per serving: *Calories 385 (From Fat 144); Fat 16g (Saturated 3g); Cholesterol 0mg; Sodium 318mg; Carbohydrate 49g (Dietary Fiber 11g); Protein 14g.*

Enjoying Cold Soups in Hot Weather

Most people think of soup as a warm, hearty hand-warmer that thaws you from the inside out in winter months. It may not have occurred to you that soup can also satisfy when temperatures soar. Summer soups, served chilled, can be a light and refreshing way to seek relief from the heat and give wilted bodies a fluid and energy boost.

Southern Sweet Onion Soup can play it both ways — hot in the winter or cold in the summer, it tastes great either way. Following this recipe are two soups that are traditionally served cold. Gazpacho is light and spicy. Cantaloupe soup, like most fruit soups, is light and sweet. Both are refreshing and healthful.

ⓣ *Southern Sweet Onion Soup*

Soft, silken tofu is the secret ingredient that makes this a "cream" soup. Serve this soup hot with a plate of seasoned, steamed greens and a whole-grain muffin in cold weather, or serve it chilled in the summertime with whole-grain crackers and a green salad.

Preparation time: *15 minutes*

Cooking time: *45 minutes*

Yield: *Six 1-cup servings*

3 tablespoons olive oil	10.5-ounce brick silken tofu
2 medium sweet onions, sliced thin	Dash ground nutmeg
4 cups vegetable broth (if unsalted, add ½ teaspoon salt)	

1 Heat the olive oil in a medium skillet over medium heat. Add the onions and cook until the onions are translucent, about 10 minutes. Remove the skillet from the heat.

2 Pour the vegetable broth into a large saucepan. Add the sautéed onions and simmer, covered, for about 30 minutes or until the onions are very soft.

3 Remove from the heat and carefully transfer the mixture to a blender.

4 Break the tofu into pieces and add it to the ingredients in the blender. Blend until smooth and creamy, about 1 minute.

5 Pour the soup into bowls and garnish with a dash of nutmeg. Serve hot or chilled.

Vary It! *If you don't mind taking the time, you can bring out the onion flavor in this soup even more by cooking the onions longer. In Step 1, cook the onions in a large skillet over low heat for 45 minutes to 1 hour until they carmelize (begin to brown and sweeten). Then add the broth to deglaze the skillet. Gently stir the onions and broth together and then carefully transfer the mixture to a blender or food processor. Add the tofu and puree until the soup is smooth and creamy. Pour the soup into a saucepan and heat through, and then serve.*

Per serving: *Calories 120 (From Fat 81); Fat 9g (Saturated 1g); Cholesterol 0mg; Sodium 671mg; Carbohydrate 8g (Dietary Fiber 2g); Protein 4g.*

Creamy Cantaloupe Soup

This dreamy, sweet summertime soup is especially good when melons are ripe and in season. This soup makes a good snack or midday pick-me-up and can even be served for breakfast.

Preparation time: *10 minutes (plus time to chill)*

Yield: *4 servings*

1 medium cantaloupe, peeled and cut into chunks

1 cup orange juice

Juice from 1 fresh lemon or lime (about 2 tablespoons)

1 tablespoon honey

1 cup plain nonfat yogurt (vegans can substitute 1 medium ripe banana)

Fresh mint leaves

1 Combine the cantaloupe, orange juice, lemon or lime juice, honey, and yogurt in a blender or food processor and puree until smooth.

2 Refrigerate until the soup is very cold — at least 1 hour. Serve in glass bowls or cups, if available, and garnish with mint leaves.

Vary It! *If you love the aroma and flavor of fresh mint with melon, tear a mint leaf into tiny pieces and add it to the blender with the other ingredients. As the soup chills, the mint will blend with the other flavors.*

Per serving: *Calories 128 (From Fat 9); Fat 1g (Saturated 0g); Cholesterol 1mg; Sodium 60mg; Carbohydrate 28g (Dietary Fiber 1g); Protein 5g.*

Figure 13-1:
Coring, seeding, and dicing a bell pepper doesn't have to be difficult; just follow these steps.

How to Core and Seed a Pepper

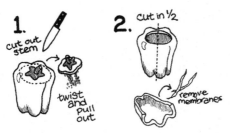

1. cut out stem — twist and pull out

2. cut in ½ — remove membranes

3. Cut into lengthwise strips

4. For cubes, hold strips together and cut crosswise

⌣ Easy Gazpacho

This spicy Spanish soup is served cold. Many variations exist, from very smooth to chunky. Adjust the "heat" according to your taste by adding more cayenne pepper and hot pepper sauce; this version is relatively mild. The soup's color and taste can vary slightly depending on the tomatoes you use, so if you like, add about a tablespoon of tomato sauce to the blender in Step 2. See the photo in this book's color section.

Preparation time: 15 minutes, plus time for bread to marinate

Yield: 5 servings

1 slice stale white bread	1 green bell pepper, chopped fine (see Figure 13-1)
2 tablespoons red wine vinegar	
1 tablespoon olive oil	1 cucumber, peeled and sliced
1 teaspoon minced garlic	¼ teaspoon cayenne pepper
28-ounce can whole peeled tomatoes	1 teaspoon hot pepper sauce
½ cup finely chopped onion	Juice of 1 fresh lemon (about 2 tablespoons)

1 Break the bread into small pieces and place it in a small cup or bowl. Pour the vinegar and oil on top and add the garlic. Mash with a fork; then set aside for at least 30 minutes.

2 Place the bread mixture in a blender and add 1 cup of the liquid from the canned tomatoes, plus the onion, green bell pepper, and cucumber (save a few tablespoons of onion and green bell pepper for garnish). Blend at low speed for 1 minute.

3 Add the remaining tomatoes and juice, cayenne pepper, hot pepper sauce, and lemon juice. Give the mixture a whirl in the blender to break up the whole tomatoes. Chill.

4 Garnish with a sprinkling of chopped onions, green bell peppers, or croutons and serve.

Per serving: Calories 99 (From Fat 27); Fat 3g (Saturated 0g); Cholesterol 0mg; Sodium 409mg; Carbohydrate 14g (Dietary Fiber 3g); Protein 3g.

Giving Tradition a Twist

Peanut soup is a mainstay in parts of West Africa, where it's usually made with chicken stock. Here, a vegetarian version remains loyal to the flavor and consistency of traditional peanut soup, but I've taken some poetic license in replacing chicken stock with vegetable broth and incorporating sweet potatoes and apples into the recipe.

☺ *West African Peanut Soup*

This very thick, creamy dish can stand alone as lunch or a snack or can be served as the first course at dinner. The flavor is overwhelmingly peanutty, so this recipe is undeniably for peanut lovers only. This delicious African soup is traditionally served for celebrations and special occasions and would work well for a North American Thanksgiving or wintertime event.

Preparation time: *15 minutes*

Cooking time: *30 minutes*

Yield: *6 servings*

1 tablespoon olive oil

1 medium onion, chopped

1 teaspoon cumin

1 pound cooked sweet potatoes, peeled and cut up (or one 15-ounce can)

1 medium tart apple (such as Granny Smith), peeled and cut up

4 cups vegetable broth

⅛ teaspoon cinnamon

½ teaspoon black pepper

¼ cup creamy peanut butter

1 Heat the oil in a large saucepan. Add the onion and cumin and cook over medium heat, stirring frequently, until the onion is translucent, about 5 minutes.

2 Add the sweet potatoes, apple, vegetable broth, cinnamon, and black pepper and continue cooking over medium heat until the mixture boils, about 4 minutes.

3 Reduce the heat and simmer for 20 to 30 minutes, or until the ingredients are soft.

4 Stir in the peanut butter. Carefully transfer the hot soup to a food processor or blender and puree until smooth.

5 Serve hot. Garnish with a dollop of sour cream or nonfat plain yogurt, chopped green onions, or chives.

Vary It! *For thinner soup, add more vegetable broth. You can also replace the sweet potatoes and apple with white potatoes and carrots in approximately the same amounts (omit the cinnamon if you do so).*

Per serving: Calories 207 (From Fat 45); Fat 9g (Saturated 1g); Cholesterol 0mg; Sodium 725mg; Carbohydrate 30g (Dietary Fiber 5g); Protein 5g.

Chapter 14

Simply Scrumptious Salads

In This Chapter

▶ Thinking creatively about salads

▶ Enjoying salads as light meals, sides, and snacks

Chilled salads — especially those made with fresh, seasonal ingredients — are refreshing in the summer months and add contrast to the temperature and texture of cooked foods in cold-weather months. In this chapter, salads move beyond the mundane and celebrate a diversity of flavors, textures, and colors.

Escaping the Iceberg Lettuce Wasteland

To many people, a salad is a bowl of anemic iceberg lettuce crowned with little more than a few shreds of carrot and a tomato wedge. Add a gob of Ranch or Thousand Island dressing, and you have a ho-hum side dish with mediocre nutritional value and nearly zero gustatory appeal. Iceberg lettuce is to salad dressing as a potato chip is to dip — not much more than a vehicle for the fat.

In this section, several well-chosen recipes show you what's possible if you think creatively and combine a variety of fresh and even canned and dried ingredients. I hope you'll agree that the results are far more appealing than the typical tossed salad.

The first three recipes use primarily fresh ingredients. Seeds and dried fruit add crunch and color. In one recipe, lavender lends an unexpected note to a mix of arugula and goat cheese. These are only three examples of the many creative options that exist for blending the fresh flavors of fruits and vegetables and other ingredients to make any number of satisfying salads.

Festive Broccoli Salad

The combination of green broccoli florets and red cherries makes this a lovely dish. The blend of flavors is unique and delicious. You may as well double the recipe — this one doesn't last. If you do happen to have leftovers, this salad tastes even better the second and third day after you prepare it.

Preparation time: *10 minutes*

Yield: *8 servings*

1 head broccoli, broken into florets (about 4 cups)	½ cup salted sunflower seed kernels
	½ cup reduced-fat or soy mayonnaise
1 cup dried cherries	2 tablespoons red wine vinegar
1 medium onion, chopped	¼ cup sugar

1 Place the broccoli, dried cherries, onion, and sunflower seed kernels in a large mixing bowl.

2 In a small bowl or cup, whisk together the mayonnaise, vinegar, and sugar to make the dressing and then pour it over the broccoli mixture.

3 Toss all the ingredients together until the broccoli mixture is covered with dressing. Chill for at least 1 hour before serving, or overnight for best flavor.

Per serving: *Calories 186 (From Fat 108); Fat 12g (Saturated 2g); Cholesterol 0mg; Sodium 110mg; Carbohydrate 20g (Dietary Fiber 2g); Protein 3g.*

Sunrise Salad

This nutrient-packed salad combines several beyond-the-ordinary ingredients to create a flavorful, filling main dish or accompaniment. Vegans can substitute chunks of soy cheese for the feta cheese if desired. Serve it with your favorite dressing — I like to make a balsamic vinaigrette or a similar olive oil–based dressing.

Preparation time: *15 minutes*

Yield: *8 servings*

6 cups mixed baby greens or Romaine lettuce	¼ cup walnuts, broken into pieces
1 cup shredded red cabbage	¼ cup feta cheese
1 cup canned garbanzo beans, drained and rinsed	Several large croutons
½ cup dried cherries	Several black olives
½ cup cherry tomato halves	

1 Toss the baby greens or lettuce, cabbage, garbanzo beans, dried cherries, cherry tomatoes, and walnuts together in a large bowl.

2 Scatter the feta cheese, croutons, and olives across the top and serve.

Vary It! *Substitute sunflower seeds for the walnuts.*

Per serving: *Calories 119 (From Fat 36); Fat 4g (Saturated 1g); Cholesterol 4mg; Sodium 91mg; Carbohydrate 17g (Dietary Fiber 4g); Protein 5g.*

THE LAST BITE

Arugula

Arugula, also known as rocket salad or roquette, is a dark, leafy green known for its distinctive sharp, spicy, peppery flavor, similar to that of mustard greens. Arugula is native to the Mediterranean and grows wild throughout southern Europe. It can be served cooked but is most popular as a salad green. Arugula is becoming very popular in the U.S. and can be found in many supermarkets.

Goat Cheese and Arugula Salad with Lavender-Vanilla Vinaigrette

The only way to describe this salad is "dreamy." If you've never tasted lavender-infused dressing, the best way to describe it is that it tastes like it smells. This recipe is adapted from one served at the Pewter Rose restaurant in Charlotte, North Carolina, where the salad has its own fan club. The recipe is not difficult to prepare, and it's worth the effort. See the color section for a photograph of this salad.

Preparation time: *45 minutes*

Yield: *6 servings*

Dressing:

5 tablespoons white wine vinegar

½ vanilla bean, split (see Figure 14-1)

¾ teaspoon untreated dried lavender

2 tablespoons clover honey

½ teaspoon salt

½ teaspoon black pepper

⅓ cup olive oil

Salad:

6 ounces goat cheese or chèvre

2 tablespoons freshly ground black pepper for dipping

¼ pound arugula, heavy stems removed

4 tablespoons pumpkin seeds, toasted

1 To make the dressing, warm the vinegar and vanilla bean in a small saucepan. Allow the vanilla bean to steep for 10 minutes.

2 Remove the pan from the heat and then remove the vanilla bean. Let the vinegar cool for 10 to 15 minutes.

3 Place the cooled vinegar in a blender or food processor and add the lavender, honey, salt, and black pepper. Blend, gradually adding the olive oil.

4 Strain the dressing through a fine mesh sieve. Set aside.

5 For the salad, divide the goat cheese or chevre into 18 portions. Roll into balls and dip one side of each ball into the pepper.

6 Arrange the arugula on 6 plates and put 3 balls of cheese on each plate. Drizzle the dressing and scatter the pumpkin seeds over the salad. Serve immediately.

The original recipe calls for double the amount of salt and goat cheese, as well as ¾ cup olive oil. It also calls for a garnish of deep-fried sweet potato strips. I adapted the recipe for this book to radically reduce the sodium, fat, and saturated fat content of the dish without unduly sacrificing flavor. Vegans can omit the goat cheese altogether and enjoy the flavorful dressing on this unique and wonderful salad.

You should be able to find vanilla bean and lavender flowers at a natural foods store, gourmet food store, or other specialty foods store. If you have trouble, see Chapter 24 for a list of online sources of ingredients.

Per serving: *Calories 290 (From Fat 216); Fat 24g (Saturated 8g); Cholesterol 22mg; Sodium 348mg; Carbohydrate 9g (Dietary Fiber 1g); Protein 10g.*

SPLITTING VANILLA BEANS

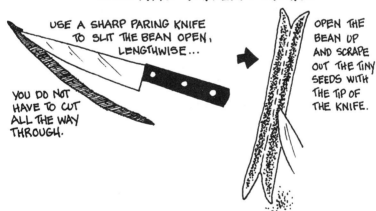

USE A SHARP PARING KNIFE TO SLIT THE BEAN OPEN, LENGTHWISE...

YOU DO NOT HAVE TO CUT ALL THE WAY THROUGH.

OPEN THE BEAN UP AND SCRAPE OUT THE TINY SEEDS WITH THE TIP OF THE KNIFE.

Figure 14-1: Splitting a vanilla bean is easy to do.

Making Substantial Salads

Salads are standard side dishes, but you can also serve them as healthful light meals or snacks. Teamed with a few whole-grain crackers, a roll, or a slice of toast, the salads that follow (including one that makes a good sandwich filling) are hearty enough to hold their own as quick and easy meals.

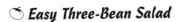

☞ Easy Three-Bean Salad

This recipe is worth doubling. It's delicious, and the leftovers taste even better after a day or two in the refrigerator. If you prefer a less-sweet salad, reduce the amount of sugar to your taste.

Preparation time: *10 minutes, plus chilling time*

Yield: *8 to 10 servings*

15½-ounce can cut green beans, drained and rinsed

15½-ounce can cut wax beans, drained and rinsed

15½-ounce can dark red kidney beans, drained and rinsed

½ cup chopped green bell pepper

½ red onion, chopped

½ cup sugar (or less, to taste)

⅔ cup vinegar

⅓ cup vegetable oil

½ teaspoon salt

2 teaspoons black pepper

1 Place the green beans, wax beans, kidney beans, green bell pepper, and red onion in a large bowl.

2 Combine the sugar, vinegar, and vegetable oil in a small bowl or cup, stir well, and pour over the bean mixture. Add the salt and black pepper and toss to coat.

3 Chill overnight. Toss again to coat the beans before serving.

Per serving: *Calories 185 (From Fat 81); Fat 9g (Saturated 1g); Cholesterol 0mg; Sodium 294mg; Carbohydrate 24g (Dietary Fiber 4g); Protein 3g.*

☙ *Tofu Salad*

If you've never tried tofu salad, you're in for a nice surprise. Many variations exist. This recipe is similar to traditional egg salad, but tofu takes the place of egg whites, and turmeric and mustard provide the color. The result is a mock egg salad that tastes and looks very much like the "real" thing. Serve it as a sandwich filling on bread, crackers, or rolls, or in a pita pocket with grated carrots. This salad also works well served on a bed of salad greens or as stuffing for a fresh, ripe tomato.

Preparation time: *10 minutes*

Yield: *6 servings*

1 pound firm tofu	*½ teaspoon black pepper*
½ teaspoon salt	*¼ teaspoon turmeric*
½ cup soy mayonnaise	*¼ cup finely chopped celery*
2 teaspoons yellow mustard	*2 green onions, finely chopped*
½ teaspoon garlic powder	

1 Mash the tofu with a fork or potato masher until crumbly.

2 Add the salt, mayonnaise, mustard, garlic powder, black pepper, and turmeric and mix well.

3 Add the celery and green onions and mix well. Chill before serving.

Per serving: Calories 110 (From Fat 63); Fat 7g (Saturated 1g); Cholesterol 0mg; Sodium 132mg; Carbohydrate 6g (Dietary Fiber 1g); Protein 6g.

☞ *Tomato and Garbanzo Bean Salad*

This is yet another recipe that you may want to double. It's absolutely delicious and tastes even better a day after you prepare it. This salad travels well and is pretty, so it's a good choice for covered dish dinners and parties — show it off in a glass salad bowl. (Look for a photo of this salad in the color section of the book.) You can assemble it up to a day ahead of time.

Preparation time: *15 minutes*

Yield: *6 servings*

Salad:

Two 15½-ounce cans garbanzo beans (chickpeas), rinsed and drained

2 cups cherry tomatoes or grape tomatoes, cut into halves

2 green onions, chopped

2 tablespoons chopped fresh basil

Dressing:

Juice of 1 fresh lemon (about 2 tablespoons)

1 tablespoon red wine vinegar

2 tablespoons olive oil

1 tablespoon salsa

¼ teaspoon paprika

¼ teaspoon tarragon

¼ teaspoon salt

½ teaspoon black pepper

1 Combine all the salad ingredients in a medium bowl and toss lightly.

2 Combine all the dressing ingredients in a small bowl or cup. Whisk together very well, and then quickly pour the dressing over the salad.

3 Cover and chill for at least 1 hour. Toss the salad gently before serving.

Per serving: *Calories 188 (From Fat 63); Fat 7g (Saturated 1g); Cholesterol 0mg; Sodium 211mg; Carbohydrate 26g (Dietary Fiber 7g); Protein 8g.*

⟳ Lentil Vinaigrette Salad

The lentils and brown rice lend a nutty flavor to this marinated vegetable dish, and the vinegar and lemon juice provide a little zip. This salad stays fresh in the refrigerator for two or three days. Take a cup to the office for a light lunch.

Preparation time: *15 minutes*

Yield: *6 servings*

Salad:	**Dressing:**
1 cup cooked brown rice	*2 tablespoons olive oil*
1 cup cooked brown lentils	*1 tablespoon red wine vinegar*
¼ cup finely shredded carrot	*Juice of ½ fresh lemon (about 1 tablespoon)*
¼ cup chopped cucumber	*½ teaspoon salt*
2 green onions, finely chopped	
¼ cup chopped green bell pepper	

1 Toss the salad ingredients together in a medium-sized bowl.

2 Combine the dressing ingredients in a small bowl or cup and whisk well. Pour over the salad and toss well to coat.

3 Chill for at least 2 hours. Toss again before serving.

Per serving: *Calories 110 (From Fat 45); Fat 5g (Saturated 1g); Cholesterol 0mg; Sodium 190mg; Carbohydrate 13g (Dietary Fiber 2g); Protein 4g.*

Adding flair to green salads

In addition to the recipes I share here, you can add flair to a basic mixed green or fresh vegetable salad in many ways. Consider the following additions:

✔ Chunks of fresh fruit such as orange, pear, or apple

✔ Slivered almonds or walnut pieces

✔ Sunflower seeds and pumpkin seeds

✔ Diced tofu

✔ Chopped dried fruits such as dried apples, pears, raisins, cherries, or figs

✔ Canned beans such as cannelloni beans (white kidney beans), garbanzo beans, and kidney beans, rinsed to remove the unsightly outer hulls

✔ Shredded red cabbage

✔ Grated carrot

Another trick to give a salad a special look is to run the tines of a fork lengthwise down the sides of a cucumber, scraping it, before slicing it into the salad. Another tip: Use the tip of a spoon to scrape away the seeds in tomato wedges before adding them to a salad. Doing so keeps globs of seeds from separating out and helps give the salad a neater appearance.

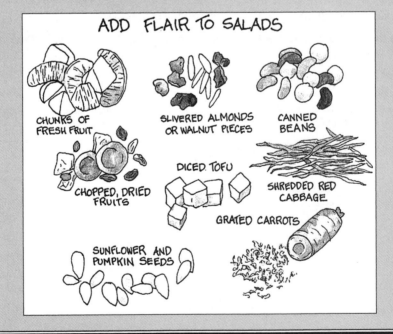

ADD FLAIR TO SALADS

CHUNKS OF FRESH FRUIT

SLIVERED ALMONDS OR WALNUT PIECES

CANNED BEANS

CHOPPED, DRIED FRUITS

DICED TOFU

SHREDDED RED CABBAGE

GRATED CARROTS

SUNFLOWER AND PUMPKIN SEEDS

Chapter 15

Entrees for Everyone

In This Chapter

▶ Preparing grain-based entrees

▶ Working with beans

▶ Incorporating pasta into main dishes

▶ Cooking with soy foods

*N*onvegetarians are often hard-pressed to visualize what a vegetarian might have for dinner. Meat-eaters tend to think of meals in terms of what type of meat they plan to eat: "I'm grilling out steaks tonight," or "Let's have fish."

What they *don't* mention is the rice or the potatoes or the salad or the vegetables — those are the side dishes, the incidentals. They aren't as important as the main course. We live in a culture for which meat is the focal point of the plate. Without it, nonvegetarians see a meal that isn't complete.

Vegetarians, on the other hand, often make a meal of any number of combinations of such foods as beans, rice and other grains, vegetables, and fruits. The "side dishes" come together on the plate, and the portions increase. The meal doesn't have to have a focal point.

On the other hand, many vegetarian main dishes do serve as entrees in vegetarian diets. This chapter introduces you to some of them. Some are foods from other cultures — often cultures in which a vegetarian tradition prevails. Others are familiar Western foods that I've modified to leave out the meat. Still others were vegetarian from the start and have been enjoyed for generations by vegetarians and nonvegetarians alike.

Making Grain-Based Entrees

Grains are rich in complex carbohydrates and protein, making them an ideal base for vegetarian entrees. Around the world, grains are blended with vegetables, herbs and spices, and other ingredients to make a wide range of flavorful, nutritious entrees.

For added flavor, some people like to use vegetable broth in place of water when they cook their grains. The recipe that follows uses quick-cooking couscous prepared with vegetable broth in place of water for extra flavor.

☺ *Tunisian Couscous*

Sarbaga Falk of Carrboro, North Carolina contributed this recipe. Sarbaga was a volunteer in the Peace Corps in Tunisia from 1970 to 1971. There she was introduced to couscous, where she saw it prepared many times and where bits of meat were typically added to the recipe. Here, she has adapted a traditional recipe to exclude the meat.

Preparation time: *20 minutes*

Cooking time: *45 minutes*

Yield: *6 servings*

2½ tablespoons olive oil

1 clove garlic, minced

1 medium onion, chopped

¼ teaspoon ground ginger

1 teaspoon cumin

¼ teaspoon turmeric

¼ teaspoon cayenne pepper

2 medium turnips, cubed

2 large carrots, sliced

2 medium potatoes (white or sweet), peeled and cubed

½ cup canned garbanzo beans, drained and rinsed

1 medium zucchini or summer squash, sliced

2 large ripe tomatoes, chopped

2 cups vegetable broth

2 cups instant couscous

Chopped fresh parsley for garnish

1 In a large skillet, heat the olive oil. Cook the garlic and onion in the oil over medium heat until the onions are translucent. Stir in the ginger, cumin, turmeric, and cayenne pepper.

2 Add the turnips, carrots, and potatoes and stir to distribute the spices. Add water to just cover the vegetables and cook for about 25 minutes or until the vegetables are nearly tender.

3 Add the garbanzo beans, zucchini, and tomatoes and cook for another 20 minutes or until all the vegetables are tender.

4 Heat the vegetable broth in a saucepan or microwave oven until boiling.

5 Place the couscous in a medium-sized bowl and add the vegetable broth. Cover and allow to set until the couscous has absorbed the broth and is tender. Fluff with a fork.

6 Serve the vegetables over a bed of couscous. Garnish with chopped parsley.

Vary It! *Add a peeled and diced medium eggplant in Step 3 for a "meaty" flavor.*

Per serving: *Calories 419 (From Fat 63); Fat 7g (Saturated 1g); Cholesterol 0mg; Sodium 446mg; Carbohydrate 77g (Dietary Fiber 8g); Protein 12g.*

The next two recipes feature brown rice combined with a variety of vegetables, herbs, and spices. One recipe contains dairy and eggs; the other is vegan.

🍅 Almond Rice Casserole

This recipe does not require you to precook the rice, although you can substitute cooked rice if you have some on hand. (If you leave out the vegetable broth because you're using precooked rice to make this dish, add ½ teaspoon salt in Step 2.) Serve this healthful dish with steamed greens and a tossed salad.

Preparation time: *15 minutes*

Cooking time: *1 hour*

Yield: *6 servings*

1 tablespoon olive oil

¾ cup diced celery

6 green onions, chopped

1 medium green bell pepper, chopped

1 cup sliced fresh mushrooms (or one 4-ounce can, drained and rinsed)

¼ cup chopped fresh parsley

½ teaspoon thyme

½ teaspoon oregano

½ teaspoon black pepper

1¼ cup uncooked brown rice (or about 5 cups cooked rice)

3¾ cup vegetable broth (omit if using precooked rice)

⅔ cup slivered almonds

1 Preheat the oven to 350 degrees.

2 Heat the olive oil in a large skillet. Cook the celery, onions, green bell pepper, mushrooms, and parsley in the oil over medium heat until the onions are translucent, about 10 minutes. Stir in the thyme, oregano, and black pepper.

3 Add the uncooked rice and cook for several minutes, mixing well. Transfer the ingredients to a lightly oiled 3-quart casserole. (If you're using precooked rice, add it in this step.)

4 Add the vegetable broth and half the almonds. Stir until the ingredients are well combined.

5 Top with the remaining almonds and bake, covered, for 1 hour or until the rice is soft and the liquid has been absorbed.

Per serving: *Calories 280 (From Fat 99); Fat 11g (Saturated 1g); Cholesterol 0mg; Sodium 646mg; Carbohydrate 39g (Dietary Fiber 5g); Protein 8g.*

Vegetarian Dinner-in-a-Dish

Garlic, onions, green bell peppers, cashews, and nutmeg are a delicious complement to the spinach and rice in this dish. I've made this savory dish lower in saturated fat and cholesterol by using reduced-fat and nonfat dairy products and egg whites instead of whole eggs.

Preparation time: *30 minutes*

Cooking time: *45 minutes*

Yield: *6 servings*

1 cup uncooked brown rice	*4 egg whites, slightly beaten*
Two 10-ounce packages frozen chopped spinach	*1 cup plain nonfat yogurt*
2 tablespoons olive oil	*½ teaspoon nutmeg*
½ medium onion, chopped	*1½ cups shredded reduced-fat mozzarella cheese*
½ medium green bell pepper, chopped	*½ cup chopped cashews*
1 clove garlic, minced	

1 Preheat the oven to 350 degrees. Cook the rice in a large saucepan according to package instructions. Set aside.

2 Heat the spinach on the stovetop or in a microwave oven until thawed and warmed, about 7 minutes. Drain well and squeeze the excess liquid out of the spinach. Set aside.

3 Heat the olive oil in a small skillet. Cook the onion, green bell pepper, and garlic in the oil over medium heat until the onion is translucent, about 3 minutes. Add to the cooked rice.

4 In a medium-sized bowl, combine the egg whites, yogurt, nutmeg, and spinach. Stir until well mixed.

5 Spread half the rice mixture in a lightly oiled 1½-quart casserole. Cover with half the spinach mixture.

6 Top with half the cheese. Repeat the rice and spinach layers (but don't add the remaining cheese yet).

7 Cover and bake for 25 minutes. Uncover and sprinkle the top with the remaining cheese and the cashews.

8 Bake, uncovered, for 10 minutes to crispen the top.

Per serving: Calories 360 (From Fat 126); Fat 14g (Saturated 4g); Cholesterol 11mg; Sodium 294mg; Carbohydrate 39g (Dietary Fiber 5g); Protein 20g.

↻ Quinoa Pilaf

This simple recipe is a tasty introduction to quinoa (pronounced "KEEN wah"), a grain that you can use in place of rice in almost any casserole or salad. Rutabaga and kohlrabi may be new to you as well. These are root vegetables that are similar in appearance to turnips. In fact, another name for kohlrabi is stem turnip. Kohlrabi has green, red, or purple skin, but the inside is white. Rutabagas have large, yellowish bulbs.

Preparation time: *15 minutes*

Cooking time: *20 minutes*

Yield: *Three 1-cup main dish servings, or six ½ cup side dish portions*

½ cup quinoa	*¾ cup cubed rutabaga or kohlrabi*
2 teaspoons olive oil	*½ cup diced zucchini*
½ medium onion, chopped	*½ cup diced yellow squash*
1 cup vegetable broth	*½ teaspoon salt*
1 cup shredded carrots	*Freshly ground black pepper (optional)*

1 Place the quinoa in a large bowl. Fill with cold water and then drain into a strainer. Repeat four times or until the water runs clear and no longer looks soapy.

2 In a 1½-quart saucepan, heat the olive oil. Over medium heat, cook the onions in the oil until translucent, about 3 minutes.

3 Add the quinoa and cook, stirring, until the quinoa makes popping sounds (about 1 to 2 minutes). Add the vegetable broth and bring to a boil.

4 Add the carrots, rutabaga or kohlrabi, zucchini, yellow squash, and salt. Reduce the heat and simmer, covered, for 15 minutes or until the broth is absorbed.

Vary It! *For additional seasoning, add minced fresh herbs in season, such as basil, sage, thyme, or tarragon.*

Per serving: *Calories 188 (From Fat 45); Fat 5g (Saturated 1g); Cholesterol 0mg; Sodium 366mg; Carbohydrate 31g (Dietary Fiber 4g); Protein 6g.*

☺ *Kamut with Mixed Vegetables*

Kamut (pronounced "kah MOOT") is a variety of wheat that has its roots in ancient Egypt. In this dish, cooked kamut is combined with beans and vegetables and lightly seasoned. A hearty serving can work as an entrée, or reduce the portion size and serve it as a side dish.

Preparation time: *15 minutes*

Cooking time: *35 minutes*

Yield: *4 servings*

2 teaspoons olive oil	*15-ounce can white kidney beans (cannelloni beans), small white beans, or navy beans*
1 medium onion, chopped	*½ cup zucchini, sliced*
2 cloves garlic, minced	*½ cup yellow squash, sliced*
1½ cups vegetable broth	*1 cup cooked kamut*
1 cup carrots, sliced	*¼ cup chopped fresh parsley*
1 cup celery, sliced	
1 bay leaf	

1 In a large saucepan, heat the olive oil. Cook the onions, and garlic in the oil over medium heat until the onions are translucent.

2 Add the broth and bring the mixture to a boil.

3 Add the carrots, celery, and bay leaf and return the mixture to a boil. Reduce the heat and simmer, uncovered, for 20 minutes; then remove and discard the bay leaf.

4 Add the beans, zucchini, squash, kamut, and parsley. Simmer, uncovered, for 10 minutes or until the vegetables are tender and the beans are hot.

Vary It! *For additional seasoning, add minced fresh herbs such as oregano, sage, thyme, or rosemary.*

Per serving: *Calories 192 (From Fat 36); Fat 4g (Saturated 0g); Cholesterol 0mg; Sodium 59mg; Carbohydrate 30g (Dietary Fiber 6g); Protein 9g.*

Creating Bean Dishes

For the bean recipes that follow, you can take advantage of the convenience of canned beans or soak dried beans the old-fashioned way. For the adventurous: Try your hand at pressure-cooking. (See Chapter 8 for more on various bean cooking methods.)

Basic Bean Burritos

You can doctor up this burrito any way you like, but here's a barebones version that virtually everyone loves. If you use whole beans, mash them with a potato masher or fork and mix until smooth in consistency. Cheese eaters can add a couple tablespoons of grated cheddar cheese or cheese alternative to the topping if desired.

Preparation time: *5 minutes*

Cooking time: *7 minutes*

Yield: *4 burritos*

2 cups canned vegetarian refried beans or plain mashed pinto beans or black beans

Four 10-inch flour tortillas

Chopped tomato, Romaine lettuce or spinach, and green onions (any combination, about 1 cup total)

¼ cup plain nonfat yogurt (vegans can use soy yogurt)

1 cup salsa

1 In a small saucepan, warm the beans over medium heat until heated through, about 7 minutes.

2 For each burrito, follow these instructions:

Lay a tortilla flat on a dinner plate. Spoon about ½ cup of the beans onto the center of the tortilla.

Fold one end of the tortilla toward the middle, and then fold the sides toward the middle. Leave the burrito on the plate with the end of the fold tucked underneath so that the burrito doesn't unroll on your plate. (See Figure 15-1.)

3 Top with salsa, chopped tomato, greens, and green onion. Add a dollop of plain yogurt and serve immediately.

Per serving: Calories 275 (From Fat 41); Fat 5g (Saturated 0g); Cholesterol 0mg; Sodium 197mg; Carbohydrate 45g (Dietary Fiber 6g); Protein 14g.

Prepping beans ahead of time

Soaking and cooking dried beans is not convenient if you want to use them for dinner that same evening. For that reason, it's a great idea to rinse, soak, drain, and store small quantities of beans in airtight containers in the freezer. When you're ready to fix a meal, you can pull a bag of beans out of the freezer and be hours ahead in prep time.

FOLDING A BURRITO

Figure 15-1:
How to fold a burrito so that it doesn't unroll on the plate.

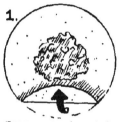

1.

FOLD ONE END OF THE TORTILLA TOWARD THE MIDDLE,

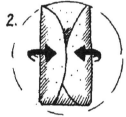

2.

AND THEN FOLD THE SIDES TOWARD THE MIDDLE.

3.

LEAVE THE BURRITO ON YOUR PLATE WITH THE ENDS TUCKED UNDERNEATH SO IT DOESN'T UNROLL ON YOUR PLATE.

Mayan Burrito

The inspiration for my very favorite burrito comes from the Flying Burrito restaurant in Chapel Hill, North Carolina, where the Flying Mayan Burrito is served. The sweet-savory combination of mashed sweet potatoes and whole black beans in the filling is addictive and sooooo nutritious. Leftover burritos are delicious reheated. You can add shredded cheddar cheese or soy cheese to the toppings if desired.

Preparation time: *10 minutes*

Cooking time: *10 minutes*

Yield: *4 burritos*

15-ounce can black beans, drained and rinsed

15-ounce can sweet potatoes (about 2 cups; if you want to use fresh, cooked sweet potatoes, be my guest, but it will take longer)

Four 10-inch flour tortillas

1 small Hass avocado, peeled and mashed

1 cup chopped Romaine lettuce

1 ripe tomato, diced

2 green onions, minced

½ cup plain nonfat yogurt

4 black olives, chopped

1 cup salsa

1 Heat the black beans in a small saucepan over low heat for about 5 minutes or until steaming hot. Alternatively, heat in a microwave oven on high for about 3 minutes.

2 Heat the sweet potatoes in a small saucepan or in a microwave oven. Mash with a potato masher or fork and stir until smooth.

3 Lay each tortilla flat on a dinner plate. Spoon about ⅓ cup of the sweet potatoes, and then the same amount of beans onto the center of the tortilla.

4 Fold one end of the tortilla toward the middle, and then fold the sides toward the middle. Leave the burrito on the plate with the end of the fold tucked underneath so that the burrito doesn't unroll on your plate.

5 Divide the remaining ingredients among the four burritos. Top each burrito with salsa, chopped lettuce, tomatoes, onions, black olives, avocado, and finally a dollop of yogurt. Serve immediately.

Per serving: *Calories 417 (From Fat 117); Fat 13g (Saturated 2g); Cholesterol 2mg; Sodium 457mg; Carbohydrate 65g (Dietary Fiber 12g); Protein 14g.*

The three recipes that follow have something in common: Each is served with rice, a common way to enjoy beans in many cultures. The first recipe hails from Latin America; the second is derived from Creole tradition. The third is a more recent creation that illustrates one of the many ways in which you can combine beans with other ingredients to arrive at an almost infinite number of delicious meals.

☉ *Cuban Black Beans*

This recipe can be served over rice as an entree or, thinned with vegetable broth, it can double as black bean soup. This flavorful, hearty dish goes well with a green salad and Fried Plantains (see Chapter 16).

Preparation time: *15 minutes*

Cooking time: *50 minutes*

Yield: *8 servings*

¼ cup olive oil

1 large onion, chopped

1 green bell pepper, chopped

2 stalks celery, including green leaves, chopped

4 garlic cloves, minced

4 cups (two 20-ounce cans) black beans, drained and rinsed (or 2 cups dried black beans, soaked or cooked in a pressure cooker)

2 teaspoons salt, or to taste

1 bay leaf

2 teaspoons ground cumin

½ teaspoon oregano

2 tablespoons lemon juice

1 In a large skillet, heat the olive oil. Cook the onions, green bell peppers, celery, and garlic in the oil over medium heat until the onions are translucent (about 10 minutes).

2 Add the beans, salt, bay leaf, cumin, oregano, and lemon juice and stir well to combine.

3 Cover and simmer for another 35 or 40 minutes, stirring occasionally to prevent sticking. Remove the bay leaf and serve over rice.

Per serving: *Calories 195 (From Fat 63); Fat 7g (Saturated 1g); Cholesterol 0mg; Sodium 593mg; Carbohydrate 25g (Dietary Fiber 9g); Protein 8g.*

☺ Creole Red Beans and Rice

This dish is a tradition in states such as Louisiana, where seasoned beans and rice are a favorite among people of mixed French, Spanish, and African descent. If you make the rice ahead of time, this dish takes very little time to prepare. Toss a salad and steam some broccoli or greens, and dinner's ready.

Preparation time: *10 minutes*

Cooking time: *15 minutes*

Yield: *8 servings*

3 tablespoons olive oil

1 large onion, chopped

3 cloves garlic, minced

½ cup chopped green bell pepper

1 stalk celery, with leaves, chopped

½ teaspoon salt

1 teaspoon cumin

1 tablespoon chili powder

½ teaspoon thyme

Two 15-ounce cans dark red kidney beans, rinsed and drained (about 3 cups)

4½ cups cooked rice

Fresh parsley for garnish

1 In a large skillet, heat the olive oil. Cook the onions, garlic, green bell pepper, and celery in the oil over medium heat until the onions are translucent, about 7 minutes. Add the salt, cumin, chili powder, and thyme and stir to combine.

2 Add the beans and mix well. Reduce the heat to low and continue cooking for several minutes until the beans are hot, stirring frequently to prevent sticking.

3 Add the rice to the bean mixture and mix all the ingredients together well. Cook for about 5 minutes to heat the rice through before serving. Garnish with sprigs of parsley.

Per serving: Calories 266 (From Fat 54); Fat 6g (Saturated 1g); Cholesterol 0mg; Sodium 164mg; Carbohydrate 45g (Dietary Fiber 7g); Protein 9g.

☻ Seasoned Cabbage and Beans

I usually serve this flavorful blend of vegetables and spices over steamed rice, but it could just as easily be paired with a baked potato or a bed of pasta. This dish is rich in dietary fiber and vitamin C.

Preparation time: *20 minutes*

Cooking time: *30 minutes*

Yield: *4 large servings*

1 tablespoon olive oil	Salt and black pepper to taste
1 medium onion, chopped	14-ounce can stewed tomatoes
2 cloves garlic, minced	½ cup water
1 red or green bell pepper, chopped	3 cups shredded cabbage
½ teaspoon paprika	15-ounce can pinto beans, drained and rinsed

1 In a large skillet, heat the olive oil over medium heat. Cook the onion, garlic, and green bell pepper in the oil until the onion is translucent, about 10 minutes.

2 Add the paprika, salt, black pepper, stewed tomatoes, and water and simmer for 5 minutes.

3 Add the cabbage and cook over low heat for 20 minutes, or until the cabbage is tender.

4 Add the beans and cook over low heat for an additional 10 minutes (or longer if you want softer cabbage).

Vary It! Substitute garbanzo beans, black beans, or white or red kidney beans for the pinto beans.

Per serving: *Calories 121 (From Fat 27); Fat 3g (Saturated 0g); Cholesterol 0mg; Sodium 410mg; Carbohydrate 21g (Dietary Fiber 6g); Protein 5g.*

ᕮ *Vegetarian Sarma*

This recipe is a makeover of a traditional Eastern European entree: cabbage rolls. In my family, we called this dish *sarma.* My Croatian grandmother prepared it the customary way, filled with ground meat and rice, but today we make it meatless. This dish looks more difficult to make than it is. Serve it with boiled potatoes and a green salad.

Preparation time: *45 minutes (including steaming the rice)*

Cooking time: *30 minutes*

Yield: *6 servings (12 cabbage rolls)*

1 large head cabbage (about 3 pounds)	*⅛ teaspoon salt*
1 medium onion, finely chopped	*⅛ teaspoon black pepper*
3 cloves garlic, minced	*½ teaspoon paprika*
2 tablespoons chopped pine nuts	*⅛ teaspoon cayenne pepper*
1½ cups cooked brown rice	*15-ounce can seasoned stewed tomatoes (Italian style or seasoned with herbs and spices)*
¼ cup chopped fresh parsley	
¼ cup golden raisins	*1 cup water or vegetable broth*
15-ounce can garbanzo beans, drained, rinsed, and mashed	

1 Wash and core the cabbage head. Place it in a large pot of boiling, salted water and cook until the leaves become soft and pliable, about 20 minutes. Remove it from the pot and gently remove 10 to 12 leaves from the cabbage and cut the core from each leaf.

2 Shred about half the remaining cabbage head in a food processor. Spread it on the bottom of a large baking dish or casserole and set aside.

3 Preheat the oven to 350 degrees.

4 In a medium skillet, heat the olive oil. Cook the onions and garlic in the oil on medium heat until the onions are translucent, about 7 minutes. Add the chopped pine nuts, rice, parsley, raisins, mashed beans, salt, black pepper, paprika, and cayenne pepper.

5 Using approximately ¼ cup filling for each cabbage leaf, place the filling at the core end of each leaf and fold the sides to envelop the filling. Roll or tuck into a neat package. Arrange the rolls over the shredded cabbage. (See Figure 15-2.)

6 Mix the water into the tomatoes and pour over the cabbage rolls.

7 Cover and bake for at least 30 minutes, or up to 45 minutes if you desire softer cabbage.

Per serving: Calories 204 (From Fat 27); Fat 3g (Saturated 0g); Cholesterol 0mg; Sodium 348mg; Carbohydrate 38g (Dietary Fiber 9g); Protein 9g.

FOLDING VEGETABLE SARMA

Figure 15-2:
Making
Vegetarian
Sarma
involves
folding the
cabbage
leaf around
the filling.

1. USE ABOUT ¼ CUP OF THE FILLING FOR EACH LEAF. PLACE AT THE CORE OF THE LEAF.

FOLD UP THE SIDES TO ENVELOPE THE FILLING.

2. ROLL OR TUCK INTO A NEAT PACKAGE AND ARRANGE OVER THE SHREDDED CABBAGE.

Combating the combustibles

Some people can eat beans with abandon and never suffer the slightest side effects. For others, a bowl of beans sets off a series of intestinal fireworks that can culminate in embarrassment at best and social isolation at worst. One of the byproducts of the digestion of beans and many other vegetables is gas, and some people produce more of it than others in response to certain foods. Beans happen to be high on the list of flatulence-producing vegetables.

Some people find that Beano, an over-the-counter product, helps ease the gas produced by bean digestion. Beano contains an enzyme that helps the body to break down the components of beans and other vegetables that cause gas. The only hitch: The company that produces

Beano recently acknowledged that its product contains fish gelatin, an ingredient that vegetarians avoid. For people with less-rigid dietary criteria, Beano may prove useful.

Exercise is another inexpensive and convenient way to help gas disperse. A long walk after dinner can be a great help in reducing intestinal gas.

The rinsing and soaking (and rinsing again) routine of preparing dried beans also can help reduce the gas-producing nature of beans. If you're using canned beans, rinsing them well before cooking not only removes the salt but also may help further reduce gas production.

Preparing Pasta Dishes

Consider that you can combine pasta with a long list of possible sauces, vegetables, cheeses, nuts, beans, herbs, and other ingredients, and it isn't hard to see that an almost infinite number of possible pasta permutations exist. The recipes that follow are a sampling.

☞ Spinach and Mushroom Manicotti

This recipe calls for manicotti noodles — long, hollow tubes of pasta that are about 4 inches long and 1 inch in diameter. Traditionally, they're cooked and then filled with a mixture of cheese and herbs and topped with a tomato-based pasta sauce. This version replaces cheese with tofu and nondairy Parmesan cheese. The result is a rich, flavorful dish with a fraction of the saturated fat and cholesterol of the original. This dish is good served with a bowl of minestrone soup, a tossed green salad, and fresh Italian bread.

Preparation time: *30 minutes or less*

Cooking time: *30 minutes*

Yield: *6 manicotti (6 small servings or 3 large servings)*

10-ounce package frozen chopped spinach, thawed	½ teaspoon black pepper
2 tablespoons olive oil	2 cups spaghetti sauce (any bottled or fresh variety)
1 medium onion, chopped	6 manicotti tubes
1 clove garlic, minced	Soy Parmesan cheese
4-ounce can sliced mushrooms, drained	1 tablespoon chopped fresh parsley
1 pound firm tofu	1 tablespoon diced black olives
Juice of 1 lemon	Chopped fresh parsley and black olives for garnish
1 teaspoon salt, if desired	

1 Preheat the oven to 350 degrees.

2 Cook the manicotti according to package directions. While the pasta cooks, drain the chopped spinach and squeeze out any remaining water. Set aside.

3 In a large skillet, heat the olive oil. Cook the garlic and onion in the oil over medium heat until the onions are translucent, about 10 minutes.

4 Chop the canned mushrooms if desired and add them to the onion mixture. Sauté for 1 additional minute.

5 Add the spinach to the onion mixture and sauté over low heat for 1 to 2 minutes, turning the contents of the skillet with a spatula to help combine them. Remove from the heat and set aside.

6 In a large bowl, place the tofu, lemon juice, salt, and black pepper. Mash well with a potato masher or fork.

7 Add the contents of the skillet to the tofu mixture. Mix well, using your hands if necessary to combine the ingredients thoroughly.

8 Oil a medium-sized rectangular baking pan or decorative casserole dish. Spoon two or three scoops of tomato sauce (about ½ cup) onto the bottom of the pan. Spread evenly.

9 Fill each manicotti tube with some of the tofu mixture. Place the manicotti side by side in the baking dish and cover with the remaining tomato sauce. (If you have extra tofu mixture left over, you can mix some of it into the tomato sauce before pouring it over the top of the manicotti.)

10 Sprinkle the tops of the manicotti lightly with soy Parmesan cheese.

11 Cover the pan loosely with aluminum foil and bake for 30 minutes. Remove the foil for the last 10 minutes of baking time.

12 Before serving, scatter chopped parsley and black olives over the top to garnish.

Vary It! *If manicotti tubes are not available, you can substitute cooked lasagna noodles. Spread the filling on noodles and roll them up instead of making filled tubes. You can also substitute chopped broccoli for the spinach if desired.*

Per serving: *Calories 277 (From Fat 81); Fat 9g (Saturated 1g); Cholesterol 0mg; Sodium 755mg; Carbohydrate 28g (Dietary Fiber 4g); Protein 13g.*

Sarbaga's Veggie Lasagne

Sarbaga Falk of Carrboro, North Carolina created this recipe while visiting friends in New York and helping out at their restaurant in Jamaica, Queens. Using jar spaghetti sauce and no-boil lasagna noodles makes the preparation a little quicker and more convenient.

Preparation time: *20 minutes*

Cooking time: *1 hour*

Yield: *10 servings*

1 jar (1 pound 9 ounces) prepared spaghetti sauce

8 ounces no-boil lasagna noodles

3 cups reduced-fat ricotta cheese

1 tablespoon olive oil

1 large head or 2 small heads broccoli

2 medium zucchini

1 large onion, chopped

4 egg whites

12 ounces shredded part-skim mozzarella cheese (3 cups)

¾ cup grated Parmesan cheese

1 teaspoon oregano

1 teaspoon thyme

¼ teaspoon dill

2 tablespoons dried parsley

½ teaspoon black pepper

1 Preheat the oven to 350 degrees.

2 Chop the broccoli and zucchini into small pieces. In a medium skillet, heat the olive oil. Cook the onions in the oil over medium heat until the onions are translucent, about 7 minutes. Add the broccoli and zucchini and steam for 2 to 3 minutes to partially cook. Remove from the heat.

3 In a medium bowl, mix the ricotta cheese, egg whites, oregano, thyme, dill, parsley, and black pepper and half the Parmesan cheese.

4 In a lightly oiled 13-x-17-inch pan, layer the lasagne as follows:

> Put a thin layer of tomato sauce on the bottom of the pan.
>
> Lay 4 uncooked lasagna noodles (or the number needed to fit pan in a single layer; break the noodles if necessary to fit).
>
> Add a layer of ricotta cheese, and then half the vegetable mixture, followed by half the mozzarella cheese.
>
> Repeat the layers, ending with a little more tomato sauce and the remaining Parmesan cheese.

5 Bake for 1 hour or until brown and bubbly.

Vary It! *If you have sun-dried tomato pesto or basil pesto on hand, spread some of that on the top of the lasagne along with the tomato sauce (or mixed in with the tomato sauce) in Step 5.*

Per serving: Calories 305 (From Fat 108); Fat 12g (Saturated 7g); Cholesterol 44mg; Sodium 618mg; Carbohydrate 26g (Dietary Fiber 4g); Protein 23g.

Pasta Primavera

Primavera means "spring style" in Italian. Primavera dishes are made with a variety of fresh vegetables. This recipe incorporates a light cream sauce — much lower in fat than the traditional pasta primavera recipe made with heavy cream.

Preparation time: *15 minutes*

Cooking time: *Less than 15 minutes*

Yield: *6 servings*

1 tablespoon olive oil	½ cup vegetable broth
1 medium onion, minced	3 tablespoons chopped fresh basil
1 clove garlic, minced	1 cup frozen peas, thawed
1 pound asparagus, trimmed and sliced diagonally in ¼-inch pieces	2 green onions, chopped
1 medium zucchini, sliced	½ teaspoon salt
1 medium carrot, sliced very thin	½ teaspoon black pepper
½ pound fresh mushrooms, sliced	1 pound hot cooked fettuccine
1 cup lowfat milk	½ cup grated Parmesan cheese
	½ cup toasted pine nuts

1 In a large skillet, heat the olive oil. Cook the onion and garlic in the oil over medium heat until the onions are translucent, about 7 minutes.

2 Add the asparagus, zucchini, carrot, and mushrooms and cook over medium heat for 2 minutes.

3 Add the milk, broth, and basil and cook over high heat until the liquid boils. Cook for about 3 minutes and then add the peas and green onions. Simmer for 1 minute.

4 Add the salt and black pepper, and then add the pasta, cheese, and pine nuts, tossing until the ingredients are well mixed. Serve immediately.

Vary It! *For a vegan version, omit the milk, broth, and cheese. Instead, toss the pasta with herbs, spices, and vegetables and an additional 2 to 3 tablespoons olive oil. Add nondairy Parmesan cheese if desired.*

Per serving: Calories 368 (From Fat 126); Fat 14g (Saturated 3g); Cholesterol 8mg; Sodium 272mg; Carbohydrate 71g (Dietary Fiber 6g); Protein 21.

⊙ *Pasta e Fagioli*

Pasta e Fagioli, which means simply "pasta with beans," is a highly nutritious, good-tasting, traditional Italian dish. This version is very simple, with just the slightest bit of olive oil, garlic, and onions to complement the mild flavor of the beans and pasta.

Preparation time: *10 minutes*

Cooking time: *Less than 15 minutes*

Yield: *4 servings*

2 tablespoons olive oil	*19-ounce can great Northern beans or cannelloni beans (white kidney beans), drained and rinsed*
½ medium onion, chopped	
2 cloves garlic, minced	*12 ounces elbow macaroni, small shells, bowtie pasta, or linguine broken into pieces*
½ cup vegetable broth	

1 In a large pot, boil water for the pasta and cook the pasta according to package instructions. Drain and set aside.

2 In a large skillet, heat the olive oil. Cook the onions and garlic in the oil over medium heat until the onions are translucent, about 7 minutes.

3 Add the broth to the skillet and bring the ingredients to a boil. Add the beans and simmer for 5 minutes, stirring frequently.

4 Add the cooked pasta to the skillet and stir to thoroughly combine with the other ingredients. Cook for 1 to 2 minutes or until heated through, stirring frequently.

Vary It! *Add additional herbs and spices, such as basil, rosemary, and/or thyme, in Step 1. Also consider adding sliced mushrooms and/or whole, peeled tomatoes (break them up with a wooden spoon after adding) in Step 3. If the dish becomes too thick (or if you're reheating leftovers), add several tablespoons of vegetable broth.*

Per serving: *Calories 547 (From Fat 81); Fat 9g (Saturated 1g); Cholesterol 0mg; Sodium 452mg; Carbohydrate 95g (Dietary Fiber 12g); Protein 27g.*

Pesto Pasta

Pesto is a sauce that's traditionally made with basil, pine nuts, Parmesan cheese, garlic, and olive oil. This dish is best in the summertime when basil is fresh and you can make a batch of pesto from scratch. Pesto is a snap to make and will fill your kitchen — and maybe your whole house — with the wonderful aroma of fresh basil. This recipe makes about double the amount of pesto that you will use for a pound of pasta. Store the leftover pesto in an airtight container for one week in the refrigerator, or freeze it in a small jar or airtight plastic bag for several months. When you can't make your own pesto, you can substitute ready-made pesto from the supermarket and have dinner ready in minutes.

Preparation time: *15 minutes*

Cooking time: *10 minutes or less for pasta*

Yield: *6 servings (about 1 cup)*

3 cups chopped fresh basil leaves, lightly packed	¼ teaspoon black pepper
	⅓ cup olive oil
4 cloves garlic	1 pound fettuccine or other pasta
4 tablespoons pine nuts	⅓ cup pine nuts
6 tablespoons Parmesan cheese or a combination of Parmesan and Romano cheeses, plus extra for garnish	6 cherry tomatoes and several sprigs parsley for garnish

1 Place the basil, garlic, pine nuts, Parmesan cheese, and black pepper in a blender or food processor. Process until well blended and smooth, and then dribble in the olive oil and continue processing until the mixture is the consistency of a smooth paste.

2 In a large pot, cook the pasta according to package instructions. Drain.

3 Combine the pesto, pine nuts, and pasta in the pot or in a large bowl and toss until the pasta is well coated. Use more or less pesto according to your preference (a ratio of about ¾ cup pesto to 1 pound pasta is typical). Add a few tablespoons of hot water to the pesto to thin it if necessary.

4 Serve immediately with grated Parmesan cheese. Garnish with cherry tomato halves and parsley.

Vary It! *If you don't have pine nuts on hand, you can substitute walnuts.*

Per serving: *Calories 337 (From Fat 126); Fat 14g (Saturated 3g); Cholesterol 79mg; Sodium 75mg; Carbohydrate 43g (Dietary Fiber 3g); Protein 11g.*

Summertime Pasta with Tomatoes and Basil

You can make this simple, light dish any time of the year, but I like to make it in the summertime when tomatoes and basil are in season and fresh. Vegans can substitute soy cheese for regular cheese or leave out the cheese entirely.

Preparation time: *15 minutes*

Cooking time: *10 minutes or less for pasta*

Yield: *6 servings*

3 cups diced Roma tomatoes (scoop out and discard most of the seeds)

½ cup chopped fresh basil

8 ounces shredded part-skim mozzarella cheese

1 cup grated Parmesan cheese

½ cup chopped walnuts

1 pound fettuccine or linguine

4 tablespoons olive oil

Freshly ground black pepper to taste

1 In a medium bowl, toss together the tomatoes, basil, mozzarella cheese, Parmesan cheese, and walnuts.

2 In a large pot, cook the fettuccine according to package instructions. Drain.

3 In the pot or in a large bowl, toss the pasta with the olive oil. Next, add the tomato mixture and toss until well combined.

4 Serve on individual plates and add freshly ground black pepper to taste. Garnish each plate with a black olive and a sprig of parsley.

Per serving: Calories 485 (From Fat 207); Fat 23g (Saturated 5g); Cholesterol 87mg; Sodium 406mg; Carbohydrate 50g (Dietary Fiber 4g); Protein 23g.

Cooking with Tofu, Tempeh, and Soy Cheese

Tofu, tempeh, and soy cheese are wonderfully helpful ingredients in vegetarian cuisine. Chapter 5 describes these nutrient-rich foods in greater detail; in this section, you can find information about cooking with these foods, as well as some tasty recipes. Go ahead, give 'em a try!

Tofu

Tofu is amazingly versatile. Because of its blandness, it picks up the flavors of whatever it's cooked with. Because of its texture, you can blend it into foods that require a smooth consistency, or you can grate, cube, chop, or crumble it into other dishes.

Tofu can be used in all the same ways that meat is used in entrees. Examples include the following:

- ✔ Mixing it with other ingredients into vegetarian burger patties, meatball, or loaves
- ✔ Adding it to a stir-fry made with vegetables and rice
- ✔ Marinating and baking it
- ✔ Grilling it on an indoor grill
- ✔ Slicing it and adding it to sandwiches
- ✔ Cubing it and adding it to salads
- ✔ Mixing it with other ingredients to make casseroles, lasagne, pasta sauce, chili, soups, and stews

Some people freeze tofu and then thaw it and use it in recipes in place of meat. Freezing tofu gives it a chewier, meatier texture that lends itself well to recipes for foods like those just listed. Firm or extra-firm tofu usually works best for recipes in which the tofu takes the place of meat.

Another tip: Boiling tofu in water for a few minutes — or steaming it over boiling water — can help it maintain its firmness and shape in recipes such as stir-fry and in marinated dishes. This step is not required, but if you decide to do it, be sure to let the tofu cool, and then pat the pieces dry before using them in the recipe.

Firm tofu is the basis for the two recipes that follow. For much more information about tofu, see Chapter 5.

☕ Chinese Vegetable Stir-Fry

In Chinese stir-fries, peanut oil is traditionally used to cook and flavor the vegetables. More convenient and just as effective for flavor is peanut butter, used here. Feel free to vary the amounts or varieties of vegetables according to your preferences and what you have on hand. This meal is highly nutritious — full of vitamins, minerals, and fiber. Leftovers aren't a problem — this dish tastes great reheated.

Preparation time: *20 minutes*

Cooking time: *15 minutes*

Yield: *4 servings*

4 tablespoons reduced-sodium soy sauce	3 carrots, thinly sliced
1 teaspoon sugar	1 cup broccoli florets
¼ teaspoon ground ginger	½ cup sliced canned water chestnuts
2 cloves garlic, minced	1 cup sliced fresh mushrooms
2 tablespoon vegetable oil	3 cups sliced bok choy (Chinese cabbage)
1 pound firm or extra-firm tofu, sliced into rectangles (approximately ¼ inch x 1½ inches)	2 cups mung bean sprouts
	1 tablespoons creamy peanut butter
1 large onion, chopped	1 tablespoon cornstarch
3 stalks celery, thinly sliced	¼ cup water

1 In a small bowl, combine the soy sauce, sugar, ginger, and garlic. Set aside.

2 In a large skillet, heat the vegetable oil over medium heat. Add the tofu and fry on both sides until browned. Remove, place on a plate lined with paper towels, and set aside.

3 Add the onion, celery, and carrots to the skillet and cook over medium heat for 3 to 4 minutes, stirring frequently.

4 Add the remaining vegetables, peanut butter, and soy sauce mixture and continue to cook for an additional 2 minutes. Stir.

5 Add the cornstarch and water and continue to cook until the liquid thickens and all the ingredients are steaming hot. Serve immediately over rice.

Per serving: Calories 238 (From Fat 117); Fat 13g (Saturated 1g); Cholesterol 0mg; Sodium 144mg; Carbohydrate 22g (Dietary Fiber 7g); Protein 13g.

☺ *Indonesian Saté*

Saté (pronounced "sah TAY") is a traditional Indonesian dish made with grilled meat and peanut sauce. This flavorful version substitutes tofu for meat. Serve it with steamed vegetables and rice. Fruit salad would make a refreshing dessert. You can use creamy peanut butter to make this recipe, but if you use crunchy peanut butter, you'll have ground nuts on top of the tofu slices — a nice touch.

Preparation time: *15 minutes (not counting time to marinate, if you choose to do so)*

Cooking time: *25 minutes*

Yield: *4 servings*

1 pound firm tofu	*2 teaspoons honey*
½ teaspoon vinegar	*¼ cup reduced-sodium soy sauce*
¼ cup peanut butter	*¼ cup boiling water*
1 tablespoon vegetable oil	*⅛ teaspoon cayenne pepper*
¼ teaspoon finely crumbled bay leaf	*¼ teaspoon ground ginger*

1 Preheat the oven to 375 degrees.

2 Lightly oil the bottom and sides of a 9-x-13-inch baking pan or shallow casserole.

3 In a small bowl or cup, whisk together the vinegar, peanut butter, oil, bay leaf, honey, soy sauce, water, cayenne pepper, and ginger, mixing well.

4 Spread a thin layer of the peanut butter mixture across the bottom of the baking pan.

5 Slice the tofu into ½-inch slabs and lay flat, one layer thick, in the baking pan. Pour the remaining sauce evenly over the top of the tofu.

6 (Optional) Let the tofu marinate in the refrigerator for 2 hours.

7 Bake at 375 degrees for 25 minutes and then serve.

Per serving: *Calories 242 (From Fat 153); Fat 17g (Saturated 3g); Cholesterol 0mg; Sodium 626mg; Carbohydrate 12g (Dietary Fiber 2g); Protein 15g.*

Making pizza with soy cheese

The last recipe in this chapter incorporates a different soy product — soy cheese — in a delicious, easy-to-make-at-home pizza. No need to order out anymore.

Soy cheese resembles cheese made from cow's milk and can be used in place of regular cheese in most recipes. Just like regular cheese, it comes in a variety of flavors and forms, including mozzarella-style, American-style, and cream cheese.

The only major drawback to soy cheese is its meltability — it doesn't melt as well as dairy cheese. For that reason, it's best used in recipes where it's mixed with other ingredients. It's less impressive as a pizza topping, although many people (such as those who are lactose-intolerant) use it that way. Soy cheese keeps in the refrigerator for two weeks to several months, depending on the variety.

Garden Pizza

Pizza is an easy food to make vegetarian — the list of possible toppings is seemingly endless. In this recipe, I show you how to take it one step further and make it vegan by using soy cheese. (Substitute regular mozzarella if you prefer.) Without all the high-fat dairy cheese, this pizza is a guiltless indulgence. This recipe makes two pizzas. You can make both pizzas at the same time, or you can save half the dough for another day. Pizza dough will keep in the freezer for up to three months.

Preparation time: *About 90 minutes (including time for dough to rise)*

Cooking time: *30 minutes*

Yield: *2 large pizzas (4 servings or 8 slices per pizza)*

Pizza Dough:

1½ teaspoons yeast

1 tablespoon honey or sugar

1¾ cup warm water (110 degrees)

1 teaspoon olive oil

½ teaspoon salt

2 cups whole-wheat flour

2 cups all-purpose flour

Pizza Toppings:

2 cups bottled pizza sauce (more or less to suit your taste)

2 cups shredded mozzarella-style nondairy cheese (or reduced-fat regular mozzarella)

2 cups combined of your choice of washed, chopped vegetables (whatever you have on hand): broccoli, mushrooms, green bell peppers, onions, black olives, pineapple chunks

Soy Parmesan cheese, if desired

1 In a large mixing bowl, dissolve the yeast in warm water (about 110 degrees) and add the honey or sugar. Add the oil and salt and stir.

2 Gradually add the flour, alternating between whole wheat and white. Mix well after each addition using a wooden spoon or your hands to make a soft dough.

3 Turn out the dough onto a floured board and knead for 5 minutes, adding more flour if needed.

4 Lightly oil the sides of the mixing bowl. Put the dough in the bowl, turn the dough over once, cover with a towel or waxed paper, and let set in a warm place for about 60 minutes.

5 While the dough rises, wash and chop the vegetables for the pizza topping. Set aside.

6 Divide the dough in half. Reserve one half for later if desired (store in the refrigerator or freezer).

7 Preheat the oven to 375 degrees.

8 Spread the dough on a 14-inch pizza pan. You can roll the dough out first on a floured surface or simply press the ball of dough onto the pizza pan and distribute it evenly by using your hands.

9 Spoon on the pizza sauce and spread it to within ½ inch of the edge of the dough.

10 Sprinkle the shredded cheese evenly over the pizza and then add the vegetable toppings.

11 Place the pizza in the oven and bake for 30 minutes, until the crust and/or cheese begins to brown lightly. Do not overcook.

12 Remove from the oven and let set for 5 minutes.

13 Cut into slices and serve. Sprinkle some Parmesan cheese on the pizza slices if desired.

Per serving: Calories 338 (From Fat 54); Fat 6g (Saturated 1g); Cholesterol 0mg; Sodium 537mg; Carbohydrate 58g (Dietary Fiber 7g); Protein 16g.

Cooking with tempeh

Similar to tofu, tempeh is relatively bland and picks up the flavors that it cooks with. In general, you can use tempeh in all the same ways you use meat — it can be crumbled or cubed and used in soups, stews, casseroles, and chili. It can also be marinated and baked or grilled. (You can find more information about tempeh in Chapter 5.)

If you're using tempeh in recipes in which it's crumbled — in salads, chili, pasta sauce, taco, or burrito filling, for example — steam it for a few minutes first over a pot of boiling water. Doing so softens it and makes it easier to crumble. Let it cool completely, and then crumble it into the recipe.

The two recipes that follow are good introductions to tempeh. Both use tempeh as an ingredient in variations of familiar foods: a tempeh-based sloppy Joe filling and a sandwich filling reminiscent of chicken salad. Don't expect these to taste exactly like their meat counterparts. They don't, but they do taste good in their own right and can be used in the same ways as their traditional cousins.

⏱ Tempeh Sloppy Joes

This is everyone's favorite alternative to burgers and hotdogs. Serve this sandwich filling on whole-grain burger buns. It's also good served on whole-grain toast. Sloppy Joe filling made with tempeh tastes similar to but not as greasy as the kind made with meat.

Preparation time: *15 minutes*

Cooking time: *20 minutes*

Yield: *4 servings*

1 tablespoon olive oil

1 clove garlic, minced

1 medium onion, chopped

½ green bell pepper, chopped

2 tablespoons reduced-sodium soy sauce

8-ounce package tempeh (any variety), crumbled into small pieces

½ cup spaghetti sauce

1 teaspoon brown mustard (or other mustard)

2 tablespoons cider vinegar

2 teaspoons sugar

4 whole-grain burger buns

1 In a medium saucepan, heat the olive oil. Add the garlic, onion, and green bell pepper and cook over medium heat until the onions are translucent, about 10 minutes. Add the tempeh and soy sauce and stir well. Cook for an additional 2 minutes.

2 Add the tomato sauce, mustard, vinegar, and sugar. Mix well and simmer for 10 minutes. Serve on whole-grain buns.

Per serving: *Calories 301 (From Fat 99); Fat 11g (Saturated 2g); Cholesterol 0mg; Sodium 634mg; Carbohydrate 39g (Dietary Fiber 3g); Protein 17g.*

☉ *Tempeh Salad*

This recipe is similar in consistency and appearance to chicken salad, but the seasonings give it a little extra kick. It makes a good sandwich filling and is also good in stuffed tomatoes or served on toast or in pita pockets.

Preparation time: *30 minutes (including time to steam tempeh)*

Yield: *Six 2-cup servings*

8-ounce package tempeh

2 stalks celery, chopped finely (leaves and stems)

¼ cup finely chopped green onions

¼ cup soy mayonnaise

2 teaspoons yellow mustard

1 teaspoon reduced-sodium soy sauce

1 clove garlic, minced

¼ teaspoon turmeric

1 Steam the tempeh over a pot of boiling water or in a vegetable steamer for about 20 minutes to soften. Let it cool; then crumble it into a medium-sized bowl.

2 While the tempeh cools, chop the onions and celery and set aside.

3 In a small bowl, whisk together the mayonnaise, mustard, soy sauce, garlic, and turmeric.

4 After the tempeh has cooled, add the chopped vegetables and the mayonnaise mixture and stir until the ingredients are well blended. Chill before serving.

Per serving: Calories 127 (From Fat 63); Fat 7g (Saturated 1g); Cholesterol 0mg; Sodium 96; Carbohydrate 9g (Dietary Fiber 0g); Protein 7g.

Chapter 16

Side Dish Spectaculars

In This Chapter

▶ Preparing vegetable sides good enough to steal the show

▶ Adding starchy side dishes that complement entrees

Sometimes, a very simple side is all that's necessary. In fact, an elaborate entree such as a layered casserole or an entree with multiple ingredients (bean burritos or vegetarian chili) often needs little more than a side of steamed broccoli or an ear of corn. On the other hand, an unexpected side dish or a side dish prepared in an unusual way can add a lot of excitement to your menu.

The recipes in this chapter are not difficult to prepare. They take just a few extra steps than, say, opening a bag of frozen mixed vegetables and heating them in the microwave does. You'll be happy that you took the extra time to make them.

Vegetable Side Dishes

The recipes that follow are made with a range of common vegetables that nearly everyone loves.

☺ Braised Sesame Greens

You can use kale or Swiss chard in this dish (pictured in the color section of the book). Both have a strong odor similar to that of cooked broccoli or cabbage. In this recipe, stir-steaming the greens gives them a milder flavor and softens them considerably, because most people find raw kale or Swiss chard too tough to eat. (Chapter 8 explains the technique of stir-steaming.)

Preparation time: *10 minutes*

Cooking time: *12 minutes*

Yield: *4 servings*

1 bunch kale or Swiss chard (about 1 pound)	*½ cup water*
1 teaspoon olive oil	*1 tablespoon sesame seeds*
1 clove garlic, minced	

1 Rinse the kale or chard leaves well, removing and discarding the thick stems (see Figure 16-1). Set aside the rinsed leaves.

2 In a skillet over low heat, cook the olive oil and garlic for 1 to 2 minutes, stirring to prevent sticking. Add the water and heat until steaming.

3 Add the greens and sesame seeds. Cover and cook over medium heat for 7 to 10 minutes or until tender.

Vary It! *You can substitute collard greens for the kale or chard in this recipe. In the photo in the color section of the book, the dish was made with red chard. Another option is to toast the sesame seeds before adding them to the recipe. To do so, preheat the oven to 350 degrees before Step 1. Spread the sesame seeds in a shallow pan and toast them in the oven for 7 to 8 minutes or until just browned.*

Per serving: *Calories 72 (From Fat 27); Fat 3g (Saturated 0g); Cholesterol 0mg; Sodium 44mg; Carbohydrate 11g (Dietary Fiber 2g); Protein 4g.*

KALE

Figure 16-1:
Rinsing and
removing
the stems
from kale.

RINSE THE LEAVES WELL
AND REMOVE THE
THICK STEMS.

☉ Scalloped Tomatoes

Brown sugar slightly sweetens this dish, taking the acidic bite out of the tomatoes.

Preparation time: *10 minutes*

Cooking time: *35 minutes*

Yield: *6 servings*

½ cup chopped onion

4 tablespoons olive oil

⅛ teaspoon nutmeg

¼ teaspoon black pepper

2 tablespoons brown sugar

1¾ cup breadcrumbs

3 cups (28 ounces) peeled whole tomatoes with no salt added

1 Preheat the oven to 350 degrees.

2 In a small skillet, heat the olive oil. Over medium heat, cook the onion in the oil until translucent. Add the nutmeg, black pepper, and brown sugar and cook over low heat for 1 additional minute.

3 Add the breadcrumbs and stir to mix well. Remove from the heat and set aside.

4 Pour the tomatoes (including the juice) into a medium bowl and break them up slightly with a wooden spoon.

5 Lightly oil an 8-x-8-inch baking pan. Spoon one-third of the breadcrumb mixture evenly over the bottom of the pan.

6 Spoon half the tomatoes over the breadcrumb mixture. Add another layer of breadcrumbs and then another layer of tomatoes, finishing with a layer of breadcrumbs. Pat the ingredients down lightly.

7 Bake for 30 minutes or until lightly browned and bubbly.

Vary It! *For extra flavor, use seasoned stuffing mix in place of the breadcrumbs.*

Per serving: *Calories 231 (From Fat 99); Fat 11g (Saturated 2g); Cholesterol 0mg; Sodium 739mg; Carbohydrate 31g (Dietary Fiber 3g); Protein 4g.*

⚲ *Roasted Roots*

Sarbaga Falk of Carrboro, North Carolina adapted this recipe from one that's served at Weaver Street Market, a co-op and natural foods store of which she is a member. This recipe is a particular favorite for potluck dinners and office lunch group gatherings, where it wins high praises for its delicious flavor that the herbs and the roasting process bring out. Peel the vegetables before cutting them. The beets stain the other vegetables a rich red color.

Preparation time: *20 minutes*

Cooking time: *55 minutes*

Yield: *8 servings*

2 carrots, sliced into 1-inch pieces	*1 bulb fennel, quartered*
1 medium turnip, sliced into 1-inch wedges	*⅓ cup olive oil*
3 to 4 beets, quartered	*4 cloves garlic (chopped or whole cloves)*
1 parsnip, cut lengthwise and then sliced	*Three 2-inch sprigs fresh rosemary, chopped*
1 medium onion, quartered	*½ teaspoon salt*
2 small leeks, split and washed	*½ teaspoon black pepper*
2 medium potatoes, cut into eighths	*5 tablespoons balsamic vinegar*

1 Preheat the oven to 350 degrees.

2 Toss the vegetables with the olive oil, garlic, rosemary, salt, and pepper. Set the fennel and leeks aside and arrange the remaining vegetables in one layer in an oiled roasting pan or on a greased cookie sheet. Do not cover.

3 Roast the vegetables for 15 minutes, and then add the fennel and leeks. Roast all the vegetables for an additional 50 minutes or until tender. Pay particular attention to the beets and make sure that they're soft before removing them from the oven.

4 Toss the vegetables with the balsamic vinegar and serve.

Per serving: *Calories 198 (From Fat 81); Fat 9g (Saturated 1g); Cholesterol 0mg; Sodium 216mg; Carbohydrate 27g (Dietary Fiber 5g); Protein 3g.*

☽ Steamed Carrot Pudding

This dish is a rich brown in color and is very pretty when made in a small pudding mold. Plan ahead because this pudding takes 2 hours to cook.

Preparation time: *15 minutes*

Cooking time: *2 hours*

Yield: *8 servings*

½ cup whole-wheat flour	*2 egg whites*
¼ teaspoon baking soda	*1 tablespoon vegetable oil*
¼ teaspoon baking powder	*½ cup grated carrots*
⅓ cup dark brown sugar, packed	*½ cup grated potatoes*
⅛ teaspoon salt	*¼ teaspoon grated lemon rind*
½ teaspoon cinnamon	*2 tablespoons chopped walnuts*
¼ teaspoon nutmeg	

1 Oil a 2½-cup casserole or a small pudding mold.

2 In a small bowl, mix the flour, baking soda, baking powder, brown sugar, salt, cinnamon, and nutmeg.

3 In a medium bowl, whisk together the egg whites and oil, and then stir in the dry ingredients. Add the carrots, potatoes, lemon rind, and walnuts and stir well. Pour the mixture into the pudding mold or casserole dish and cover tightly with foil.

4 Heat several cups of water to boiling.

5 Place a wire rack on the bottom of a deep pot, such as a large stockpot. Set the mold or casserole on the rack, and then add boiling water to the pot until the water is halfway up the side of the mold or casserole (see Figure 16-2).

6 Cover the pot and let the pudding simmer on low to medium heat for 2 hours.

7 Remove the pudding from the pot and let it cool on a rack until it's lukewarm. Unmold the pudding over a plate or serving dish. Serve warm or chilled.

Vary It! *Use pecans in place of walnuts. Omit the lemon rind if you're not a fan of lemon flavor.*

Per serving: *Calories 103 (From Fat 27); Fat 3g (Saturated 0g); Cholesterol 0mg; Sodium 110mg; Carbohydrate 17g (Dietary Fiber 1g); Protein 2g.*

A RACK FOR STEAMED CARROT PUDDING

DEEP POT

PLACE A WIRE RACK ON THE BOTTOM OF A DEEP POT. SET THE MOLD ON THE RACK. ADD BOILING WATER TO THE POT UNTIL HALFWAY UP THE SIDE OF THE MOLD.

MOLD OR CASSEROLE

RACK

BOILING WATER

Figure 16-2: Setting up a rack for Steamed Carrot Pudding.

🍅 *Green Beans and Walnuts*

Simply seasoned, this side dish is flavorful and easy to make. See the color section of this book for a photo.

Preparation time: *15 minutes*

Cooking time: *5 minutes*

Yield: *4 servings*

1 pound fresh green beans	*½ cup coarsely broken walnuts*
2 to 3 tablespoons water	*¼ teaspoon salt (optional)*
1 tablespoon olive oil	*¼ teaspoon white or black pepper, or to taste*
1 clove garlic, minced	

1 Clean the green beans and place them in a microwave-safe bowl. Add the water, cover, and steam in the microwave on high until the beans are just tender but bright green, about 2 minutes. Remove from the microwave oven, drain, and set aside.

(***Note:*** If you don't use a microwave oven, steam the vegetables in a medium pot. Heat 1 cup water in the pot until boiling. Add the beans, cover, and steam for several minutes until the beans are just tender but bright green, about 5 minutes.)

2 In a medium skillet over medium heat, cook the olive oil and garlic for 1 minute.

3 Add the beans, walnuts, salt (if desired), and pepper and cook for an additional 3 minutes or until the mixture is hot.

Per serving: *Calories 163 (From Fat 117); Fat 13g (Saturated 1g); Cholesterol 0mg; Sodium 8mg; Carbohydrate 11g (Dietary Fiber 5g); Protein 4g.*

Starchy Sides

These side dishes are stick-to-your ribs substantial — filling and delicious.

♨ Seasoned Home Fries

This is the ultimate easy recipe — there's no measuring, and it comes out great every time. You can leave out or reduce the amount of cayenne pepper if you like your food less spicy. These potatoes are hugely popular with everyone I serve them to, and the leftovers are good reheated. The cayenne pepper and paprika give the potatoes a nice coppery color.

Preparation time: *10 minutes*

Cooking time: *40 minutes*

Yield: *About 8 servings*

6 medium white potatoes

Several shakes each of garlic powder, oregano, cayenne pepper, and paprika

Vegetable oil spray or olive oil

1 Preheat the oven to 350 degrees.

2 Coat a baking sheet with vegetable oil spray or a thin layer of olive oil.

3 Wash the potatoes. Leaving the peels on, cut the potatoes into wedges and place them in a mixing bowl. (Small potatoes can be quartered. Cut fist-sized potatoes into 6 or 8 wedges each.)

4 Sprinkle the potato wedges with several shakes of each of the spices, more or less to your taste. Toss to coat.

5 Spread the potatoes in a single layer on the baking sheet. Spray the tops with a thin film of vegetable oil spray, or brush with olive oil.

6 Bake for about 40 minutes or until the potatoes are soft. Serve plain, with ketchup or salsa, or with malt vinegar for dipping.

Per serving (based on 6 medium potatoes): Calories 117 (From Fat 9); Fat 1g (Saturated Fat 0g); Cholesterol 0mg; Sodium 6mg; Carbohydrate 26g (Dietary Fiber 2g); Protein 2g.

☉ Rosemary-Roasted Red Potatoes

Another easy recipe. This dish is very aromatic and will give your home a wonderful fragrance.

Preparation time: *10 minutes*

Cooking time: *40 minutes*

Yield: *8 servings*

6 to 8 medium red potatoes (the size of a small fist)	*Three 3-inch sprigs fresh rosemary, chopped*
2 tablespoons dried parsley flakes	*2 tablespoons olive oil*

1 Preheat the oven to 350 degrees. Oil a 9-x-13-inch baking dish.

2 Wash the potatoes. Leaving the peels on, cut the potatoes into wedges and place them in a mixing bowl.

3 Add the parsley, rosemary, and olive oil and toss well to coat.

4 Dump the seasoned potatoes into a baking dish and spread evenly. Scrape any remaining herbs from the mixing bowl into the baking dish.

5 Bake, uncovered, for 40 minutes or until the potatoes are soft.

Per serving: *Calories 144 (From Fat 36); Fat 4g (Saturated 1g); Cholesterol 0mg; Sodium 8mg; Carbohydrate 26g (Dietary Fiber 2g); Protein 2g.*

☺ Family-Style Baked Beans

These traditional New England–style beans have a thick, dark, sweet sauce flavored with maple syrup and molasses.

Preparation time: *15 minutes*

Cooking time: *1 hour*

Yield: *6 servings*

3 cups (30 ounces) canned Great Northern beans or navy beans, drained

½ cup pure maple syrup

¼ cup molasses

2 tablespoons ketchup or tomato paste

1 teaspoon dry mustard

¼ teaspoon white pepper

1 medium onion, chopped

2 cloves garlic, minced

1 Preheat the oven to 350 degrees. Oil a 3-quart casserole.

2 Combine all the ingredients in a mixing bowl and stir to mix well.

3 Transfer the mixture to a casserole dish. Cover and bake for 45 minutes. After 45 minutes, uncover and continue to bake for an additional 15 minutes or until the top is browned and bubbly.

Per serving: *Calories 222 (From Fat 9); Fat 1g (Saturated 0g); Cholesterol 0mg; Sodium 296mg; Carbohydrate 49g (Dietary Fiber 7g); Protein 8g.*

☉ *Easy Baked Sweet Potatoes*

These potatoes are moist with a sweet-tart flavor.

Preparation time: *2 minutes*

Cooking time: *10 minutes*

Yield: *2 servings*

2 medium sweet potatoes or yams, scrubbed clean	*2 tablespoons brown sugar*
2 tablespoons water	*Juice from 1 fresh lime (about ¼ cup)*

1 Cut off the ends of the sweet potatoes with a paring knife and pierce each potato with a fork in several places.

2 Place the potatoes in a shallow, microwave-safe dish, add the water, and cover. Heat in the microwave on high for 10 minutes, or until the potatoes are soft when pierced with a fork.

(***Note:*** If you're cooking on the stovetop instead, place the potatoes in a small pot and cover with water. Bring the potatoes and water to a boil, lower the heat, cover, and let simmer on low to medium heat for about 30 minutes or until the potatoes are tender.)

3 Remove the potatoes from the oven and place them on a plate. Slice each potato lengthwise and fold it open into two halves.

4 Sprinkle each sweet potato with 1 tablespoon brown sugar, and then drizzle lime juice on top.

Vary It! *Add 2 tablespoons crushed pineapple to each potato in Step 4.*

Per serving: *Calories 160 (From Fat 0); Fat 0g (Saturated 0g); Cholesterol 0mg; Sodium 15mg; Carbohydrate 39g (Dietary Fiber 4g); Protein 2g.*

⏱ *Fried Plantains*

Plantains look like large bananas, but they taste starchy rather than sweet. They can be eaten green (unripe) or yellow (ripe). This simple recipe calls for ripe yellow plantains. You can serve them as a side dish with such entrees as Cuban Black Beans (see Chapter 15) and vegetable soups and stews.

Preparation time: *5 minutes*

Cooking time: *10 minutes*

Yield: *4 servings*

2 ripe yellow plantains

2 tablespoons vegetable oil or butter

1 Peel the plantains and slice them into ¼-inch circles or diagonally into ¼-inch slices.

2 Heat the butter or oil in a large skillet. Add the plantains, arranging them in a single layer in the skillet. Fry on both sides until golden brown and hot, about 10 minutes total. Serve.

Vary It! *Before frying, dip the plantain slices into flour or breadcrumbs. For a slightly sweet version, add 1 tablespoon brown sugar with the butter or oil in Step 2.*

Per serving: *Calories 169 (From Fat 63); Fat 7g (Saturated 1g); Cholesterol 0mg; Sodium 4mg; Carbohydrate 29g (Dietary Fiber 2g); Protein 1g.*

Maple Baked Acorn Squash

The inside of an acorn squash is deep yellow or orange, in vivid contrast to the green, sometimes mottled exterior. Maple syrup and brown sugar add sweetness to this warming wintertime dish.

Preparation time: *5 minutes*

Cooking time: *30 minutes*

Yield: *2 servings*

1 medium acorn squash	*2 tablespoons dark brown sugar*
2 teaspoons butter	*2 tablespoons pure maple syrup*

1 Preheat the oven to 350 degrees.

2 Cut the squash in half. Scoop out and discard the seeds and strings.

3 Put 1 teaspoon of the butter, 1 tablespoon of the maple syrup, and 1 tablespoon of the brown sugar in the center of each squash half.

4 Place the squash halves in a small, oiled baking dish and fill the dish ½ inch high with water.

5 Cover the dish loosely with foil and bake for 30 minutes or until the squash is soft.

Vary It! *Vegans or anyone seeking to limit saturated fat intake can leave the butter out of this recipe entirely. Add a couple tablespoons of finely minced Granny Smith apple to each squash half in Step 3 if desired.*

Per serving: *Calories 208 (From Fat 36); Fat 4g (Saturated 3g); Cholesterol 11mg; Sodium 53mg; Carbohydrate 45g (Dietary Fiber 4g); Protein 2g.*

☺ Tabbouleh

Lemon juice gives this Middle Eastern dish its tangy flavor, and mint provides its characteristic fragrance. Tabbouleh can be served as a side dish with sandwiches and burgers, or it can be paired with hummus in a pita pocket. See the color section for a photo.

Preparation time: *20 minutes, including time to cook bulgur wheat and let it cool*

Cooking time: *20 minutes*

Yield: *6 servings*

2 cups water	*¼ cup chopped fresh mint leaves*
1 cup bulgur wheat	*½ cup chopped fresh parsley*
¼ cup olive oil	*½ cup canned garbanzo beans, drained and rinsed*
Juice of 1 large lemon (about ¼ cup)	*2 medium tomatoes, finely chopped*
½ teaspoon salt	
3 green onions, chopped (white and green parts)	

1 Bring the water to a boil in a saucepan. Add the bulgur wheat, reduce the heat to low, cover, and simmer until the bulgur absorbs all the water, about 8 to 10 minutes.

2 Remove the bulgur wheat from the stovetop and set aside to cool for about 15 minutes.

3 In a medium bowl, combine the cooled bulgur wheat and the remaining ingredients and toss well.

4 Chill the tabbouleh for at least 2 hours before serving. It's best when you chill it overnight. Toss again before serving.

Vary It! *Leave out the mint or reduce the amount of mint if you're not a big fan.*

Per serving: *Calories 238 (From Fat 90); Fat 10g (Saturated 1g); Cholesterol 0mg; Sodium 206mg; Carbohydrate 34g (Dietary Fiber 7g); Protein 5g.*

Chapter 17

A Bounty of Breads and Rolls

In This Chapter

▶ Using grains to make breads and rolls

*I*n Chapter 5, I cover everything you need to know about grains and how to use them as the basis for entrees. In this chapter, you use both whole and processed grains to make a variety of breads and rolls.

Bread is sometimes called "the staff of life" — it's a dietary staple around the world. Teamed with a cup of soup, a salad, or a chunk of cheese, a slice of good, hearty bread is often all you need to round out a meal.

Savory Breads

The recipes that follow include both whole and processed grains. Although it's best for health's sake to choose whole-grain breads and cereals as often as possible, that doesn't mean that you can't also enjoy breads made with refined flour every now and then.

Many bread recipes work best when you use a combination of whole and refined flours. Whole grains lend a rich, nutty flavor to breads, while refined flours help lighten the texture. Together, they can be an ideal blend.

Country Cornbread

This cornbread is flavorful and moist — similar to spoonbread in consistency. Serve it warm alongside Vegetarian Chili with Cashews (see Chapter 15), with vegetable stews and casseroles, or in combination with such dishes as Family-Style Baked Beans, Braised Sesame Greens, and Scalloped Tomatoes (all in Chapter 16).

Preparation time: *10 minutes*

Cooking time: *30 minutes*

Yield: *4 servings*

2 tablespoons olive oil	½ teaspoon baking soda
¾ cup cornmeal	½ teaspoon salt
2 egg whites	½ cup chopped onion
1½ cups plain nonfat yogurt	¼ teaspoon black pepper

1 Preheat the oven to 425 degrees. Oil a 1-quart casserole or skillet.

2 Combine all the ingredients in a medium-sized bowl and stir until completely mixed.

3 Pour the batter into a casserole or skillet and bake for 30 minutes or until set. Do not overcook.

Vary It! *Add ¼ cup chopped sun-dried tomatoes.*

Per serving: *Calories 210 (From Fat 72); Fat 8g (Saturated 1g); Cholesterol 2mg; Sodium 554mg; Carbohydrate 27g (Dietary Fiber 2g); Protein 9g.*

☞ Cheese Bread

This flavorful bread is low in fat and contains no saturated fat or cholesterol if you make it with soy cheese.

Preparation time: *30 minutes, plus rising time of at least 1 hour*

Cooking time: *60 minutes*

Yield: *2 loaves (24 slices)*

6 cups all-purpose flour	*1 tablespoon olive oil*
1½ teaspoons salt	*¾ cup cheddar-style soy cheese (or other cheese substitute)*
1 tablespoon granulated sugar	
1 package (¼ ounce) active dry yeast	*1 tablespoon black pepper*
1¾ cups warm water	

1 Stir together the flour, salt, sugar, and olive oil in a medium mixing bowl.

2 Combine the yeast and water in a small cup and stir until the yeast is dissolved.

3 Pour the yeast mixture into the flour and mix thoroughly in an electric mixer with a dough hook, in a food processor, or with your hands.

4 Remove the dough from the bowl, turn onto a floured surface, and knead for 10 minutes (or knead for 10 minutes by machine). Figure 17-1 shows the proper technique for kneading bread dough.

5 Cover with a towel or waxed paper and let rise in a warm place until doubled in size, about 1 hour.

6 On a floured surface or in the bowl of a food processor or mixer with a dough hook, combine the cheese and black pepper and then knead the dough into the cheese mixture. Continue kneading for 6 or 7 minutes until the cheese and pepper are well incorporated into the dough.

7 Divide the dough into 2 loaves. Place each ball into an oiled 9-x-5-x-3-inch loaf pan. Cover the loaf pans and let the dough rise for 30 minutes to 1 hour, until it reaches to just above the top of the loaf pan. Preheat oven to 350 degrees.

8 Bake for 60 minutes or until the bread is browned on top and sounds hollow when thumped with your knuckles.

9 Remove from the oven, let cool, and serve.

Vary It! *Add 2 teaspoons chopped dill or other favorite herb in Step 6.*

Per serving: Calories 148 (From Fat 18); Fat 2g (Saturated 0g); Cholesterol 0mg; Sodium 194mg; Carbohydrate 25g (Dietary Fiber 1g); Protein 6g.

THE PROPER WAY TO KNEAD DOUGH

1. MIX THE WET + DRY INGREDIENTS TOGETHER TO FORM A CRUMBLY MASS.

2. PUSH THE DOUGH DOWN AND AWAY FROM YOU WITH YOUR PALMS.

TRANSFER TO A LIGHTLY FLOURED SURFACE.

3.

Figure 17-1:
How to knead bread dough with your hands so that your breads come out perfect every time.

LIFT THE DOUGH AND GIVE IT A QUARTER TURN. FOLD OVER, KNEAD AND GIVE IT ANOTHER QUARTER TURN. KEEP REPEATING THE PROCESS.

THE DOUGH WILL APPEAR SMOOTH AND ELASTIC WHEN IT HAS BEEN KNEADED WELL.

Whole-Wheat Crescent Rolls

These rolls fill the house with the delicious aroma of yeast bread and make any meal special. Their texture is soft and slightly chewy. They freeze well and are good left over for two or three days. The addition of whole-wheat flour makes these rolls more nutritious and flavorful than rolls made with only white, refined flour. It also gives them a nice light brown color. You can find a picture of these rolls in the color section of this book.

Preparation time: *15 minutes, plus 2 hours for the dough to rise*

Cooking time: *20 minutes*

Yield: *32 rolls*

1 package (¼ ounce) active dry yeast	*1 teaspoon salt*
¼ cup warm water	*2 egg whites*
¾ cup warm milk	*¼ cup vegetable oil*
2 tablespoons sugar	*1½ cups whole-wheat flour*
2 tablespoons honey	*2 cups all-purpose flour*

1 In a large mixing bowl, dissolve the yeast completely in the water.

2 Add the milk, sugar, honey, salt, egg whites, oil, and whole-wheat flour. Stir until all the ingredients are well combined and the dough is smooth.

3 Add the all-purpose flour and mix until the dough forms a ball. If the dough is too sticky to handle, add several more tablespoons of flour as necessary.

4 Place the dough on a floured surface and knead for several minutes until it's smooth and elastic.

5 Oil a large bowl with olive oil. Place the dough ball in the bowl, and then turn it over once so that you lightly coat the top of the dough ball with oil. Cover with a towel or waxed paper and let the dough rise in a warm place until doubled in size, about 2 hours.

6 Punch down the dough ball with your fist; then divide the ball into 2 pieces.

7 Place the dough balls one at a time on a floured surface. Roll each piece of dough into a circle approximately 12 inches in diameter. Lightly brush each circle with vegetable oil or butter. With a sharp knife, cut the circle in half, and then in quarters, continuing until you have 16 wedges of dough. (See Figure 17-2.)

8 Preheat the oven to 350 degrees. Beginning at the wide end of each wedge, roll the dough into a crescent shape, ending by pressing the tip onto the roll. Set each roll on a lightly oiled baking sheet and bend the ends slightly to give the roll a crescent shape.

9 Cover and let the rolls rise for about 30 minutes before baking. Bake for 15 minutes or until the rolls are lightly browned. Do not overcook.

Per serving: Calories 74 (From Fat 18); Fat 2g (Saturated 0g); Cholesterol 0mg; Sodium 80mg; Carbohydrate 12g (Dietary Fiber 1g); Protein 2g.

MAKING WHOLE-WHEAT CRESCENT ROLLS

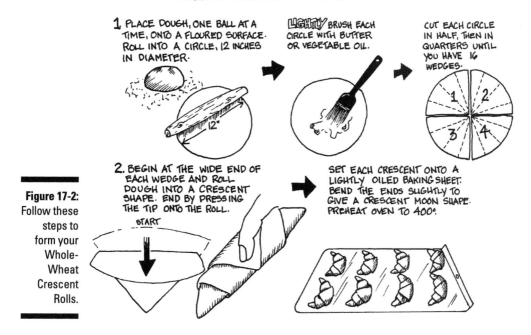

Figure 17-2: Follow these steps to form your Whole-Wheat Crescent Rolls.

1. PLACE DOUGH, ONE BALL AT A TIME, ONTO A FLOURED SURFACE. ROLL INTO A CIRCLE, 12 INCHES IN DIAMETER.

LIGHTLY BRUSH EACH CIRCLE WITH BUTTER OR VEGETABLE OIL.

CUT EACH CIRCLE IN HALF, THEN IN QUARTERS UNTIL YOU HAVE 16 WEDGES.

2. BEGIN AT THE WIDE END OF EACH WEDGE AND ROLL DOUGH INTO A CRESCENT SHAPE. END BY PRESSING THE TIP ONTO THE ROLL.

START

SET EACH CRESCENT ONTO A LIGHTLY OILED BAKING SHEET. BEND THE ENDS SLIGHTLY TO GIVE A CRESCENT MOON SHAPE. PREHEAT OVEN TO 400°.

☺ *Karen's Brown Bread*

This high-protein bread is dense, rich, and a beautiful dark brown color.

Preparation time: *10 minutes*

Cooking time: *1 hour*

Yield: *1 loaf (12 slices)*

1½ cups graham flour	*1½ cup plain soymilk*
1 cup all-purpose flour	*½ cup blackstrap molasses*
½ teaspoon salt	*1 cup chopped walnuts*
1 teaspoon baking soda	*8 ounces chopped dates*
2 teaspoons baking powder	

1 Preheat the oven to 400 degrees.

2 In a mixing bowl, stir together the flours, salt, baking soda, and baking powder.

3 Add the soymilk and molasses and stir well to blend. Stir in the walnuts and dates.

4 Spread the batter in an oiled 9-x-5-x-3-inch loaf pan. Bake for 60 minutes. Serve warm.

Per serving: *Calories 260 (From Fat 81); Fat 9g (Saturated 1g); Cholesterol 0mg; Sodium 290mg; Carbohydrate 46g (Dietary Fiber 4g); Protein 6g.*

Honey Wheat Beer Bread

This bread is soft, slightly sweet, and golden brown, and it's remarkably quick to prepare. Yeast is unnecessary because the beer gives the bread its lift. Note that dark beer gives the bread a richer color, but it also may lend a stronger beer flavor. See the color section of this book for a photograph of Honey Wheat Beer Bread.

Preparation time: *10 minutes*

Cooking time: *45 minutes*

Yield: *1 loaf (12 slices)*

2 cups self-rising flour (see note)	*1 teaspoon baking powder*
¾ cup whole-wheat flour	*¼ cup honey*
¼ cup toasted wheat germ	*12 ounces beer (light or dark)*

1 Preheat the oven to 350 degrees.

2 Combine the flours, wheat germ, and baking powder in a mixing bowl and stir well.

3 Add the honey and beer and blend well.

4 Pour the batter into an oiled and floured 9-x-5-x-3-inch loaf pan. Bake for 40 minutes or until lightly browned. Serve warm.

Self-rising flour is all-purpose flour with salt and baking soda mixed into it. Many people keep it on hand for biscuit making.

Per serving: *Calories 142 (From Fat 9g); Fat 1g (Saturated 0g); Cholesterol 0mg; Sodium 300mg; Carbohydrate 29g (Dietary Fiber 2g); Protein 4g.*

Sweet Breads

The recipes in the preceding section were for savory breads. The recipes in this section are for sweeter breads — quick breads and muffins — as well as a recipe for traditional cinnamon rolls, which are good *any*time.

In some of the savory recipes, yeast provided the lift. In the quick breads and muffins that follow, baking powder and baking soda serve that purpose and help shorten the preparation time.

☺ Date Bran Muffins

These dense, flavorful muffins make a good breakfast bread or snack. The bran cereal adds a hefty dose of dietary fiber, and the dates add flavor and sweeten the muffins.

Preparation time: *15 minutes*

Cooking time: *25 minutes*

Yield: *10 muffins*

1 cup plain soymilk	*½ teaspoon baking soda*
1 tablespoon vinegar	*⅓ cup packed brown sugar*
1½ cups bran cereal	*½ ripe banana, mashed*
1 cup all-purpose flour	*¼ cup vegetable oil*
2 teaspoons baking powder	*¾ cup chopped dates*

1 Preheat the oven to 400 degrees.

2 Pour the soymilk into a bowl and add the vinegar. Stir; then add the bran cereal. Set this mixture aside for a few minutes to let the bran absorb the milk.

3 In a large bowl, combine the flour, baking powder, baking soda, and brown sugar.

4 Add the banana and oil to the soymilk and cereal mixture and stir well to combine. Then add this mixture to the dry ingredients and stir until the ingredients are just moistened.

5 Stir in the dates. The batter will be stiff.

6 Oil muffin tins or line them with paper, and divide the batter among 10 muffins.

7 Bake for 25 minutes or until the muffins are browned and set.

Per serving: *Calories 202 (From Fat 54); Fat 6g (Saturated 1g); Cholesterol 0mg; Sodium 180mg; Carbohydrate 37g (Dietary Fiber 4g); Protein 3g.*

Pear Bread

This rich breakfast or dessert bread is low in saturated fat and contains no cholesterol. You can peel the fruit or leave the peel on.

Preparation time: *15 minutes*

Cooking time: *1 hour*

Yield: *1 loaf (12 slices)*

½ cup vegetable oil	*½ teaspoon salt*
1 cup sugar	*½ teaspoon baking soda*
1 teaspoon pure vanilla extract	*1 teaspoon baking powder*
1 tablespoon powdered vegetarian egg replacer	*¼ teaspoon nutmeg*
¼ cup water	*¼ cup plain nonfat yogurt*
2 cups all-purpose flour	*1 large pear, chopped*

1 Preheat the oven to 350 degrees.

2 In a mixing bowl, combine the oil, sugar, and vanilla.

3 Mix the powdered egg replacer with the water until dissolved. Whisk into the oil and sugar mixture.

4 In a separate bowl, combine the flour, salt, baking soda, baking powder, and nutmeg. Mix well.

5 Mix the dry ingredients into the oil and sugar mixture, alternating with the yogurt. Stir in the pears.

6 Pour the batter into a greased 9-x-5-x-3-inch loaf pan and bake for 1 hour until golden brown on top.

Vary It! Substitute coarsely chopped apple for the pear.

Per serving: Calories 235 (From Fat 81); Fat 9g (Saturated 1g); Cholesterol 0mg; Sodium 187mg; Carbohydrate 36g (Dietary Fiber 1g); Protein 3g.

⟡ Zucchini Bread

This is another good breakfast or snack bread in the summer, when zucchini is in season and abundant. The recipe makes two loaves — serve one and freeze the other. You can find a photo of this bread in the color section of the book.

Preparation time: *30 minutes*

Cooking time: *1 hour*

Yield: *2 loaves (24 slices)*

2 cups sugar	*2 cups all-purpose flour*
1 cup vegetable oil	*¼ teaspoon baking powder*
4½ teaspoons powdered vegetarian egg replacer	*2 teaspoons baking soda*
	3 teaspoons cinnamon
6 tablespoons water	*1 teaspoon salt*
3 teaspoons vanilla	*1 cup chopped walnuts*
2 cups coarsely grated unpeeled zucchini, packed	

1 Preheat the oven to 350 degrees.

2 Combine the sugar, oil, egg replacer, water, and vanilla in a large bowl. Add the zucchini and mix well.

3 In a separate bowl, combine the flour, baking powder, baking soda, cinnamon, and salt. Stir to blend the dry ingredients well.

4 Add the dry ingredients to the zucchini mixture. Mix well. Stir in the nuts.

5 Pour into two greased and floured 9-x-5-x-3-inch loaf pans. (Make sure that the pans are well greased!) Bake for 1 hour or until the tops of the loaves are golden brown.

Vary It! *If you prefer a lighter, less oily bread, reduce the amount of vegetable oil to ¾ cup.*

Per serving: *Calories 215 (From Fat 108); Fat 12g (Saturated 1g); Cholesterol 0mg; Sodium 207mg; Carbohydrate 25g (Dietary Fiber 1g); Protein 2g.*

○ Carob Chip Banana Bread

The combination of banana and carob makes this is a sweet, richly flavored bread for Sunday brunch or dessert. If you prefer, you can substitute regular ol' chocolate chips for the carob chips in this recipe.

Preparation time: *15 minutes*

Cooking time: *60 to 70 minutes*

Yield: *1 loaf (12 slices)*

½ cup vegetable oil	1 teaspoon baking powder
1 cup sugar	½ teaspoon baking soda
1 tablespoon powdered vegetarian egg replacer	½ teaspoon salt
	6 ounces carob chips (about 1 cup)
4 tablespoons water	½ cup chopped walnuts
2 ripe bananas, mashed	
2 cups all-purpose flour	

1 Preheat the oven to 350 degrees.

2 In a medium bowl, whisk together the oil, sugar, egg replacer, and water. Add the bananas and blend well with an electric mixer.

3 In a separate bowl, combine the flour, baking powder, baking soda, and salt. Add this mixture to the banana mixture gradually, beating well between additions.

4 Stir in the carob chips and walnuts.

5 Pour the batter into an oiled 9-x-5-x-3-inch loaf pan and bake for 60 to 70 minutes or until the bread is golden brown. When cool enough to handle, remove from the pan.

Vary It! *Substitute milk chocolate chips, semisweet chocolate chips, or butterscotch chips for the carob chips.*

Per serving: *Calories 344 (From Fat 153); Fat 17g (Saturated 5g); Cholesterol 0mg; Sodium 184mg; Carbohydrate 44g (Dietary Fiber 2g); Protein 5g.*

THE LAST BITE

The charm of carob

Carob powder is made from the dried pods of the carob tree, indigenous to the Mediterranean. It resembles cocoa in flavor and color, but it contains no caffeine. You can use it measure for measure in place of cocoa in recipes. Likewise, carob chips have the advantage of containing no saturated fat and can be used in place of chocolate chips in recipes.

Old-Fashioned Cinnamon Rolls

These rolls (pictured in the color section of this book) are soft and chewy and sweet and will fill your home with the welcoming fragrance of cinnamon and freshly baked bread. Egg whites replace whole eggs in this version to reduce saturated fat and cholesterol without sacrificing flavor.

Preparation time: *45 minutes, plus an hour and 45 minutes for dough to rise*

Cooking time: *20 minutes*

Yield: *24 rolls*

Rolls:

1 cup whole-wheat flour

3 cups all-purpose flour

1 package (¼ ounce) active dry yeast

1 cup plain soymilk or milk

¾ cup sugar

¼ cup vegetable oil

1 teaspoon salt

4 egg whites

¼ cup butter

2 teaspoons cinnamon

Glaze:

1 cup powdered sugar

½ teaspoon vanilla

2 tablespoons soymilk or milk

1 In a large mixing bowl, combine the whole-wheat flour, 1 cup of the all-purpose flour, and the yeast and set aside.

2 Combine the soymilk, ¼ cup of the sugar, the oil, and the salt in a saucepan and heat on low until warm (no more than 110 degrees, or just warm to the touch). Stir to blend, and then add to the flour and yeast mixture. Whisk in the egg whites.

3 Beat on high speed for about 4 minutes, stopping occasionally to scrape down the sides.

4 Stir in enough (most) of the remaining all-purpose flour to make a stiff dough.

5 Remove the dough from the mixing bowl and set it on a floured surface. Knead the dough for about 10 minutes, adding more flour by the tablespoon as needed to prevent sticking. When you're finished kneading, the dough should be smooth and elastic.

6 Set the dough in an oiled bowl, and then turn it to oil the top of the dough ball. Cover with a towel or waxed paper and let rise in a warm place until doubled in size, about 1 hour.

7 After the dough has doubled, punch it down and divide it into two pieces. Roll each piece of dough into a rectangle about ¼ inch thick.

8 Melt the butter and brush it onto each rectangle of dough. In a small cup, mix the cinnamon and the remaining ½ cup sugar and sprinkle the mixture evenly over both rectangles of dough.

9 Roll up the rectangles, starting at the widest ends. Pinch the ends shut with your fingers and press the seams into the dough. (See Figure 17-3.)

10 Cut the rolls into 1-inch pieces and place the pieces cut side down in two oiled baking dishes or 9-inch round nonstick pans. Cover each dish with a towel or waxed paper and let the rolls rise in a warm place until doubled in size, about 45 minutes. Preheat the oven to 375 degrees.

11 Bake for 20 minutes or until the rolls are slightly browned. Do not overcook.

12 While the rolls are baking, prepare the glaze by mixing the confectioner's sugar, vanilla, and 1 tablespoon of the soymilk. Add additional soymilk in increments of 1 teaspoon until the glaze is thick but pourable. Drizzle the glaze over the warm rolls and serve.

Vary It! *Add ½ cup chopped walnuts or the same amount of raisins or currants to the filling in Step 8.*

Per serving: *Calories 163 (From Fat 45); Fat 5g (Saturated 2g); Cholesterol 5mg; Sodium 134mg; Carbohydrate 27g (Dietary Fiber 1g); Protein 3g.*

ASSEMBLING OLD-FASHIONED CINNAMON ROLLS

1. REMOVE DOUGH FROM BOWL AND SET ON A FLOURED SURFACE.

KNEAD DOUGH FOR ABOUT 10 MINUTES. ADD MORE FLOUR BY TABLESPOON AS NEEDED TO PREVENT STICKING.

WHEN YOU'RE FINISHED KNEADING, DOUGH SHOULD BE SMOOTH + ELASTIC.

2. SET THE DOUGH IN AN OILED BOWL AND TURN DOUGH SO THE TOP IS OILED. COVER WITH A TOWEL OR WAXED PAPER AND LEAVE IN A WARM PLACE UNTIL DOUBLED (ABOUT 1 HOUR).

3. WHEN DOUGH HAS DOUBLED IN VOLUME, PUNCH IT DOWN AND DIVIDE INTO 2 PIECES.

ROLL EACH PIECE OF DOUGH INTO A RECTANGLE ABOUT ¼" THICK.

4. MELT THE BUTTER + BRUSH INTO EACH RECTANGLE OF DOUGH. MIX THE SUGAR + CINNAMON AND SPRINKLE EVENLY OVER THE TWO RECTANGLES.

5. ROLL UP THE RECTANGLES STARTING AT THE WIDEST ENDS.

PINCH THE ENDS SHUT WITH YOUR FINGERS. PRESS THE SEAMS INTO THE DOUGH.

6. CUT THE ROLLS INTO 1 INCH THICK PIECES AND PLACE THEM CUT SIDE DOWN INTO AN OILED BAKING DISH. COVER THE DISHES WITH A TOWEL OR WAXED PAPER. LET RISE UNTIL DOUBLED, ABOUT 45 MINUTES. PREHEAT OVEN TO 375°.

Figure 17-3: Old-Fashioned Cinnamon Rolls are worth the extra effort they require (and they really aren't that difficult to make!).

Chapter 18

Desserts

In This Chapter

▶ Using tofu as a dairy substitute in delicious desserts
▶ Preparing fabulous pies, cakes, cookies, and more
▶ Making puddings with soymilk in place of cow's milk

*P*eople often think of desserts as caloric extravagances — not much in the way of nutrition in exchange for the calories. That's not always the case, however, as many of the recipes in this chapter prove.

The keys to making wholesome, good-tasting desserts include minimizing the use of fat-laden dairy products such as butter, cream cheese, and cream or whole milk, as well as reducing the amounts of oil and sugar. Mixing whole-grain flour with all-purpose flour when possible is also a good idea. You'll notice that fruit is a major component of many of the recipes in this chapter, boosting fiber and phytochemical content and reducing the calories of some desserts.

Remember, desserts should be enjoyed. Although some of the desserts in this chapter are higher in calories than others and should be viewed as once-in-a-while indulgences, most can be worked into a health-supporting diet anytime.

Substituting Tofu for the Dairy Products in Desserts

You can use silken soft tofu to make a wide range of desserts, spreads, sauces, fillings, and toppings. It's smooth and creamy when blended with liquid ingredients. Numerous recipes in this book show the range of possibilities for using tofu, but generally it can be used in many recipes that traditionally call for cream cheese, sour cream, whipped cream, and milk.

Tofu can replace dairy products (and eggs) in recipes for

- ✔ Puddings, custard, and pie filling
- ✔ Cheesecake
- ✔ Pastry fillings
- ✔ Whipped topping
- ✔ Smoothies

Pies

These two pies are festive and are good choices for holidays and special occasions.

⌀ Maple Pecan Pumpkin Pie

Tofu replaces the eggs and milk in this pumpkin pie recipe. The filling is thick, rich, and smooth.

Preparation time: _15 minutes_

Cooking time: _40 minutes_

Yield: _One 9-inch pie (8 slices)_

15-ounce can pumpkin (about 2 cups)

8 ounces silken firm tofu

½ cup pure maple syrup

½ teaspoon ground ginger

1 teaspoon cinnamon

¼ teaspoon nutmeg

1 tablespoon flour

9-inch pie shell

¼ cup chopped pecans

1 Preheat the oven to 350 degrees.

2 Place the pumpkin, tofu, maple syrup, ginger, cinnamon, nutmeg, and flour in a blender or food processor and process until smooth.

3 Pour the pumpkin mixture into the pie shell.

4 Sprinkle the chopped nuts evenly over the top of the pie.

5 Bake for about 40 minutes, or until set. Cool and then serve.

Per serving: Calories 236 (From Fat 99); Fat 11g (Saturated 2g); Cholesterol 0mg; Sodium 137mg; Carbohydrate 31g (Dietary Fiber 3g); Protein 5g.

 Tortoni Pie

A blend of cherries, chocolate, and rum gives this rich pie a festive appearance and flavor.

Preparation time: *25 minutes (including time for the ice cream to soften)*

Freezing time: *60 minutes*

Yield: *One 9-inch pie (8 servings)*

½ gallon Rice Dream vanilla or other nondairy ice cream substitute	¼ cup cherry juice (from the jar of maraschino cherries)
¼ cup rum	6 ounces chocolate or carob chips
1 tablespoon pure vanilla extract	9-inch ready-made chocolate crumb crust
1 small jar maraschino cherries, drained and chopped (reserve cherry juice)	

1 Leave the ice cream out at room temperature until slightly softened, about 10 minutes.

2 In a large mixing bowl, combine the ice cream, rum, vanilla, cherries, cherry juice, and chocolate chips. Stir with a large spoon until the ingredients are well blended and the mixture is smooth.

3 Pour the ice cream mixture into the pie shell. Cover with foil and place in the freezer until hardened, about 1 hour.

Per serving: Calories 558 (From Fat 216); Fat 24g (Saturated 8g); Cholesterol 0mg; Sodium 312mg; Carbohydrate 73g (Dietary Fiber 4g); Protein 6g.

Cakes

The recipes that follow completely or partially eliminate eggs and dairy products, greatly reducing the levels of saturated fat and cholesterol with delicious results.

☉ Island Upside-Down Cake

This cake is very moist and has a wonderful soft, springy texture. The blend of bananas, pineapple, coconut, and pecans is scrumptious, and the fragrance is divine.

Preparation time: *20 minutes*

Cooking time: *45 to 55 minutes*

Yield: *8 servings*

¼ cup butter

½ cup sugar

20-ounce can unsweetened pineapple rings, drained (reserve juice)

1 ripe banana, mashed

1 tablespoon powdered vegetarian egg replacer blended with 4 tablespoons water

1 cup plain or vanilla soymilk mixed with 1½ teaspoons vinegar

¾ cup brown sugar

2 tablespoons vegetable oil

1 teaspoon pure vanilla extract

1¼ cups all-purpose flour

½ teaspoon baking soda

½ teaspoon baking powder

½ teaspoon salt

1 Preheat the oven to 350 degrees.

2 In an 8-x-8-inch baking pan over low heat on the stovetop, melt the butter over low heat. Add the sugar, stir, and continue to cook for a few minutes until the sugar has completely dissolved into the butter.

3 Add about 5 tablespoons of the reserved pineapple juice to the butter and sugar mixture. Stir until completely blended, remove the pan from the heat, and set it aside.

4 Arrange 6 pineapple rings on the bottom of the baking pan in two lines of three rings each (see Figure 18-1).

5 In a mixing bowl, combine the banana, egg replacer, soymilk, brown sugar, oil, and vanilla. Mix until well blended and smooth.

6 Add the flour, baking soda, baking powder, and salt to the banana mixture. Mix until well blended and smooth.

7 Pour the batter over the pineapple rings in the baking pan. Bake for 40 to 50 minutes or until the cake is set in the middle and lightly browned.

8 Remove the cake from the oven and cool in the pan for 15 minutes. When the pan is cool enough to handle, invert the cake onto a serving plate. Cut into 8 squares and serve warm.

Per serving: *Calories 379 (From Fat 117); Fat 13g (Saturated Fat 5g); Cholesterol 16mg; Sodium 329mg; Carbohydrate 64g (Dietary Fiber 2g); Protein 3g.*

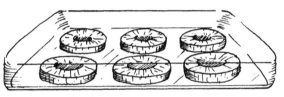

Figure 18-1: Arranging the pineapple rings for Island Upside-Down Cake. ARRANGE 6 PINEAPPLE RINGS ON THE BOTTOM OF THE BAKING PAN IN 2 LINES OF 3 RINGS EACH.

☼ Cocoa Pinks

This recipe is adapted from a dessert that has been a family favorite since I was a child. These cupcakes have a not-too-sweet, comforting cocoa flavor. The cocoa gives them a rosy brown color on the inside.

Preparation time: *30 minutes*

Cooking time: *25 minutes*

Yield: *About 22 cupcakes*

½ cup whole-wheat flour

2½ cups all-purpose flour

1 tablespoon cocoa

1 teaspoon salt

¾ cup vegetable oil

1¼ cup sugar

1 tablespoon powdered vegetarian egg replacer blended with 4 tablespoons water

1 teaspoon pure vanilla extract

1 teaspoon baking soda

1 cup cold water

6 ounces (1 cup) semi-sweet chocolate chips

½ cup chopped walnuts

Confectioner's sugar

1 Preheat the oven to 375 degrees.

2 In a small bowl, combine the flours, cocoa, and salt, stir to blend, and then set aside.

3 In a large mixing bowl, cream the oil and sugar together, and then add the egg replacer and vanilla.

4 In a cup, combine the baking soda and water and stir to dissolve.

5 Add the baking soda mixture alternately with the dry ingredients to the creamed mixture, beginning and ending with the dry ingredients, blending well on low speed after each addition.

6 Stir half the chocolate chips and nuts into the batter.

7 Line muffin tins with paper liners and fill each a little more than half full with batter.

8 Sprinkle the remaining chocolate chips and nuts over the tops of the cupcakes.

9 Bake for about 25 minutes. The cupcakes should appear done but no more than very lightly browned. Be careful not to overcook them, or they'll become dry.

10 After the cupcakes cool, sift confectioner's sugar over the tops.

Per cupcake: Calories 234 (From Fat 108); Fat 12g (Saturated 3g); Cholesterol 0mg; Sodium 165mg; Carbohydrate 29g (Dietary Fiber 1g); Protein 3g.

Company Apple Cake

This cake is moist and slightly sweet. It's large, so consider freezing half for later. It is a nice dish to serve to overnight guests in the morning or with coffee or tea in the afternoon.

Preparation time: *30 minutes*

Cooking time: *1 hour and 10 minutes*

Yield: *16 slices*

5 large Granny Smith apples, peeled and sliced

2⅓ cups sugar

2 teaspoons cinnamon

1 cup vegetable oil

3 teaspoons pure vanilla extract

¼ cup orange juice

4 egg whites

½ cup tofu

3 cups all-purpose flour

3 teaspoons baking powder

1 Preheat the oven to 350 degrees.

2 In a medium bowl, combine the apples, ⅓ cup of the sugar, and the cinnamon. Toss until the apple slices are well coated with sugar and cinnamon.

3 In a larger bowl, combine the oil, vanilla, orange juice, egg whites, and tofu. Blend until the tofu is well incorporated into the mixture and the mixture is smooth. Add the flour, the remaining sugar, and the baking powder. Mix until all the ingredients are well blended.

4 Oil a tube pan or Bundt pan, and then pour one-third of the batter into the pan. Then add half the apples, another third of the batter, the rest of the apples, and the rest of the batter.

5 Bake for 1 hour and 10 minutes, or until a toothpick inserted into the center of the cake comes out clean. The cake will be well browned.

Per serving: Calories 350 (From Fat 126); Fat 14g (Saturated 2g); Cholesterol 0mg; Sodium 92mg; Carbohydrate 53g (Dietary Fiber 2g); Protein 4g.

Decadent Chocolate Tofu Cheesecake

Tofu makes a fabulous replacement for cream cheese in cheesecake recipes. This cheesecake has a rich chocolate flavor and a smooth, creamy texture. I adapted it from a recipe in *Tofu Cookery,* by Louise Hagler (The Book Publishing Company). You may want to double the recipe for a party. You can also use a ready-made 9-inch graham cracker crust (which holds the same volume as the 8-inch springform pan used in this recipe). See the photo in this book's color section.

Preparation time: *30 minutes*

Cooking time: *40 minutes (plus 2 hours to chill)*

Yield: *8 servings (1 pie)*

Filling:	*Crust:*
1¼ pounds firm tofu	*1¼ cups graham cracker crumbs*
1½ cups sugar	*1 tablespoon sugar*
3 ounces (3 squares) semi-sweet baking chocolate	*⅓ cup butter or margarine*
1 teaspoon pure vanilla extract	
½ teaspoon pure almond extract	
⅛ teaspoon salt	

1 Place the tofu in a clean sink, cover it with waxed paper and a heavy weight, and let it drain for 20 minutes. While the tofu drains, make the crust.

2 For the crust, combine the graham cracker crumbs and sugar in a medium bowl. Melt the butter or margarine in a saucepan over low heat, and then add it to the crumb mixture. Stir until blended, and then press the crumbs into the bottom and sides of an 8-inch nonstick springform pan. Set aside.

3 In a blender or food processor, blend the drained tofu, ¼ pound at a time, with 1 cup of the sugar, adding ¼ cup sugar with each addition of tofu. Process until the ingredients are well blended.

4 Pour the tofu-sugar mixture into a bowl. Preheat the oven to 350 degrees.

5 In a double boiler or saucepan, melt the chocolate. While the chocolate is melting, place the graham cracker crust in the oven and cook for about 8 minutes; then remove, set aside, and let cool.

6 After the chocolate has melted, add it to the tofu mixture.Mix in the vanilla, almond extract, salt, and remaining ½ cup sugar. Blend well.

7 Pour the mixture into the graham cracker crusts and bake for about 40 minutes. When the cheesecake is done, it will be slightly risen on the edges with small cracks on the surface. The middle will not have risen, but it will be springy to the touch and will have a dry, firm appearance. Chill the cheesecake for at least 2 hours after baking.

Vary It! *Top the cheesecake with fresh raspberries or thaw a bag of frozen raspberries, mix them with a few tablespoons of sugar, and spread them on top of the cheesecake. You can also top the cheesecake with canned cherries.*

Per serving: *Calories 510 (From Fat 153); Fat 17g (Saturated 5g); Cholesterol 0mg; Sodium 310mg; Carbohydrate 84g (Dietary Fiber 3g); Protein 9g.*

Cookies

Everyone loves cookies — they're easy to make and convenient to eat at the kitchen table with a glass of milk or soymilk, or you can grab a couple to eat on the go. Freeze half a batch of any of the cookies in this section. You'll be glad to have them handy a few weeks down the road.

Charleston Benne Wafers

These diminutive cookies (pictured in the color section of this book) are a Southern tradition. They get their name from the benne seeds, or sesame seeds, that they contain. They're about an inch to an inch and a half in diameter and are light and sweet.

Preparation time: *20 minutes*

Cooking time: *10 minutes per batch*

Yield: *8 dozen cookies*

⅓ cup sesame seeds	*½ teaspoon vanilla*
2 egg whites	*¼ cup butter*
¾ cup packed light brown sugar	*½ cup all-purpose flour*

1 Preheat the oven to 350 degrees.

2 Spread the benne seeds in a shallow pan and toast in the oven for 7 to 8 minutes or until just browned. Do not overcook. Set aside. Reduce the oven temperature to 325 degrees.

3 In a mixing bowl, beat the egg whites until stiff. Add the brown sugar, vanilla, butter, and flour and mix well. Fold in the toasted benne seeds.

4 Drop the cookie dough by the half teaspoon onto lightly greased cookie sheets. These cookies are meant to be very small, so use a measuring spoon if necessary to get the right amount of dough. Bake for 10 minutes or until lightly browned. Watch carefully or the edges will get too dark.

Per cookie: *Calories 16 (From Fat 9); Fat 1g (Saturated 0g); Cholesterol 1mg; Sodium 7mg; Carbohydrate 2g (Dietary Fiber 0g); Protein 0g.*

☁ Oatmeal-Cherry Cookies

These cookies are chewy and thick. The cherries are a nice surprise. You can find a photo in the color section of this book.

Preparation time: *20 minutes*

Cooking time: *12 minutes per batch*

Yield: *36 large cookies*

1 cup butter	½ teaspoon salt
1 cup packed dark brown sugar	½ teaspoon baking soda
½ cup sugar	½ teaspoon baking powder
2 large eggs	1 teaspoon cinnamon
1 teaspoon pure vanilla extract	2 cups rolled oats
¾ cup whole-wheat flour	1 cup dried cherries
¾ cup all-purpose flour	½ cup chopped walnuts or pecans

1 Preheat the oven to 350 degrees. In a large mixing bowl, cream the butter and sugars. Add the eggs and vanilla and beat until light and fluffy.

2 In a separate bowl, combine the flours, salt, baking soda, baking powder, and cinnamon. Add the dry mixture to the butter mixture and beat until combined.

3 Stir in the oats, cherries, and nuts and blend well.

4 Drop the cookie dough by the tablespoonful onto lightly greased cookie sheets. Bake for 12 minutes or until lightly browned.

Per serving: Calories 127 (From Fat 63); Fat 7g (Saturated 4g); Cholesterol 15mg; Sodium 119mg; Carbohydrate 15g (Dietary Fiber 1g); Protein 2g.

○ Date Squares

These are Dad's favorite cookies. They're wholesome and satisfying. The outside of the cookie is soft and moist, and the inside is sweet and chewy. See the color section for a photo.

Preparation time: *20 minutes*

Cooking time: *30 minutes*

Yield: *25 squares*

2¼ cups chopped dates	*½ teaspoon baking soda*
½ cup sugar	*¾ cup packed brown sugar*
½ cup water	*1½ cups rolled oats*
2 tablespoons lemon juice	*½ cup vegetable oil*
1½ cups all-purpose flour	

1 In a medium saucepan, combine the dates, sugar, water, and lemon juice. Cook over medium heat until the dates are soft. Set aside and let cool for 20 minutes.

2 Preheat the oven to 350 degrees.

3 In a mixing bowl, combine the flour, baking soda, brown sugar, and oatmeal. Then add the oil and mix until the ingredients are well blended.

4 Press half the flour mixture into the bottom of an oiled 8-x-8-inch pan.

5 Cover the flour layer with the date mixture and then sprinkle with the remaining flour mixture. Press down lightly with your fingers.

6 Bake for 30 minutes or until lightly browned. Cool for 15 minutes, and then cut into squares and remove from the pan.

Per serving: *Calories 168 (From Fat 45); Fat 5g (Saturated 1g); Cholesterol 0mg; Sodium 29mg; Carbohydrate 31g (Dietary Fiber 2g); Protein 2g.*

Carob Chipsters

A slightly healthier version of chocolate chip, these drop cookies are chewy and moist.

Preparation time: *30 minutes*

Cooking time: *10 to 12 minutes per batch*

Yield: *About 6 dozen cookies*

¾ cup butter, softened

½ cup packed brown sugar

½ cup granulated sugar

1 tablespoon powdered vegetarian egg replacer mixed with ¼ cup water

1 teaspoon pure vanilla extract

1¼ cups all-purpose flour

¾ cup whole-wheat flour

¼ teaspoon salt

1 teaspoon baking soda

½ teaspoon baking powder

½ teaspoon cinnamon

2 cups rolled oats

1½ cups (12 ounces) carob chips

1 Preheat the oven to 350 degrees.

2 In a mixing bowl, cream the butter, sugars, egg replacer, and vanilla until smooth.

3 In a separate bowl, mix together the flours, salt, baking soda, baking powder, and cinnamon. Add to the butter mixture and mix well.

4 Stir in the oats. The batter will be very stiff.

5 Add the carob chips and mix thoroughly using clean hands.

6 Drop the dough by rounded teaspoonfuls about 3 inches apart on an ungreased cookie sheet. Bake each batch for 10 to 12 minutes or until the cookies are lightly browned.

Per serving: *Calories 84 (From Fat 36); Fat 4g (Saturated 3g); Cholesterol 5mg; Sodium 50mg; Carbohydrate 11g (Dietary Fiber 1g); Protein 2g.*

☼ *Swedish Molasses Cookies*

These thin, crisp molasses cookies are often baked at Christmastime and cut into shapes. Make them year-round for a light, low-fat dessert or snack. To store these cookies for later, cover them tightly.

Preparation time: *15 minutes, plus chilling time (2 hours or overnight)*

Cooking time: *15 minutes*

Yield: *About 7 dozen cookies*

1 tablespoon baking soda

¼ cup hot water

¾ cup plain soymilk

1 cup molasses

1½ teaspoons powdered vegetarian egg replacer mixed with 2 tablespoons water

1 tablespoon ginger

1 tablespoon cinnamon

½ teaspoon salt

1 cup vegetable oil

5 cups all-purpose flour

1 In a mixing bowl, combine the baking soda and water and stir until the baking soda has dissolved. Add the remaining ingredients in the order listed and blend thoroughly.

2 Cover the dough tightly with plastic wrap and chill in the refrigerator for at least 2 hours, or overnight.

3 Preheat the oven to 375 degrees.

4 Roll out the dough on a lightly floured table to about ⅛ inch thick and cut it into circles or other shapes by using a floured knife or 2 inch cookie cutter.

5 Place the cookies on greased or ungreased cookie sheets and bake for 15 minutes or until lightly browned. Remove from the cookie sheets, let cool, and serve.

Per serving: *Calories 71 (From Fat 27); Fat 3g (Saturated 0g); Cholesterol 0mg; Sodium 62mg; Carbohydrate 11g (Dietary Fiber 0g); Protein 1g.*

Fruit Desserts

Fruit desserts tend to be lower in saturated fat and cholesterol and higher in fiber than cakes, pies, and cookies are. The recipes in this section will satisfy your sweet tooth and make a nutritional contribution to boot.

Pear Cranberry Crisp

This beautiful dish is sweet, tart, and totally satisfying. The cranberries add a festive color and flavor, so this dish works well as a simple but lovely dessert for holidays and other gatherings.

Preparation time: *20 minutes*

Cooking time: *40 minutes*

Yield: *12 servings*

Filling:

6 large, soft, ripe pears, peeled, cored, and sliced

1½ cups fresh or frozen cranberries

¾ cup sugar

2 tablespoons flour

Topping:

1 cup rolled oats

½ cup packed brown sugar

⅓ cup flour

¼ cup butter

½ cup chopped pecans

1 Preheat the oven to 375 degrees. Oil a 9-x-13-inch baking dish.

2 In a large bowl, combine the pears, cranberries, sugar, and flour. Toss to coat the fruit. Spread the fruit over the bottom of the baking dish.

3 In a small bowl, combine the oats, brown sugar, flour, and butter. Using a fork or pastry blender, combine the ingredients until the mixture is crumbly and the butter is well incorporated. Stir in the pecans.

4 Sprinkle the topping evenly over the fruit and pat it down with your fingers.

5 Bake for 40 minutes or until the fruit is bubbly and the topping is browned. Serve warm or chilled.

Vary It! *Use tart apples in place of the pears and walnuts in place of the pecans.*

Per serving: *Calories 267 (From Fat 72); Fat 8g (Saturated 3g); Cholesterol 11mg; Sodium 48mg; Carbohydrate 48g (Dietary Fiber 5g); Protein 4g.*

Baked Apples

Baked apples are quick and convenient to make when you already have the oven heated to bake a casserole or loaf of bread. They keep in the refrigerator for up to three days, and they're good any time of the day or night, warm with ice cream or cold for breakfast or as a snack.

Preparation time: *10 minutes*

Cooking time: *1 hour*

Yield: *4 servings*

4 large tart apples	*1 tablespoon butter*
½ cup packed brown sugar	*½ cup apple juice (optional)*
1 teaspoon cinnamon	

1 Preheat the oven to 350 degrees.

2 Wash and core the apples, stopping the coring just before the bottom of the apple (so that the hole doesn't go all the way through). Using a paring knife, cut away the peel from the top to about one-third of the way down each apple (see Figure 18-2).

3 In a small dish or cup, combine the brown sugar and cinnamon. Spoon one-quarter of the mixture into the center of each apple.

4 Divide the butter into quarters and put one chunk in the center of each apple.

5 Set the apples in an 8-inch-x-8-inch baking dish or 1-quart casserole and add water or apple juice to a depth of about ¼ inch.

6 Bake, uncovered, for 1 hour or until the apples are soft. Serve warm or chilled.

Per serving: Calories 177 (From Fat 36); Fat 4g (Saturated 2g); Cholesterol 8mg; Sodium 38mg; Carbohydrate 39g (Dietary Fiber 4g); Protein 0g.

1. WASH AND CORE THE APPLES.

USE A PARING KNIFE TO CUT AWAY THE PEEL FROM THE TOP TO ABOUT 1/3 DOWN.

2. IN A SMALL DISH, COMBINE THE BROWN SUGAR AND CINNAMON. SPOON 1/4 OF THE MIXTURE INTO THE CENTER OF EACH APPLE.

3. DIVIDE THE BUTTER INTO 4 CHUNKS AND PUT 1 INTO THE CENTER OF EACH APPLE.

4. SET THE APPLES IN A BAKING DISH OR CASSEROLE. ADD WATER TO A DEPTH OF ABOUT 1/2 INCH.

Figure 18-2:
Filling
Baked
Apples.

☞ Berry Cobbler

This recipe comes from one of my favorite vegetarian cookbooks, *The Peaceful Palate*, by Jennifer Raymond (Heart & Soul Publications). It's delicious, easy to make, and far lower in fat than a berry pie. It's one of the staple desserts at my house. You can use whatever type of berries you like, or a mixture of berries.

Preparation time: *15 minutes*

Cooking time: *25 minutes*

Yield: *9 servings*

5 to 6 cups fresh or frozen berries (boysenberries, blackberries, raspberries, or a mixture)

3 tablespoons whole-wheat flour

½ cup plus 2 tablespoons sugar

1 cup whole-wheat pastry flour

1½ teaspoons baking powder

¼ teaspoon salt

2 tablespoons vegetable oil

½ cup soymilk or rice milk

1 Preheat the oven to 400 degrees.

2 Spread the berries in a 9-x-9-inch baking dish. Mix in the whole-wheat flour and ½ cup of the sugar.

3 In a separate bowl, mix the pastry flour and the remaining 2 tablespoons sugar with the baking powder and salt.

4 Add the oil to the flour mixture and mix it with a fork or your fingers until the mixture resembles coarse cornmeal.

5 Add the soymilk or rice milk and stir to combine.

6 Spread this mixture over the berries (don't worry if they're not completely covered) and bake for about 25 minutes or until golden brown.

Vary It! *For a real treat, top the hot cobbler with a spoonful of nondairy ice cream.*

Per serving: *Calories 304 (From Fat 36); Fat 4g (Saturated 0g); Cholesterol 0mg; Sodium 141mg; Carbohydrate 68g (Dietary Fiber 5g); Protein 3g.*

☞ *Summertime Strawberry Shortcake*

You can make this refreshing warm-weather dessert with other seasonal fruits or even fruit salad in place of strawberries when strawberries aren't in season. Top with whipped topping or a scoop of sorbet or ice cream if desired. See the color section of this book for a photo.

Preparation time: *20 minutes*

Cooking time: *20 minutes*

Yield: *8 servings*

1 quart strawberries, sliced lengthwise, plus extra berries for garnish

¾ cup plus 2 tablespoons sugar

2 cups all-purpose flour

3 teaspoons baking powder

½ teaspoon salt

⅓ cup vegetable oil

1 cup plain or vanilla soymilk

Confectioner's sugar

1 Preheat the oven to 450 degrees. Oil an 8-inch-round cake pan.

2 In a mixing bowl, toss the strawberries with ¾ cup of the sugar. Cover and refrigerate.

3 In another mixing bowl, combine the flour, baking powder, salt, oil, and the remaining 2 tablespoons sugar and mix with a fork until crumbly. Add the soymilk and stir just enough to dampen the dry ingredients.

4 Scoop the batter into the pan and press it in evenly with your fingers.

5 Bake for about 20 minutes or until browned.

6 Allow the cake to cool enough to handle. Slice the cake in half lengthwise. Cool completely. Just before serving, arrange the sugared fruit between the two layers of cake. Top with more strawberries and a sprinkling of sifted confectioner's sugar.

Per serving: Calories 315 (From Fat 90); Fat 10g (Saturated 1g); Cholesterol 0mg; Sodium 314mg; Carbohydrate 52g (Dietary Fiber 3g); Protein 4g.

Cooking Puddings with Soymilk

As Chapter 5 explains, you can use soymilk in all the ways that you use cow's milk in cooking, and in exactly the same proportions. So if a recipe calls for 2 cups of milk, you can use 2 cups of soymilk instead. Substituting soymilk reduces the fat content of the recipe without sacrificing flavor or texture — and who isn't looking to do that? In desserts, vanilla soymilk works great, adding a sweeter flavor than cow's milk or plain soymilk would.

Soymilk replaces cow's milk in these three pudding recipes. You get the same creamy texture without all the saturated fat that whole cow's milk would add.

Rustic Apple Bread Pudding

The cubes of bread give this pudding a pleasing, lumpy-bumpy texture. The fragrance and flavor of cinnamon and apples make it a comfort food that you can enjoy any time of day.

Preparation time: *15 minutes*

Cooking time: *60 minutes*

Yield: *6 servings*

4 slices whole-grain bread, cut into 1-inch cubes

½ cup raisins or chopped dates

1 cup unsweetened applesauce

½ teaspoon ground cinnamon

1 teaspoon pure vanilla extract

⅓ cup packed light brown sugar

4 egg whites

2½ cups vanilla soymilk

Confectioner's sugar

1 Preheat the oven to 350 degrees. Lightly oil an 8-x-8-x-2-inch baking pan.

2 Spread the bread cubes evenly in the pan. Sprinkle the raisins on top.

3 In a blender or food processor, blend the applesauce, cinnamon, vanilla, brown sugar, egg whites, and soymilk thoroughly.

4 Pour the mixture evenly over the bread cubes and raisins. Allow the pudding to set for 10 or 15 minutes before baking.

5 Bake for 60 minutes or until the pudding is set in the middle and lightly browned.

6 Dust with a sprinkling of powdered sugar and serve warm or chilled.

Vary It! *Omit the raisins or dates and serve topped with sliced fresh strawberries or peaches, blueberries, or raspberries when they're in season. If you prefer refined to rustic, substitute 3 cups French bread cubes for the whole-grain bread.*

Per serving: *Calories 260 (From Fat 36); Fat 4g (Saturated 0g); Cholesterol 0mg; Sodium 200mg; Carbohydrate 50g (Dietary Fiber 3g); Protein 8g.*

☽ Chocolate Almond Tapioca Pudding

This dessert combines two favorite comfort foods: chocolate pudding and tapioca pudding. Soaking the tapioca before cooking gives it time to absorb some of the soymilk and helps prevent the scorching that sometimes happens when tapioca beads settle on the bottom of the pan.

Preparation time: *25 minutes*

Cooking time: *10 minutes*

Yield: *6 to 8 servings*

¾ cup sugar

3 tablespoons quick-cooking tapioca

2¾ cups plain or vanilla soymilk

1½ teaspoons powdered vegetarian egg replacer mixed with 2 tablespoons water

¼ cup semi-sweet chocolate chips

½ teaspoon pure almond extract

¼ cup slivered almonds

1 In a medium saucepan, combine the sugar, tapioca, soymilk, and egg replacer. Stir and then let soak for 5 minutes.

2 Add the chocolate squares. Cook over medium heat, stirring constantly, until the mixture comes to a full boil (about 10 minutes). Remove from the heat.

3 Stir in the almond extract. Let cool for 20 minutes, and then stir again.

4 Spoon the pudding into 6 serving cups or 1 serving bowl. Sprinkle with the almonds and serve warm or chilled.

Per serving: *Calories 264 (From Fat 90); Fat 10g (Saturated 3g); Cholesterol 0mg; Sodium 57mg; Carbohydrate 41g (Dietary Fiber 2g); Protein 5g.*

Rice Pudding

This version of rice pudding requires no eggs because it thickens in the pan as the rice absorbs the liquid in the recipe. The result is a rich, creamy rice pudding that's simple to make and requires minimal time in supervising the stovetop.

Preparation time: *5 minutes (plus time to chill, if desired)*

Cooking time: *50 minutes*

Yield: *6 servings*

3 cups vanilla soymilk	*¼ teaspoon ground cinnamon*
½ cup long-grain white rice	*¼ teaspoon ground nutmeg*
¼ teaspoon salt	*¼ cup sugar*
1 tablespoon butter	

1 In a medium saucepan over high heat, bring the soymilk to a boil, stirring constantly (about 5 minutes).

2 Add the rice, salt, butter, cinnamon, nutmeg, and sugar and stir to combine. Reduce the heat to low and cover.

3 Cook, covered, for about 45 minutes or until all the liquid has been absorbed. Lift the lid and stir every 15 minutes, covering again tightly each time you remove the lid.

4 After all the liquid has been absorbed, remove the pudding from the heat. Cool to warm, and then serve or place in the refrigerator to chill for at least 2 hours before serving.

__Per serving:__ Calories 180 (From Fat 45); Fat 5g (Saturated 1g); Cholesterol 5mg; Sodium 82mg; Carbohydrate 30g (Dietary Fiber 0g); Protein 4g.

Chapter 19

Hooray for Holidays!

- -

In This Chapter

▶ Preparing festive vegetarian meals

▶ A sampling of special holiday recipes

- -

Recipes in This Chapter

▶ Cheese and Nut Loaf

▶ Stuffed Squash

▶ Golden Creamed Potatoes with Mushroom Gravy

↻ Wilted Spinach with Garlic and Pine Nuts

▶ Chocolate Bourbon Pecan Pie

*H*olidays are made special by the family and friends we share them with; their historical, spiritual, or other significance; and the traditions that surround them. Chief among those traditions, of course, is food!

In with the New . . . Traditions!

There are no rules about what must be served on a particular holiday or special occasion. Christmas dinner may mean antipasto and ravioli to one family and tofu turkey with all the trimmings to another. It's all a matter of tradition — what has become familiar to you and your family or friends over the years. Many of the recipes in this book are well suited to special-occasion meals. They're colorful and aromatic, or they make use of seasonal foods that evoke a particular mood or season. Pear Cranberry Crisp, for instance (see Chapter 18), may bring late autumn and the winter holidays to mind.

If you're new to a vegetarian diet and your traditions still center on foods of animal origin, don't fret. Choose the aspects of special-occasion meals that still fit and find replacements for those that don't. For example, most of a traditional Thanksgiving dinner is already vegetarian. Mashed potatoes, candied sweet potatoes, green peas, cranberry sauce . . . these foods can stay on the menu. You can easily swap the turkey for the Cheese and Nut Loaf or Stuffed Squash recipes in this chapter — or any of a number of other main dishes. To supplement your menu, think Whole-Wheat Crescent Rolls (Chapter 17), Festive Broccoli Salad (Chapter 14), or Green Beans and Walnuts (Chapter 16). Use your imagination and think about the foods that you enjoy most. Over time, these will become your new traditions, as dear to you as the old ones once were.

Making Holiday Meals Special

When you read over the following recipes, think about what makes holiday meals special for you. Do you eat special-occasion meals in the dining room rather than the kitchen? Do you place candles or a centerpiece on the table? Do you use your best linen tablecloth and set out the fine china?

The way you present the food can set the tone of the meal. Just serving foods on platters or attractive serving dishes and garnishing them nicely can set a meal apart from the everyday routine. You can serve the recipes in this chapter anytime, but if you reserve them for special occasions and serve them with flair, they say "Holiday!"

Cheese and Nut Loaf

This hearty dish, pictured in the book's color section, is reminiscent of meatloaf in texture and has a nutty flavor. It's festive if it's presented on a platter garnished with parsley and cherry tomatoes. A family tradition at Thanksgiving and Christmas dinners for over 20 years, we now make two loaves in order to ensure that we have some left over. Leftovers are wonderful reheated or eaten cold in a sandwich.

Preparation time: *20 minutes*

Cooking time: *30 minutes*

Yield: *8 servings*

2 tablespoons olive oil

1 large onion, chopped fine

½ cup water

1½ cups whole-wheat breadcrumbs, plus extra for topping

2 cups grated reduced-fat cheddar cheese

1 cup chopped walnuts

Juice of 1 fresh lemon (about 2 tablespoons)

6 egg whites (or vegetarian egg replacer equal to 3 eggs)

Parsley, bell pepper rings, and cherry tomato halves for garnish

1 Preheat the oven to 400 degrees.

2 In a large skillet, heat the olive oil. Over medium heat, cook the onions in the olive oil until they're translucent.

3 Add the water and breadcrumbs and mix well. Remove from the heat.

4 Add the cheese, walnuts, lemon juice, and egg whites and mix well.

5 Scoop the mixture into a greased 9-x-5-x-3-inch loaf pan or a casserole dish. Top with a sprinkling of breadcrumbs.

6 Bake for about 30 minutes or until golden brown.

7 Turn out onto a platter and garnish with parsley sprigs and cherry tomatoes or slices of red and yellow bell peppers. This may also be served with ½ cup ketchup mixed with ½ cup salsa.

Vary It! *Experiment with this recipe by replacing part of the walnuts with an equal amount of chopped water chestnuts, or replacing a portion of the cheese with an equal portion of grated carrots.*

Per serving: *Calories 260 (From Fat 180); Fat 20g (Saturated 3g); Cholesterol 0mg; Sodium 509mg; Carbohydrate 11g (Dietary Fiber 1g); Protein 11g.*

Stuffed Squash

Stuffed squash (or pumpkin) makes a festive main course for holiday meals, as well as being a convenient and colorful centerpiece for the table. (See the color section for a photo.) Any kind of squash will do, but acorn and butternut squash are the most commonly found in supermarkets. This recipe shows you how to make one large, stuffed squash, enough for four ample servings (¼ squash each). Double or triple the recipe as needed to make enough servings to feed the number of guests you'll be serving. You can also use the filling to make several small (3 to 4 inch) individual stuffed pumpkins instead if you prefer.

Preparation time: *1 hour (including time to prebake squash)*

Cooking time: *20 minutes*

Yield: *4 servings*

1 butternut squash, cut in half, seeds and strings removed (or use two small acorn squashes for four individual servings — see Figure 19-1 for an illustration of both types of squash)

2 tablespoons olive oil

1 medium onion, chopped

½ cup sliced fresh mushrooms

1 clove garlic, minced

¼ cup finely minced celery (leaves and stem)

¼ teaspoon black pepper

2 tablespoons minced fresh parsley

½ teaspoon sage

½ teaspoon thyme

Juice of 1 lemon (about 2 tablespoons)

¼ cup diced, peeled Granny Smith apple

¼ cup chopped walnuts

¼ cup golden raisins

3 slices whole-wheat bread, coarsely crumbled

¾ cup grated reduced-fat cheddar cheese (use nonfat cheese or a mix to lower the saturated fat content further)

1 Preheat the oven to 350 degrees.

2 Cut the squash in half. Scoop out and discard the seeds and strings.

3 Place the squash halves in a small, oiled baking dish and fill the dish ½ inch high with water. Place the baking dish in the oven and bake, covered loosely with foil, for 30 minutes or until the squash is soft.

4 While the squash is baking, heat the olive oil in a small skillet. Cook the onions, mushrooms, garlic, and celery in the oil until the onions are translucent. Stir in the black pepper, parsley, sage, thyme, and lemon juice and remove from the heat.

5 Transfer the onion mixture to a mixing bowl. Add the apples, walnuts, raisins, bread, and cheese. Mix until well combined.

6 Remove the squash from the oven after about 30 minutes, when it's tender but still firm (don't let it cook so much that it falls apart when you move it).

7 Transfer the squash cut side up to a decorative baking dish or casserole if desired. Otherwise, carefully pour out the water in the pan. Then fill each squash half with half the stuffing mixture and press down lightly.

8 Cover tightly with foil and bake the squash for another 20 minutes or until the cheese is melted and the stuffing is browned.

Per serving: Calories 412 (From Fat 162); Fat 18g (Saturated 5g); Cholesterol 15mg; Sodium 320mg; Carbohydrate 56g (Dietary Fiber 11g); Protein 12g.

Figure 19-1:
These two common types of squash are great for stuffing.

Golden Creamed Potatoes with Mushroom Gravy

Yukon Gold potatoes lend a rich color to this dish. The gravy goes well on the potatoes as well as over Cheese and Nut Loaf (you can find the recipe earlier in this chapter).

Preparation time: *15 minutes*

Cooking time: *30 minutes*

Yield: *8 servings*

Potatoes:

5 pounds Yukon Gold potatoes, peeled and cut into 2-inch chunks (or halved if they're small)

¼ cup melted butter

1 cup plain soymilk or skim milk

¼ teaspoon salt

¼ teaspoon black pepper

Mushroom Gravy:

1 tablespoon olive oil

1 pound mushrooms, thinly sliced

1 medium onion, chopped

2 tablespoons flour

1 vegetable bouillon cube

¼ teaspoon salt (if using a sodium-free bouillon cube, otherwise omit)

¼ teaspoon black pepper

1 cup plain soymilk or skim milk

1 Place the potatoes in a pot and fill with cold water to cover them. Cover and cook over medium-high heat until boiling; then reduce the heat, tilt the cover to allow steam to escape, and simmer for 30 minutes or until the potatoes are tender.

2 While the potatoes are cooking, prepare the Mushroom Gravy. Heat the olive oil in a medium skillet. Over medium heat, cook the mushrooms and onions in the olive oil until the onions are translucent, about 5 minutes.

3 Add the flour and crumble the bouillon cube into the skillet. Add the salt (if needed) and pepper and stir.

4 Add the soymilk. Cook and stir for 2 to 3 minutes, until the gravy thickens and the ingredients are well blended. Pour into a small pitcher or serving dish and set aside until the potatoes are ready. If you don't serve it immediately, the gravy may need to be reheated in a microwave oven, or you can hold it on the stovetop, warming, until ready to eat.

5 When the potatoes are done, drain them. In a large bowl, combine the potatoes, butter, milk, salt, and pepper. Mash with a potato masher until smooth and well blended. Use a wooden spoon to help blend the ingredients if necessary. Transfer to a serving dish and serve with Mushroom Gravy.

Vary It! *Add 1 tablespoon chopped parsley or chives in Step 5.*

Per serving: *Calories 378 (From Fat 90); Fat 10g (Saturated 4g); Cholesterol 16mg; Sodium 309mg; Carbohydrate 66g (Dietary Fiber 6g); Protein 8g.*

☕ *Wilted Spinach with Garlic and Pine Nuts*

This dish is delicious by itself as a side, or as an entree served on a bed of fettuccine or linguine with freshly grated Parmesan cheese and a diced Roma tomato on top. It's pictured in the color section of this book.

Preparation time: 15 minutes

Cooking time: 15 minutes

Yield: 4 servings

¼ cup pine nuts	2 cloves garlic, minced
1 large bunch spinach (about 1 pound)	¼ teaspoon salt
1 tablespoon olive oil	¼ teaspoon black pepper

1 Place the pine nuts in a dry skillet and cook over low heat for several minutes until the nuts are browned, about 4 minutes. Stir frequently and watch carefully to prevent burning. Remove from the pan and set aside.

2 Wash the spinach well and remove the stems. Set aside (do not spin dry; leave it wet).

3 In a large skillet, heat the olive oil. Add the garlic, salt, and pepper and cook over medium heat for a minute or two, until the garlic is slightly softened and the ingredients are mixed.

4 Add the spinach, tossing it with the oil and garlic seasoning. Cover and cook over medium heat for about 1 minute or until all the leaves are wilted.

5 Add the pine nuts and toss with the spinach. Arrange the spinach on individual plates or in a serving bowl.

Vary It! *Substitute coarsely chopped walnuts for the pine nuts.*

Per serving: *Calories 90 (From Fat 72); Fat 8g (Saturated 1g); Cholesterol 0mg; Sodium 260mg; Carbohydrate 2g (Dietary Fiber 9g); Protein 4g.*

Chocolate Bourbon Pecan Pie

Rich and chocolatey — the ultimate holiday dessert. Serve it with a scoop of vanilla low-fat ice cream or nondairy frozen dessert to reduce the damage; this one is high in fat. You can see what this pie looks like in the color section of this book.

Preparation time: *20 minutes*

Cooking time: *50 minutes*

Yield: *One 9-inch pie (6 servings)*

6 egg whites (or vegetarian egg replacer equal to 3 eggs)

1 cup sugar

¼ teaspoon salt

¼ cup melted butter

1 cup light corn syrup

1 cup pecan halves

3 tablespoons bourbon

5 ounces (about ¾ cup) chocolate chips

1 unbaked 9-inch pie shell

1 Preheat the oven to 375 degrees.

2 In a medium mixing bowl, combine the egg whites or egg replacer, sugar, salt, butter, and corn syrup. Beat until smooth and creamy.

3 Stir in the pecan halves, bourbon, and chocolate chips.

4 Pour the mixture into the pie shell. Bake for 50 minutes or until a toothpick inserted into the center comes out clean. Serve warm or chilled.

Vary It! *Substitute 1 teaspoon vanilla for the bourbon. Add a handful of coconut flakes.*

Per serving: *Calories 546 (From Fat 234); Fat 26g (Saturated 8g); Cholesterol 16mg; Sodium 348mg; Carbohydrate 75g (Dietary Fiber 2g); Protein 6g.*

Chapter 20

Menus Made Easy

· ·

In This Chapter

▶ Retooling your menu-planning skills for meals without meat

▶ Planning menus for main meals, light meals, and snacks

▶ Menu-planning ideas for special occasions

· ·

*F*eeling comfortable with a new eating style takes time and practice. If you're switching to a vegetarian diet, don't be too hard on yourself if you draw a blank when it comes to deciding what to make for dinner. Over time, meal planning will become much easier as you master and refine new skills.

Make a list of all the vegetarian foods you currently enjoy. Many of foods that nonvegetarians enjoy are vegetarian — vegetable lasagne, bean burritos, and vegetable pizza, for example. Work these foods into your weekly menus. Then experiment with the recipes in this book and others to find some new favorite dishes. As you begin incorporating them into your menus on a regular basis, menu planning will become easier. Before long, you won't need to refer to recipes as you put your meals together.

Good luck as you begin the adventure!

Breakfast

Whether you have a little time or a lot, there's always enough time to grab *something* to eat before you run out the door. Breakfast can be as simple as a bowl of cereal or a muffin and juice. When you have more time, treat yourself to pancakes or hot cereal. Beginning the day with something nutritious gives you an energy boost that benefits you all day long.

Have coffee or tea with breakfast if you like, but remember that caffeine should be limited — at least once in a while, drink water instead.

Monday

Date Bran Muffins (see Chapter 17)
Half a grapefruit

Tuesday

Oats and Apples with milk or vanilla soymilk (see Chapter 11)
Whole-wheat toast with jelly
Orange juice

Wednesday

Morning Miso Soup (see Chapter 11)
English muffin with apple butter
Tomato juice

Thursday

Zucchini Bread (see Chapter 17)
Whole banana
Orange juice

Friday

Whole-grain cereal with milk or soymilk
Sunshine in a Cup (see Chapter 10)

Saturday

Old-Fashioned Cinnamon Rolls (see Chapter 17)
Fresh fruit salad
Pineapple-orange juice

Sunday

Peppers and Tofu Scrambler (see Chapter 11)
Seasoned Home Fries (see Chapter 16)
Whole-wheat toast with jelly
Freshly squeezed orange juice

Main Meals

The menus that follow are hearty and satisfying, and the leftovers are perfect candidates for lunches or snacks. Rely on water as your main beverage.

Monday

Cuban Black Beans and rice (see Chapter 15)
Fried Plantains (see Chapter 16)
Braised Sesame Greens (see Chapter 16)
Island Upside Down Cake (see Chapter 18)

Tuesday

Tempeh Sloppy Joes (see Chapter 15)
Roasted Roots (see Chapter 16)
Berry Cobbler (see Chapter 18)

Wednesday

Vegetarian Chili with Cashews (see Chapter 15)
Santa Fe Cornbread (see Chapter 17)
Festive Broccoli Salad (see Chapter 14)
Rustic Apple Bread Pudding (see Chapter 18)

Thursday

Garden Pizza (see Chapter 15)
Easy Three-Bean Salad (see Chapter 14)
Carmel Apple Smoothie (see Chapter 10)

Friday

Greek Lentil Soup (see Chapter 13)
Pasta Primavera (see Chapter 15)
Sunrise Salad (see Chapter 14)
Hard roll with Roasted Garlic Spread (see Chapter 12)
Fresh fruit

Saturday

Fresh Avocado and Lime Dip with tortilla chips (see Chapter 12)

Mayan Burrito (see Chapter 15)

Steamed broccoli

Butterscotch Pudding (see Chapter 18)

Sunday

Goat Cheese and Arugula Salad with Lavender-Vanilla Vinaigrette (see Chapter 14)

Pesto Pasta (see Chapter 15)

Whole-Wheat Crescent Rolls (see Chapter 17)

Summertime Strawberry Shortcake (see Chapter 18)

Light Meals and Snacks

Most light meals and snacks have one thing in common: They're quick. Prepare the foods for the menus in this section ahead of time so that they're ready when you need a quick meal. Most of them will keep in the refrigerator for several days.

Monday

Easy Gazpacho (see Chapter 13)

Whole-grain crackers

Tuesday

Creamy Cantaloupe Soup (see Chapter 13)

Tofu Salad (see Chapter 14) on whole-wheat bread

Wednesday

Date Squares (see Chapter 18)

Brown Bear Cocoa (see Chapter 10)

Thursday

Tomato and Garbanzo Bean Salad (see Chapter 14)

Spicy Black Bean Dip (see Chapter 12) with breadsticks or sliced Cheese Bread (see Chapter 17)

Friday

Hummus (see Chapter 12) with pita bread wedges

Jasper (see Chapter 10)

Saturday

Savory Mushroom Tofu Quiche or Traditional Savory Mushroom Quiche (see Chapter 11)

Fresh fruit salad

Sunday

Karen's Brown Bread (see Chapter 17)

Family-Style Baked Beans (see Chapter 16)

Green pepper and carrot sticks

Menus for Special Occasions

New traditions take time to create. However, you don't have to wait for good food. The menus that follow combine delicious vegetarian dishes to celebrate various special occasions. With this book to help you, plus a little imagination and forethought, you can develop your own holiday menus. All you need now is a room full of hungry guests!

Thanksgiving Feast

Sunrise Salad (see Chapter 14)

Splendid Stuffed Squash (see Chapter 19)

Golden Creamed Potatoes with Mushroom Gravy (see Chapter 19)

Green Beans and Walnuts (see Chapter 16)

Candied sweet potatoes

Cheese Bread (see Chapter 17) with Roasted Garlic Spread (see Chapter 12)

Maple Pecan Pumpkin Pie (see Chapter 18)

Coffee or tea

Christmas Dinner

Cheese and Nut Loaf (see Chapter 19)
Baked potatoes with butter and chives
Wilted Spinach with Garlic and Pine Nuts (see Chapter 19)
Festive Broccoli Salad (see Chapter 14)
Whole-Wheat Crescent Rolls (see Chapter 17)
Seasonal fruit salad
Tortoni Pie (see Chapter 18)
Chocolate Bourbon Pecan Pie (see Chapter 19)
Coffee or tea

July 4th Celebration

Veggie burgers and hotdogs on buns
Family-Style Baked Beans (see Chapter 16)
Easy Three-Bean Salad (see Chapter 14)
Watermelon
Oatmeal-Cherry Cookies (see Chapter 18)
Carob Chipsters (see Chapter 18)
Jasper (see Chapter 10)

Valentine's Day Dinner

Goat Cheese and Arugula Salad with Lavender-Vanilla Vinaigrette (see Chapter 14)
Spinach and Mushroom Manicotti (see Chapter 15)
Rosemary Roasted Red Potatoes (see Chapter 16)
Scalloped Tomatoes (see Chapter 16)
Italian bread
Decadent Chocolate Cheesecake (see Chapter 18)
Coffee or tea

Finding vegan Passover recipes

Many foods are restricted during Passover. If you're vegan, finding vegetarian Passover recipes that also omit dairy products and eggs is an added challenge. It can be done, however, and the results might amaze you.

For example, you can make pancakes and muffins with matzo meal and bananas in place of eggs. Apple latkes served with applesauce are also possible, minus the eggs. You can make delicious knishes, kugel, casseroles, stuffed cabbage, fruit pies — even eggless macaroons — acceptable for Passover but free of animal ingredients.

If you're looking for ideas for vegetarian and vegan Passover and Rosh Hashanah meals, I recommend two books that contain recipes plus menu-planning tips and ideas:

✔ *The Lowfat Jewish Vegetarian Cookbook,* by Debra Wasserman (Vegetarian Resource Group)

✔ *No Cholesterol Passover Recipes,* Revised Edition, by Debra Wasserman (Vegetarian Resource Group)

Part V

The Part of Tens

"First it was the cattle, now it's a tempeh mutilation. I just wish I knew what these weird other-worldly vegetarian aliens wanted."

In this part . . .

This part contains four top-ten lists selected especially for aspiring vegetarian cooks. These chapters include pointers on the advantages of a vegetarian eating style, a list of recommended vegetarian cookbooks, ten great Web sites, and ten online sources of vegetarian foods and ingredients.

Chapter 21

Ten Reasons to Cook Vegetarian

In This Chapter

▶ The health and nutritional advantages of eating a vegetarian diet

▶ The practical aspects of vegetarian cooking

*V*eteran vegetarian cooks will tell you that planning and preparing meat-free meals offers infinite opportunities for creative expression and opens a window on the world of healthy traditions from other cultures. If the sheer joy and experience of eating good food isn't enough, however, this chapter gives you ten more reasons to make it vegetarian tonight.

Vegetarians Have Less Coronary Artery Disease

Vegetarians have reduced rates of death and disability from heart disease. There may be many reasons for this fact, but chief among them is that vegetarians tend to eat more antioxidant-rich fruits and vegetables, more folate and phytochemicals, more dietary fiber, and less saturated fat, cholesterol, and animal protein than nonvegetarians do. The result is cleaner arteries and fewer heart attacks. Vegetarian diets have even been shown to halt and reverse severe coronary artery disease.

Vegetarians Have Lower Rates of Some Forms of Cancer

For many of the same reasons, vegetarians also suffer less from certain types of cancer than nonvegetarians do. For example, vegetarians have lower rates of lung cancer and colorectal cancer. Vegetarians also may be at a reduced risk for breast cancer.

Vegetarians Are More Likely to Be of Normal Weight

Vegetarians tend to be closer to their ideal weights and have lower body mass indexes than nonvegetarians do. Obesity is a major public health problem in the United States, but vegetarians as a group are much less likely to be affected.

Vegetarians Are Healthier Overall

Vegetarians are less likely to have high blood pressure and Type II diabetes. Vegetarian diets also protect and prolong the life of the kidneys.

Vegetarian Diets Protect the Planet

Plant-based diets help conserve precious topsoil, trees, and forests. As compared to meat-based diets, vegetarian diets help conserve water as well and reduce the pollution of rivers and streams by pesticides, herbicides, and fertilizers used to grow animal feed. When you eat meatless meals, you also contribute to a reduction in pollution from the nitrogenous fecal waste produced by animals raised for meat.

Meat-Free Diets Are More Humane

Let's face it: Vegetarian diets are more compassionate. Animals have feelings, and they suffer unnecessarily because of our meat habit. Albert Schweitzer said, "Until he extends his circle of compassion to include all living things, man will not himself find peace." By choosing a meatless diet, you take a stand for nonviolence.

Vegetarian Cooking Can Save You Big Money

Sure, you can rack up big bills if you rely on gourmet vegetarian food products. But vegetarian cooking doesn't have to cost a lot. In fact, the typical meatless meal costs less to prepare than a meal that includes meat. Cut down on cheese and other dairy products, and you'll save even more. Exactly how much depends on your specific food choices. Look at your food bill and see for yourself which foods cost you the most.

Vegetarian Cooking Is Cleaner

Vegetarian cooking means less frying and roasting and less grease to wash off counters, stovetops, sinks, and ovens. In fact, some pots, pans, and utensils may need only a quick rinse after you use them. In contrast, when raw meat, eggs, and dairy products come into contact with cooking utensils and preparation surfaces, those items need to be washed thoroughly with soap and water and often need to be disinfected as well.

Vegetarian Meals Mean More Variety

How many different types of meat do nonvegetarians eat? Most people build meals around chicken, beef, or fish in some form. For those who are trying to avoid red meat, meals are often a monotonous rotation of chicken and fish, chicken and fish, chicken and fish.

Vegetarians, on the other hand, enjoy an almost infinite number of colorful, interesting, and delicious dishes, many of which hail from cultures outside our own. With vegetarian cooking, the sky is the limit. Rarely is there a need for repetition unless you just happen to love a particular food. Rather than three or four mainstays, the staples for vegetarians include dozens of different grains and beans and hundreds of varieties of fruits and vegetables.

Vegetarian Meals Make You Feel Better

For many people, the most compelling feature of vegetarian cooking is that eating plant-based meals makes them feel so much better. Many people who switch from a nonvegetarian diet to a meatless diet report that they feel "lighter" and have more energy. Don't take my word for it, though. Try it yourself and see if they're right.

Chapter 22

Ten Practical Vegetarian Cookbooks

In This Chapter

▶ Ten vegetarian cookbooks that have uniquely useful properties

▶ Things to consider as you add to your own collection

*E*veryone has favorite cookbooks; in this chapter, I tell you about some of mine. The collection I've chosen is by no means exhaustive. Many, many good vegetarian cookbooks are available. However, those that made my list did so because they have special qualities that make them particularly good choices for the majority of cooks. These are the cookbooks that *vegetarians* like. They're the ones that are most likely to become dog-eared from use. Not all the cookbooks listed here are published by mainstream publishers. A few are classics. One is self-published. Many have resulted in sequels that are also good choices.

Enjoy!

Bean Banquets

By Patricia Gregory; published by Woodbridge Press

This unassuming paperback contains a fine collection of delicious recipes that feature a wide range of beans and peas used in 200 traditional recipes from around the globe. I'm sure you'll find several new favorite recipes in this cookbook.

Lean, Luscious and Meatless

By Bonnie Hinman and Millie Synder; published by Prima Publishing

This chunky, spiral-bound book is packed with consistently good-tasting, easy-to-prepare recipes that include complete nutritional analyses. Some recipes call for eggs or dairy products, but animal ingredients are not a dominant feature, and you can easily make substitutions.

Several other cookbooks by Hinman are also excellent, including *The Meatless Gourmet: Easy Lowfat Favorites* (Prima Publishing) and *The Meatless Gourmet: Favorite Recipes from Around the World* (Prima Publishing).

Moosewood Cookbook, Revised Edition

By Mollie Katzen; published by Ten Speed Press

Moosewood is a charming book, hand-lettered by Katzen, who is an accomplished artist. In this revised edition of the classic, the recipes have been updated a bit to reduce the dependence on dairy products and eggs. Katzen has published several other excellent cookbooks as well, including *Mollie Katzen's Vegetable Heaven* (Hyperion) and *The Enchanted Broccoli Forest* (Ten Speed Press).

Both *Moosewood* and *Laurel's Kitchen* (see the following section) have been criticized for the saturated fat content of their recipes. These books were written at a time when American vegetarian cooking meant heavy use of milk, cheese, eggs, sour cream, and yogurt. However, the redeeming value of these cookbooks is in their lighthearted, wholesome approach to vegetarian cooking and recipes that have wide appeal. Foods are delicious and can easily be modified to lower the saturated fat content. (See Chapter 9 for information about adapting recipes.)

The New Laurel's Kitchen

By Laurel Robertson, Carol Flinders, and Brian Ruppenthal; published by Ten Speed Press

This is the revised edition of the classic *Laurel's Kitchen*. The recipes are comfy and familiar, are easy to prepare, and call for common ingredients. The authors take care to fully describe cooking techniques and ingredients. Note that the recipes freely use eggs and dairy products, so if you're a vegan, you will need to make the appropriate substitutions.

The Peaceful Palate, Revised Edition

By Jennifer Raymond; published by Heart and Soul Publications

Many vegetarians love this self-published gem of a cookbook. The revised edition has a cheerful, beautiful cover; a convenient, lay-flat binding; and an appealing 8½-x-11-inch size. The recipes are vegan, good tasting, and easy to prepare, using common ingredients.

Simply Vegan, Third Edition

By Debra Wasserman and Reed Mangels, PhD, RD; published by The Vegetarian Resource Group

In contrast to *Laurel's Kitchen* and *Moosewood, Simply Vegan* is a collection of recipes that contain no animal ingredients whatsoever. The food is very plain and easy to prepare, and the recipes rarely contain more than a handful of ingredients. The book includes an excellent, comprehensive discussion of vegan nutrition.

Soy of Cooking

By Marie Oser; published by John Wiley & Sons

This book is beautifully illustrated with color photos of many of the recipes. The dishes are relatively easy to make and include complete nutritional analyses. The front of the book contains a comprehensive discussion of soy foods, and the recipes make use of a variety of soy products.

Tofu Cookery, Revised Edition

By Louise Hagler; published by The Book Publishing Company

Another classic, this one devoted to cooking with tofu. The recipes in this book should lay to rest any notion you have that the only way to eat tofu is in a stir-fry. The fabulous array of salads, main dishes, breads, desserts, and more will surprise you if you're a newcomer to soy cookery. The accompanying full-page, color photos are eye-poppers. The recipes are easy to follow, with short lists of common ingredients. And this is one of those wonderful tall, skinny paperback books that lay open easily on the kitchen counter.

The Vegetarian Hearth

By Darra Goldstein; published by HarperCollins

This beautiful book is devoted to recipes "for the cold season." It's an elegant collection of vegetarian recipes — not all vegan — representing wintertime traditions from around the world. A plus: The ingredient lists are fairly short, and the recipes are uncomplicated.

Vegetarian Times Complete Cookbook

By the editors of *Vegetarian Times;* published by Hungry Minds, Inc.

This cookbook contains a very good collection of more than 600 recipes, as well as tips for menu planning.

Chapter 23

Ten Helpful Web Sites to Check Out

. . . .

. . . .

*I*f the material in this book has whetted your appetite for more information about vegetarian nutrition and cooking, the Web is a great place to mine for materials. I list some of the best online sources in this chapter. You can find free recipes, answers to questions about health and nutrition, cooking tips, additional resources for vegetarian cooks, and more.

Vegetarian and Vegan Nutrition Information

The Vegetarian Resource Group (VRG) is a nonprofit organization that educates the public about vegetarianism and the interrelated issues of health, nutrition, ecology, ethics, and world hunger. The organization publishes the bimonthly *Vegetarian Journal*.

Go to www.vrg.org/nutrition for links to articles and other resources from the VRG on the nutritional aspects of plant-based diets, including information about protein, calcium, and iron in the diet, as well as dietary advice for pregnant and nursing mothers, school-aged children, and older adults.

Free Recipes

For a fabulous collection of international vegetarian recipes, visit the International Vegetarian Union at www.ivu.org/recipes. You'll find hundreds of vegetarian recipes from Africa, Latin America, the Caribbean, Europe, North America, and India, as well as dozens of delectable holiday recipes.

The International Vegetarian Union (IVU) is a nonprofit organization made up of other member organizations. Member organizations advocate vegetarianism and are governed exclusively by vegetarians. The IVU receives support from individuals, families, and organizations — vegetarian or not — that support the IVU's aims and objectives.

Vegetarian Cooking Demos

The North American Vegetarian Society's annual Vegetarian Summerfest is held in July, usually on the campus of the University of Pittsburgh at Johnstown. Go to www.navs-online.org for information about this year's event. Participants in Vegetarian Summerfest attend cooking classes and demos given by well-known vegetarian chefs. They also attend lectures and take part in other activities. Summerfest is a family event, drawing vegetarians and nonvegetarians alike from all over the United States, Canada, and even overseas. The vegan meals served all week in the university cafeteria have a reputation for being a highlight of the conference.

Vegetarian Cooking for Families

The Vegetarian Resource Group also offers information about raising vegetarian children, veg-friendly cookbooks for kids, tips for making wholesome baby food from scratch, and other vital information about cooking for families. Go to www.vrg.org/family.

Hidden Animal Ingredients

Another Vegetarian Resource Group site provides answers to a long list of frequently asked questions about the sources of ingredients commonly listed on food labels. Go to www.vrg.org/nutshell/faqingredients.htm for the answers to such questions as

✔ What are agar agar and guar gum?

✔ Why are some cheeses labeled "vegetarian" and others are not?

✔ What is chewing gum made of?

✔ Why won't some vegans eat white sugar?

Nutrient Analysis of Foods

A database of the nutrient composition of a huge range of foods is available online from the U.S. Department of Agriculture's Agricultural Research Service. Check it out at `www.nal.gov/fnic/cgi-bin/nut_search.pl`.

This database is extremely simple to use. Just type in the name of the food you want nutrient information about and press Enter. You're linked to a list of possible products. Choose the one you want, and a full report of the food's nutritional composition is only a couple more clicks away.

Vegetarian Phrases for Travelers

Sampling vegetarian foods in other countries can be a source of inspiration that you can take home to your own kitchen. The International Vegetarian Union maintains a site where you can look up a long list of phrases in dozens of languages. Visit `www.ivu.org/phrases`.

Animal Rights

People for the Ethical Treatment of Animals (PETA) maintains a site that explores the ethical side of food choices. Go to `www.meatstinks.com` for a free vegetarian starter kit, recipes, fact sheets, and more.

Transitioning to Meat-Free

Go to `www.vrg.org/nutshell/nutshell.htm` for helpful information about making the transition from a meat-based diet to a meat-free one. At this Web site, you can find sample vegetarian recipes as well as tips for replacing meat, eggs, and dairy products in other recipes.

Cooking School

The Vegetarian Society of the United Kingdom offers a cooking school called Cordon Vert for aspiring vegetarian chefs. Visit the Society's site at www.vegsoc.org for information about the school, as well as free recipes.

Chapter 24

Ten Online Sources of Ingredients

*V*egetarian cooking doesn't require fancy ingredients or specialty products. You can find everything you need at your local supermarket. But natural foods stores do carry interesting and versatile products that aren't yet commonly available in mainstream stores. If you happen to live near a large natural foods store, that's great. If you don't, you'll love the convenience of ordering online. The Web retailers listed in this chapter stock a variety of vegetarian and vegan foods and other products, including books, clothing, accessories, household cleaners, cosmetics, and cruelty-free personal care products.

Note: If you're new to the Internet, you should know that sites often change without notice. Those that I list here were up and running at the time of writing. Others may have sprouted since then, and some may have vanished. That's the nature of the Net!

Dixie Diner

Dixie Diner is an online retailer that specializes in soy foods. Visit it at www.dixiediner.com. The company sells more than 100 soy-based food items and takes pride in developing and marketing "health food that tastes like junk food."

Ener-G Foods

This company makes Ener-G Egg Replacer, a versatile, convenient, vegan powdered egg replacer. If you can't find this product at a store near you, you can order it directly from the company. The Ener-G Web site also markets other vegetarian specialty products. You can order products singly or by the case. Shop at www2.digimktg.com/enrg/default.html.

The Mail Order Catalog

The Mail Order Catalog is a long-established business that's familiar to many vegetarians as a favorite mail-order source of well-known and beloved vegetarian cookbooks, books about vegetarianism, and specialty food products. The Tennessee-based business now offers online ordering as well at www.healthy-eating.com. Happy shopping!

Mountain Ark

Mountain Ark specializes in organic, vegan, vegetarian, and kosher foods, with an emphasis on macrobiotics. Visit the online store at www.mountainark.com. Shop here for shoyu, tamari, miso, sea vegetables, natural sweeteners, dried fruits and snacks, noodles, seeds and nuts, grains, and more.

NoMeat.com

As you might guess, you won't find any meat being sold at this site. Instead, this site specializes in a wide range of meat alternative products. See for yourself at www.nomeat.com. Look here for vegetarian sandwich meats, burgers, steaks, and patties, as well as breakfast meats, gravies, chili, and more.

Pangea

Pangea is a Washington, D.C.–based vegan store specializing in vegan products of all sorts. The online store sells vegan foods, sweets, shoes and boots, belts, wallets, bags, jackets, body care products, cookbooks, candles, neckties, vitamins, cat and dog products, and more. Shop at www.pangeaveg.com.

Toboggan Hill Farm

Visit Toboggan Hill Farm at www.tobogganhill.com/index2.htm to shop for vegan specialty food products, personal care products, cat and dog supplies, dietary supplements, and household cleaning products.

Vegetarian Market Place

At vegetarianmarketplace.com, you can find a wide range of vegetarian foods, personal care products, books, and other vegetarian products.

Whole Foods Market

Another full-service online source of vegetarian foods and specialty products is www.wholefoods.com. This is the online version of the big natural foods store chain. You can find everything here. See you in a week.

World Food Supply

This site specializes in all sorts of dehydrated foods, such as fruits, vegetables, soups, and meat substitutes. Check it out at www.worldfoodsupply.com.

Metric Conversion Guide

· ·

*N*ote: The recipes in this cookbook were not developed or tested using metric measures. You may see some variation in quality when converting to metric units.

Common Abbreviations

Abbreviation(s)	What It Stands For
C, c	cup
g	gram
kg	kilogram
L, l	liter
lb	pound
mL, ml	milliliter
oz	ounce
pt	pint
t, tsp	teaspoon
T, TB, Tbl, Tbsp	tablespoon

Volume

U.S Units	Canadian Metric	Australian Metric
¼ teaspoon	1 mL	1 ml
½ teaspoon	2 mL	2 ml
1 teaspoon	5 mL	5 ml
1 tablespoon	15 mL	20 ml

(continued)

Volume *(continued)*

U.S Units	Canadian Metric	Australian Metric
¼ cup	50 mL	60 ml
⅓ cup	75 mL	80 ml
½ cup	125 mL	125 ml
⅔ cup	150 mL	170 ml
¾ cup	175 mL	190 ml
1 cup	250 mL	250 ml
1 quart	1 liter	1 liter
1½ quarts	1.5 liters	1.5 liters
2 quarts	2 liters	2 liters
2½ quarts	2.5 liters	2.5 liters
3 quarts	3 liters	3 liters
4 quarts	4 liters	4 liters

Weight

U.S. Units	Canadian Metric	Australian Metric
1 ounce	30 grams	30 grams
2 ounces	55 grams	60 grams
3 ounces	85 grams	90 grams
4 ounces (¼ pound)	115 grams	125 grams
8 ounces (½ pound)	225 grams	225 grams
16 ounces (1 pound)	455 grams	500 grams
1 pound	455 grams	½ kilogram

Measurements	
Inches	*Centimeters*
½	1.5
1	2.5
2	5.0
3	7.5
4	10.0
5	12.5
6	15.0
7	17.5
8	20.5
9	23.0
10	25.5
11	28.0
12	30.5
13	33.0

Temperature (Degrees)	
Fahrenheit	*Celsius*
32	0
212	100
250	120
275	140
300	150
325	160
350	180

(continued)

Temperature (Degrees) *(continued)*

Fahrenheit	Celsius
375	190
400	200
425	220
450	230
475	240
500	260

Index

• *U* •

• *V* •

FOR DUMMIES
BOOK REGISTRATION

We want to hear from you!

Visit **dummies.com** to register this book and tell us how you liked it!

- ✔ Get entered in our monthly prize giveaway.

- ✔ Give us feedback about this book — tell us what you like best, what you like least, or maybe what you'd like to ask the author and us to change!

- ✔ Let us know any other *For Dummies* topics that interest you.

Your feedback helps us determine what books to publish, tells us what coverage to add as we revise our books, and lets us know whether we're meeting your needs as a *For Dummies* reader. You're our most valuable resource, and what you have to say is important to us!

Not on the Web yet? It's easy to get started with *Dummies 101: The Internet For Windows 98* or *The Internet For Dummies* at local retailers everywhere.

Or let us know what you think by sending us a letter at the following address:

For Dummies Book Registration
Dummies Press
10475 Crosspoint Blvd.
Indianapolis, IN 46256

™

**BESTSELLING
BOOK SERIES**